Understanding Bollywood

This book offers an introduction to popular Hindi cinema, a genre that has a massive fan base but is often misunderstood by critics, and provides insight on topics of political and social significance.

Arguing that Bollywood films are not realist representations of society or expressions of conservative ideology but mediated texts that need to be read for their formulaic and melodramatic qualities and for their pleasurable features like bright costumes, catchy music, and sophisticated choreography, the book interprets Bollywood films as complex considerations on the state of the nation that push the boundaries of normative gender and sexuality. The book provides a careful account of Bollywood's constitutive components: its moral structure, its different forms of love, its use of song and dance, its visual style, and its embrace of cinephilia. Arguing that these five elements form the core of Bollywood cinema, the book investigates a range of films from 1947 to the present in order to show how films use and innovate formulaic structures to tell a wide range of stories that reflect changing times. The book ends with some considerations on recent changes in Bollywood cinema, suggesting that despite globalization the future of Bollywood remains promising.

By presenting Bollywood cinema through an interdisciplinary lens, the book reaches beyond film studies departments and will be useful for those teaching and studying Bollywood in English, sociology, anthropology, Asian studies, and cultural studies classes.

Ulka Anjaria is Professor of English at Brandeis University, where she writes and teaches on South Asian literature and film. She is the author of *Realism in the Twentieth-Century Indian Novel: Colonial Difference and Literary Form* (2012) and *Reading India Now: Contemporary Formations in Literature and Popular Culture* (2019), and is the editor of *A History of the Indian Novel in English* (2015).

D0488072

Understanding Bollywood
The Grammar of Hindi Cinema

Ulka Anjaria

Routledge
Taylor & Francis Group

LONDON AND NEW YORK

First published 2021
by Routledge
2 Park Square, Milton Park, Abingdon, Oxon OX14 4RN

and by Routledge
52 Vanderbilt Avenue, New York, NY 10017

Routledge is an imprint of the Taylor & Francis Group, an informa business

© 2021 Ulka Anjaria

The right of Ulka Anjaria to be identified as author of this work has been asserted by them in accordance with sections 77 and 78 of the Copyright, Designs and Patents Act 1988.

All rights reserved. No part of this book may be reprinted or reproduced or utilised in any form or by any electronic, mechanical, or other means, now known or hereafter invented, including photocopying and recording, or in any information storage or retrieval system, without permission in writing from the publishers.

Trademark notice: Product or corporate names may be trademarks or registered trademarks, and are used only for identification and explanation without intent to infringe.

British Library Cataloguing-in-Publication Data
A catalogue record for this book is available from the British Library

Library of Congress Cataloging-in-Publication Data
Names: Anjaria, Ulka, 1979- author.
Title: Understanding Bollywood : the grammar of Hindi cinema /
Ulka Anjaria.
Description: Abingdon, Oxon ; New York, NY : Routledge, 2021. |
Includes bibliographical references and index.
Identifiers: LCCN 2020041173 (print) | LCCN 2020041174 (ebook) |
ISBN 9780367260668 (hardback) | ISBN 9780367265441 (paperback) |
ISBN 9780429293726 (ebook)
Subjects: LCSH: Motion pictures--India--History. |
Motion pictures, Hindi--India.
Classification: LCC PN1993.5.I8 A783 2021 (print) |
LCC PN1993.5.I8 (ebook) | DDC 791.430954--dc23
LC record available at https://lccn.loc.gov/2020041173
LC ebook record available at https://lccn.loc.gov/2020041174

ISBN: 978-0-367-26066-8 (hbk)
ISBN: 978-0-367-26544-1 (pbk)
ISBN: 978-0-429-29372-6 (ebk)

Typeset in Bembo
by Taylor & Francis Books

To Naseem and Rehaan, and to all the fans, past and future

Contents

List of figures   xi
Acknowledgments   xv

Introduction   1

What is Bollywood? 3
Origins, size, and stature 7
Language 7
The question of realism 11
The fan and the critic 13

PART I   15

1   Structure   17

Genre 17
The moral universe 19
Repetition and coincidence 24
Character types 26
Kinship 27
Fictive kinship 29
The lost-and-found plot 30

2   Love   33

The lover 33
Love and destiny 38
Love as intoxication 39
Madness, obsession, and self-annihilation 41

Love as crossing borders 45
Separation 45
Erotics 46
Love's enemy 50
Losing faith in love 53
Love after marriage 54
Love these days 55

3   Song and dance   58

Playback singing 59
Circulation 62
Understanding the song sequence: diegesis 63
Song-and-dance sequences 64
Lyrics 66
Songs and emotions 70
The love song 71
Erotics 74
Female sexual desire 76
Prohibited desire 79
Lust and the item number 81

4   Visual style   84

Morality and visual style 84
Color 85
Costumes 86
Locations 94
Sets and the role of artifice 96
Gestures and expressions 100
The tableau and the fourth wall 102
Angles, zooms, and pans 107
Editing 108
Montage 109
Choreography and picturization 110
Kitsch and visual style 114

5   Cinephilia   117

Cinephilia and the star 119
Fandom 120
Double roles, twin plots, and cameos 126

Film titles 128
Intertextuality 130
The affectionate parody 135
The technology of filmmaking 136

PART II 139

6 Nationalism 141

The nation as mother 142
Corruption and capitalism 145
Police corruption and the vigilante 148
The secular nation 151
Partition and the question of Pakistan 154
Kashmir and the margins of the nation 159
Love and the nation 160
The nation and the diaspora 162

7 Gender and sexuality 168

Gender roles 169
Homosociality and male friendship 172
Female friendship 177
Love triangles 178
Relationships with no name 181
Mothers and sons 182
Queer Bollywood 184

PART III 191

8 The future of Bollywood 193

The multiplex 193
Bollywood no more? 194
Hatke cinema 195
Blockbusters 196
Social reform films 198
Questioning good and evil 198
Female-centered films 200
The impact of #MeToo 202

New masculinities 203

The future of Bollywood 206

Notes   207
Works cited   214
Index   221

List of figures

0.1 A page of a recent Hindi newspaper featuring Bollywood news. The term "Bollywood" is written at the top of the page in English, suggesting that even though it's not a word that developed alongside the genre, it is widely used today across languages. © Savera India Times, Daman, April 20, 2017. 4

0.2 The film's title is written in Roman (English), Devanagari (Hindi), and Nastaliq (Urdu) scripts and presented within one frame during the credits in *Padosan* (1968). This was standard practice for most of the twentieth century. 8

2.1 Chandni's face reappears through the paint on Rohit's wall, suggesting the indestructibility of their love, in *Chandni* (1989). 39

2.2 Shamu and Radha share a moment of intimacy after he puts a set of bangles on her wrist, in *Mother India* (1957). 47

2.3 Ravi and Meena share an intimate moment on two sides of a changing room wall, in *Waqt* (1965). 48

2.4 Arun and Vandana overhear an erotic encounter in the next room, leading them to make love for the first time, in *Aradhana* (1969). 49

3.1 Every time he sees Chandni, Ram hears music and his body makes the Bollywood lover's classic gesture, against his own volition, in *Main Hoon Na* (2004). 73

3.2 Erotic love amidst dramatic landscapes in "Suraj Hua Maddham," from *Kabhi Khushi Kabhie Gham* (2001). 76

3.3 Simran, singing about her dreams in the rain, in *Dilwale Dulhania Le Jayenge* (1995). 78

3.4 Zaara fantasizes about Veer in "Main Yahan Hoon," from *Veer-Zaara* (2004). 78

3.5 The item dancer is not impressed with the men who try to objectify her, in *Bunty Aur Babli* (2005). 82

3.6 Gabbar Singh (second to the left) is so fixated on the dance that he does not notice the arrival of our heroes to his camp, in *Sholay* (1975). 82

4.1 Sharmila Tagore in a glamorous sari with a sleeveless blouse, in fashion in the 1960s, in *An Evening in Paris* (1967). 88

4.2 Sharmila Tagore dresses up as a poor woman in order to meet a man who doesn't just want her for her money, in *An Evening in Paris* (1967). 89

4.3 In a double role in *An Evening in Paris* (1967), Sharmila Tagore also plays Suzy, a cabaret dancer. 89

4.4 Deepa enjoying the water in *An Evening in Paris* (1967). 90

4.5 Mumtaz's iconic sari drape in *Brahmachari* (1968). 90

4.6 Dimple Kapadia's look in *Bobby* (1973) sparked new fashion trends. 91

4.7 Madhuri Dixit and her iconic jeweled sari in *Hum Aapke Hain Koun* (1994). 91

4.8 With his bouffant and cravat, Dev Anand was a male style icon of the 1960s, here in *Guide* (1965). 92

4.9 Amitabh Bachchan in *Kabhi Kabhie* (1976). 93

4.10 A new, male, street aesthetic in *Rangeela* (1995). 93

4.11 Arun and Vandana declare their love in front of a dramatic, mountainous landscape in *Aradhana* (1969). 95

4.12 The striking landscape of Pangong Lake is a fitting backdrop for the inventive choreography of "Satrangi Re" in *Dil Se* (1997). 96

4.13 The long shot captures Raj's alienation in a wealthy house that lacks familial love, in *Bobby* (1973). 97

4.14 The extravagant palace set in *Mughal-e-Azam* (1960). 98

4.15 Chandramukhi's costumes were just some of the extravagant designs on the set of *Devdas* (2002). 99

4.16 Arms outstretched to the sides: this is one of superstar Shah Rukh Khan's signature gestures – here in *Kal Ho Naa Ho* (2003). 101

4.17 Sridevi as the reincarnation of a female snake in *Nagina* (1986). 102

4.18 One of actor Sridevi's goofy expressions in the song "Hawa Hawai" in *Mr. India* (1987). 103

4.19 The tableau renders the love triangle in spatial form, in *Sangam* (1964). 104

4.20 The mother stands at the crux of the familial conflict in *Deewaar* (1975). 105

4.21 The three brothers, separated as young boys, donate blood to a woman whom they later discover is their mother, in *Amar Akbar Anthony* (1977). 106

4.22 Breaking the fourth wall in *Chalti Ka Naam Gaadi* (1958). 106

4.23 The opulence of the Raichand mansion suddenly becomes lonely and alienating when Rahul is disowned by his father for marrying his true love, in *Kabhi Khushi Kabhie Gham* (2001).   107

4.24 A song-and-dance sequence seen through a bird's eye shot that highlights the symmetry of the dance, in *Kuch Kuch Hota Hai* (1998).   111

4.25 Complex footwork and gestures distinguish the mujra performance "In Aankhon Ki Masti," in *Umrao Jaan* (1981).   113

4.26 The Raichand mansion in *Kabhi Khushi Kabhie Gham* (2001), where Rahul arrives by helicopter.   116

5.1 A frame from the Indian Police Foundation's video on how to stop the spread of Covid-19, narrated by three well-known Bollywood police. © Indian Police Foundation.   118

5.2 In *Billu Barber* (2009), the fictional star Sahir Khan, played by Shah Rukh Khan, is greeted in the village with a display of posters from many of his past films, which are in fact real posters of past Shah Rukh Khan films.   120

5.3 Superstar Aryan Khanna faces off with Gaurav, his devoted fan, in *Fan* (2016), with Shah Rukh Khan playing both roles.   126

5.4 Multiple stars had cameos in the "Deewanagi" song sequence in *Om Shanti Om* (2007). Pictured here: Sanjay Dutt, Saif Ali Khan, and Salman Khan, along with the film's star, Shah Rukh Khan.   129

5.5 Nandita dancing to the wet sari song in *Mr. India* (1987) while the sequence, originally starring Sridevi, is screened in the background, in *Gunday* (2014).   132

5.6 Not just the stars, but camera operators, costume designers, makeup artists, lighting technicians, and many others get a shout-out in the credits sequences of Farah Khan's films. Here, a frame from the end credits of *Main Hoon Na* (2004).   137

6.1 Om wears a necklace featuring the symbols of India's three main religions in *Om Shanti Om* (2007).   152

7.1 Rohit and Lalit enjoy an afternoon sharing their love stories with one another, in *Chandni* (1989).   173

7.2 Best friends Bala and Bikram share a drink as they watch a dance performance, in *Gunday* (2014).   174

7.3 "Khana-peena saath hai, marna-jeena saath hai" ("We'll eat and drink together, live and die together"); close male friendship in *Sholay* (1975).   175

7.4 Close friends Neena and Sheela share an intimate moment during a song in *Andaz* (1949) while Dilip accompanies them on the piano.   177

7.5 While showering together, Shekhar drops a bar of soap and jokingly asks his brother Amit to pick it up, in *Silsila* (1981).   180

7.6   The pre-wedding celebrations in *Hum Aapke Hain Koun* (1994)
      include a queer dance.   186
7.7   Mannu seduces Dhingra while in drag, in *Duplicate* (1998).   187
7.8   Sam's mother gifts Kunal the bangles that she was saving for her
      daughter-in-law, in *Dostana* (2008).   188
8.1   The half-dressed male body offers the possibility of alternative
      viewing positions to the heterosexual male gaze, here in *Ghajini*
      (2008).   205
8.2   Shah Rukh Khan is the "item girl" in "Dard-e-Disco" in *Om
      Shanti Om* (2007).   205

Acknowledgments

I had the pleasure of presenting from this project at the Great Indian Fandom Conference hosted by the Godrej Culture Lab in Mumbai in September, 2019, alongside Paromita Vohra, whose delightful writings on Hindi cinema constantly challenge scholarly assumptions and platitudes. Thanks to Paromita, Parmesh Shahani, Saniya Shaikh, and the entire team at Godrej for such a wonderful conference, which included many against-the-grain conversations on film, fandom, and queerness. The students in my Bollywood class over the years have inspired me with their open minds and their enthusiasm for all things Bollywood. From Brandeis, thanks to my research assistant Paige Eggebrecht and to the Theodore and Jane Norman Faculty Research Grant from Brandeis University for supporting the research for this book. Thank you to Natalie Foster and Jennifer Vennall at Routledge for guiding this book through production. Thank you to Rehaan and Naseem for watching films with me, and to Jonathan for the encouragement to write this book and the long conversations about film, *mazaa*, and what it means to be a scholar. My father, Shailendra Anjaria (1946–2020), passed away before he saw this book in print, and before I was able to convince him that Bollywood movies are worth watching. I was hoping this was the book to finally change his mind.

Introduction

Bollywood is a huge and influential genre of popular films, based in Mumbai (formerly known as Bombay), India. It includes tens of thousands of films, with an output of several hundred a year, millions of fans, many die-hard superfans, and significant global recognition. It has, like any cinema, some spectacularly good films, some terrible ones, and many that lie somewhere in between. Sometimes it is made fun of for being over-the-top, unrealistic, and melodramatic. Even in India – even by people who regularly watch Bollywood films – embarrassment is sometimes evident around the quality and aesthetics of the genre.

This book is an attempt to name and describe the various conventions used by Bollywood films in order to see how they work on their own terms. Understanding the moral structure, the song-and-dance sequences, the at-times hyperbolic visual style, and other aspects of these films helps provide us with a shared vocabulary to watch and understand Bollywood films with a well-informed literacy of their conventions, rather than contrasting it to Hollywood, or to international arthouse cinema, with which it has little in common. Knowing the grammar of Bollywood films[1] is useful for those who are familiar with the genre *and* for those who have never seen a Bollywood film. For the former, it can help defamiliarize conventions that might be seen as self-evident and illuminate the relationship of an individual film to larger patterns across time. For the latter, this book offers a vocabulary to begin to understand a genre that might at first glance seem radically unfamiliar. In both cases, I attempt to refute claims of Bollywood's lack of sophistication to see the underlying structures on which films make meaning.

The book is divided into three parts. The first is comprised of five chapters, each of which describes a major convention of Bollywood: its moral structure, its idea of love, its use of song and dance, its visual style, and its self-referential, cinephilic, qualities. Without understanding these basic building blocks of Bollywood cinema, we cannot begin to understand how Bollywood relates to historical, social, and political questions in twentieth- and twenty-first-century India. Part II begins to make those links, reading Bollywood films not simplistically as social artifacts or as straightforward representations of reality, but rather as commentaries on social and political issues, which can only be understood *by means of* the conventions discussed in Part I. My claim is that like any popular genre, we need to understand Bollywood films as mediated texts with their own, in-built logic, rather than simply as representations of social realities. However, once we understand what this logic is, we can see how films offer at times quite surprising perspectives on political and social issues in the world around us. In Part II, I focus on two topics that have dominated the study of Bollywood for the past two decades: nationalism; and gender and sexuality. Using the grammar and vocabulary developed in Part I, Chapters 6 and 7 look at how we might think more deeply about what it means for a film to be "nationalist," "patriarchal," or "heteronormative." And Part III, the book's epilogue, is a brief discussion of the future of Bollywood cinema, in a contemporary India which appears to have drastically changed in recent decades. The chapter discusses new trends in twenty-first-century Bollywood cinema while also hypothesizing on the genre's future.

This book is not comprehensive; it does not – no book can! – cover every single Bollywood film, nor even every single successful or famous film. It does not delve into film production or the political economy of marketing and distribution, in part because that has been done so comprehensively by others.[2] Rather, it tries to name conventions, find general patterns across decades and styles, and give examples of how these conventions and patterns work and are innovated on. Its chapter divisions are analytic rather than classificatory, and I have included several cross-references so that readers can make various connections across the chapters. Ideally, understanding the grammar of Bollywood cinema will not only help readers make sense of the individual films mentioned here, but give a larger sense of the genre as a whole, which will inform an understanding of films they see in the future as well. The goal is to identify patterns across the board and thus begin to recognize where films deviate from them and how those deviations might be meaningful.

While many academics and critics put singular emphasis on what has changed in Bollywood, especially in relation to India's increasing embrace of capitalism and consumerism over the last several decades, this book is more interested in seeing what has persisted. The book's last chapter addresses some possible directions for the future of Bollywood, but otherwise, I emphasize continuity over change and the persistence of conventions rather than their dramatic upheaval. In doing so, I attempt to loosen the hold of the social sciences over the study of Bollywood's social relevance, maintaining that we miss a lot when we read films only as sociological or cultural phenomena or as reflections of contemporary realities. While gleaning the politics of films can be important, I suggest that we need to understand how films work as narratives and visual texts *before* we interpret them as forms of social commentary.

This book is wide in its historical range but centers on individual films that help us understand the grammar of Bollywood over the last seventy-odd years. I cover films from approximately 1947 until 2019 coming from the Bombay industry, with 1947 marking the date of India's independence. There were many important pre-independence films – with India's first feature film, Dadasaheb Phalke's *Raja Harishchandra*, released in 1913 – but because it was in the 1950s that Bollywood cinema acquired many of its current characteristics and became a pan-Indian phenomenon, this book focuses on the post-independence era.[3]

What is Bollywood?

Bollywood is a relatively new term that likely means different things to different people. Popularly in the US and UK, the term is associated with blingy and brightly colored costumes or a particular dance style. In India, the term is less common, with more specific terms like "Bombay cinema" or "Hindi popular cinema" being preferred. In many parts of India, a Bollywood movie is simply called a *"picture"* (an English word incorporated into Hindi and used colloquially even by non-English speakers) or a *"fillum,"* a vernacularization of "film." By contrast, for film critics, Bollywood references the recent globalization and "gentrification"[4] of the industry that extends beyond the actual films themselves, including marketing, branding, stage shows, global fan followings, and reality shows, such that "Bollywood [is] a culture industry, and … the Indian cinema [is] only a part, even if culturally a significant one, of that industry."[5] Some Indian film personalities, most famously superstar Amitabh Bachchan, have criticized the term Bollywood for its implicit suggestion that Hindi cinema is derivative of Hollywood.[6] And indeed, the term was originally used dismissively. For instance, in 1961, in an article critical of contemporary Indian writers, Mulk Raj Anand wrote: "Some of the most important younger talent was soon absorbed in Bollywood, Mollywood and Collywood, writing indifferent dialogue for bad films and decorating the awkward situations with catchy tunes."[7] This criticism of film writing and the dismissive use of the terms Bollywood, Mollywood, and Collywood express Anand's disdain for the popular cinema – a disdain that remains somewhat embedded in the term itself.[8]

Yet, despite this dubious origin, a look at the use of the term Bollywood in the *Times of India* shows its gradual incorporation into the mainstream over the decades. While in the 1960s it was used sparingly and dismissively, as in the example above, by the late 1980s it is used more casually and without denigration, and by the first few years of the 1990s it seems to have become widespread in the English media, shorn of its negative connotation, as a catchy, shorthand descriptor of the Bombay film industry.[9] Indeed today, Bollywood is used in both English and India's bhashas (Figure 0.1) and commonly describes not so much an industry (as with Hollywood) as a genre and style of filmmaking with relatively consistent thematic, narrative, and formal features.[10] In critics' eagerness to condemn recent changes in the economy that they see to have influenced Hindi cinema and turned it into a marketing phenomenon, they often overlook consistent and recurring patterns, tropes, and other features that do seem to indicate a certain solidity of the genre throughout the decades. Thus, for the purposes of this book, I use Bollywood synonymously with Bombay cinema, as referring to Hindi-language popular films based in Mumbai.[11]

Figure 0.1 A page of a recent Hindi newspaper featuring Bollywood news. The term "Bollywood" is written at the top of the page in English, suggesting that even though it's not a word that developed alongside the genre, it is widely used today across languages. © Savera India Times, Daman, April 20, 2017.

Bollywood cinema includes a large body of films that both operate along consistent formal, narrative, and thematic features, and simultaneously exhibit a significant amount of heterogeneity.[12] Obviously when we're talking about such a huge industry, there is so much variation that for every rule, there is an exception. This book is mostly about the rules: what Bollywood films tend to do, the assumptions they operate on, and the language and visual conventions many of them use, all of which are essential for understanding the meaning of individual films. Likewise, only by understanding the conventions can we begin to analyze when and why films deviate from these conventions; throughout the book, I have tried to point out important exceptions to any conventions I delineate, or examples where newer films poke fun at the conventions of older ones.

Indeed, despite significant variations, there is a set of identifiable conventions that unite Bollywood films and make it possible to talk about Bollywood as a whole in a way that might not always be possible for other industries or national products. Bollywood films are often known as "masala" films, referring to the mix of flavors that makes Indian food so tasty.[13] That means that whereas Hollywood films tend to get classified by genre – comedy, romantic comedy, horror, thriller, action, and so on – many Bollywood films contain several or even all of the above. Of course, they do so to different degrees, so some predominantly action films will have only a brief, undeveloped romance plot, and many romantic films have just a few fight scenes. Comedy also exists to various degrees in many films, but there are some films that are heavily comedic, and even action or romance in those films are presented in a light-hearted tone. All of these sub-genres merit attention. However, this book focuses mostly on the three-hour, masala melodramas – the most popular and widespread type of Bollywood film – in order to begin unpacking how to understand them and what they mean.

Bollywood films are 2.5–3.5 hours long, divided in half by an interval; they include a formulaic narrative broken up by several song-and-dance sequences in which the actors or guest performers lip-synch to songs solely written for the film, often accompanied by a complex choreographed dance sequence. Bollywood films rarely develop character interiority, meaning they do not present complex characters with psychological depth, but use formulaic conventions to establish "good" and "bad" characters, with no reason given for their having these qualities.[14] We rarely see characters undergo any transformation; rather, plot is affected by external forces. In this way, Bollywood films could be said to be melodramatic, in the sense of abiding by a theatrical logic that focuses on external presentations of emotion rather than character depth or interiority. Aesthetically, Bollywood is characterized by excess: extravagant song sequences, brightly colored costumes, shiny jewelry, expansive sets, heightened emotions, hyperbolic gestures, swelling music, thrilling chases, beautiful actors, and unbelievable plots. It evinces a striking disregard for realism: thus bad guys are really, really bad and good guys are really, really good, and there are few shades of grey; fight scenes look unabashedly fake; songs are lip-synched rather than sung by the actors; and storylines are implausible. Bollywood's lack of realism – its lack of *interest* in realism – has made its films the butt of jokes for Indians and foreigners alike. In India, more educated viewers in particular are embarrassed by the absurdity of the genre, and some Indians refuse to watch Bollywood films altogether, preferring art cinema or international cinema. In the west, Bollywood is seen as unsophisticated and is often decried as low-budget or purely commercial. The idea that Bollywood film directors will do "anything" to make a profitable film is a dismissive exaggeration that is thrown around both in India and abroad.

But aside from these pockets of skeptics, Bollywood is hugely popular. In India, films have an enormous fan following across religious, age, and gender divides. Going to see a "*picture*" can be a family outing on a Sunday afternoon, it can be something friends do after (or instead of!) college, or the setting for a romantic date. Indian cinemas are full of crying babies, toddlers, parents, grannies, friends, and lovers; film-watching is a collective and pleasurable experience, even since the arrival of satellite television in 1992 and the ubiquity of pirated DVDs, which make it possible for people to watch films from the comfort of their living rooms. Many people see every, or almost every, film, and repeated viewings, whether in the cinema or at home, are common. Clips from song-and-dance sequences are shown on television before a film's release, so by the time a movie appears in the theater, audiences often can already hum the tunes.

Movie stars have massive fan followings, evident in posters hung up in bedrooms, gossip magazines, and organized fan clubs, both in person and online. When highly anticipated films are released, audience members line up in front of cinema halls to pose and take photographs with the life-size cardboard cut-outs of their stars placed out front. When superstar Amitabh Bachchan was wounded on the sets of *Coolie* in 1982, fans embarked on pilgrimages to pray for his recovery. Even today, fans congregate outside film stars' houses in Mumbai to take photos and linger, for the small chance a star will appear, or to greet the star on their birthday or on a holiday, when they sometimes emerge to wave to crowds of waiting fans.

Bollywood films have also had fan followings outside of India. The USSR hosted its first Indian film festival in 1954, attended by superstars Dev Anand, Raj Kapoor, and Nargis, which propelled Bombay films to popularity there for the next several decades.[15] Since then, Bollywood has had a significant following in Nigeria, the Middle East, and across the global South.[16] One scholar records that "in 1975–77 … statistics show that Indian films were exported to Africa, the Arab states, Trinidad, Guyana and Barbados, Burma, Hong Kong, Indonesia, Iran, Malaysia, Singapore, Sri Lanka and Thailand."[17] In many of these countries, Indian cinema represented an alternative to European and American hegemony in the arts, and Bollywood's melodramatic quality – its unrealistic plots, its stock characters, and the conflict it stages between love and family – made it broadly accessible to a range of audiences. More recently, interest in Bollywood is growing in China, where superstar Aamir Khan in particular has a massive fan following, and where his films *3 Idiots* (2009), *Dangal* (2016), and *Secret Superstar* (2017) were very successful at the box office.[18] Turkey and Peru also have many Bollywood fans.[19] Bollywood films are screened in cinema halls in the UK and the US, although the films that do financially well in those countries are generally seen by Indian and Pakistani audiences. Bollywood has generated very little interest among non-South Asian audiences in the west, except perhaps as a source of kitsch, in Bollywood dance classes or bhangra competitions. There have been only a few attempts to remake Bollywood films in English for a wider audience,[20] as with *Guide*, a successful 1965 film whose star, Dev Anand, tried to remake it in a shorter, English version the same year,[21] but which earned little critical or box office success.

The popularity of global streaming channels like Netflix and Amazon Prime has expanded the potential audiences of Bollywood films. Now viewers in Mexico, South America, and Europe can watch Bollywood films with good-quality subtitles. The Bollywood film *3 Idiots* (2009) was remade in Mexico as *Tres Idiotas* (2017) and other similar global circulations are likely to follow.

Origins, size, and stature

The first Indian feature film ever made was *Raja Harishchandra* (1913), a silent film made by Dadasaheb Phalke, known as the founder of Indian cinema. The first Bombay films were mythological films, telling the stories of Hindu gods, but romance became popular in the 1920s and social realism in the 1930s.[22] The first talkie, *Alam Ara*, was released in 1931. This was also the first film to have song sequences; thus, song and dance were central to Bollywood from its outset.[23]

Indian independence in 1947 coincided with Partition, the breakup of the Indian subcontinent into two independent countries, India and Pakistan, as the result of the long-standing political alienation of India's Muslims. Several important Bollywood figures left India for Pakistan in the succeeding years, causing a significant loss for the industry. Notable among these were actor and playback singer Noor Jehan, actor Swarnalata and her producer husband Nazir, screenwriter Saadat Hasan Manto, and filmmaker Shaukat Hussain Rizvi.[24] Some Muslim stars who remained in India feared for their bankability and changed their names to Hindu-sounding names, such as the superstar Dilip Kumar, who was born Muhammad Yusuf Khan.[25]

After independence Bombay cinema reached a much wider audience and started to address contemporary political, economic, and social concerns. However, throughout its history Bollywood has been seen as a lowbrow genre, even within India, and in India's early years film songs were not even allowed to be played on All-India Radio, the state-sponsored radio station, because they were considered unrefined, in contrast to Hindustani classical music.[26] Listeners could try to gain a signal from Radio Ceylon in neighboring Sri Lanka, where Bollywood songs were popular.

Currently, there are around 200 releases in Hindi cinema each year. These films vary widely in terms of theme and box office success. Many films are "flops," meaning they did not break even at the box office; 85 percent of films do not make a profit.[27] Non-flop films are categorized as hit, superhit, and blockbuster, depending on their level of profit.

Budgets range significantly. Whereas today, the average budget for a Hollywood production is $70–90 million, films in India are made on significantly smaller budgets. Even *Thugs of Hindostan* (2018), one of the most expensive Bollywood films ever made, had a budget of around $30 million, and the average budget for Bollywood is much less, averaging around $2–7 million.

Language

Bollywood refers to films made in Hindi, one of the most widely spoken and understood languages of India. More accurately, the cinema's language should be described as Hindustani, which is a spoken language that includes vocabulary derived from both Sanskrit and Persian and thus reflects the mixed cultural heritage – Hindu and Muslim – that characterizes India's diverse past. In the nineteenth century, the status of Hindustani started to be contested as Hindus tried to claim "Hindi" – Hindustani written in the Devanagari script and shorn of many Persio-Arabic words – as the language of India's Hindu majority, which eventually led to Urdu – written in the Nastaliq script and shorn of its Sanskrit vocabulary – being politicized as a Muslim language, even though grammatically, the two are identical.[28] This split between Hindi for Hindus and Urdu for Muslims only widened with the subcontinent's Partition in 1947. Now, Hindi is widely spoken in India, Urdu is the official language of Pakistan, and Hindustani is nowhere officially acknowledged, though it is widely spoken by people of both countries, and, indeed, is the language of Bollywood films.

While these language debates have been taking place in the political sphere, the cinema is where Indians can enjoy the secular, pan-religious heritage that is being weakened elsewhere. Even in the decades following Partition, films had multi-religious and multi-ethnic production teams and dialogues were spoken in a heterogenous language that was widely comprehensible. Most films and film posters proudly presented their titles in all three scripts: Roman, Devanagari, and Nastaliq, corresponding to English, Hindi, and Urdu, respectively (Figure 0.2). Although currently this practice is rarer, some filmmakers continue to do it, as seen in the opening credits of *Main Hoon Na* (2004).

Figure 0.2 The film's title is written in Roman (English), Devanagari (Hindi), and Nastaliq (Urdu) scripts and presented within one frame during the credits in *Padosan* (1968). This was standard practice for most of the twentieth century.

Bollywood is India's most well-known film industry, but by no means its only one. India has hundreds of languages, and 22 official ones, many of which have their own cinematic traditions. Hindi cinema makes the most films per year, but film industries in Kannada, Tamil, Telugu, Malayalam, and Bengali are also prolific and popular. Of these, Hindi cinema reaps the largest box office share at 44 percent.[29] Hindi is widely understood beyond Mumbai, making Bollywood closest to what could be a national cinema; however, the status of Hindi continues to be contested, and in some regions of India, such as the South and the Northeast, Hindi is seen as a form of cultural domination that is widely resented and resisted. Thus, Bollywood is popular across India, but not universally so. There is significant crossing between the different popular film industries; for instance, several famous Bollywood stars began their careers in South Indian cinema. Waheeda Rehman began in Telugu films before she became a Bollywood superstar. Sridevi began her career as a child star in Tamil, Telugu, Malayalam, and Kannada films[30] and stayed with South Indian cinema even as her career blossomed in Bollywood, becoming "one of the first crossover stars in Indian cinema."[31] Rekha and Hema Malini also began in South Indian cinema. Amrish Puri has acted in Hindi, Kannada, Punjabi, Telugu, and Tamil cinema. Deepika Padukone first acted in Kannada films and is now one of the biggest stars in Bollywood. Beyond South India, Shreyas Talpade and Sonali Kulkarni began in Marathi films and then moved to Bollywood.

Bollywood is also distinct from the various traditions of art cinema that have flourished in India since the 1950s, often known as parallel cinema.[32] Prominent parallel film directors include Satyajit Ray, who made several internationally recognized films in Bengali, Ritwik Ghatak, Mrinal Sen, M.S. Sathyu, K.N.T. Sastry, and Mani Kaul. Contemporary directors who might be seen as working in this tradition include Shyam Benegal, Aparna Sen, Mira Nair, Rituparno Ghosh, Sudhir Mishra, and Kiran Rao. Parallel cinema is more realistic than Bollywood, usually does not employ generic features like song-and-dance sequences, and is much more legible within an international arthouse aesthetic.

Despite being in Hindi, Bollywood also reflects India's linguistic diversity. Songs tend to be in Hindustani, but carry traces of Urdu poetic forms. If there is a second dominant language in Bollywood, it is Punjabi, due in no small part to the significant number of Punjabi directors in the industry.[33] There are many songs which mix Punjabi with Hindi, like "Shava Shava" in *Kabhi Khushi Kabhie Gham* (2001) and "Lohri" in *Veer-Zaara* (2004). This is rarer with other Indian languages, although it does happen: *Secret Superstar* (2017) has a Gujarati-English song, "I'll Miss You," and "Jiya Jale Jaan Jale" in *Dil Se* (1997) mixes Hindi with Malayalam. In addition, Bengali, Marathi, Gujarati, and Tamil characters often sprinkle their Hindi with bits of those languages, usually just a few words so they remain comprehensible to a wide range of viewers. More rarely, linguistic difference becomes part of a film's plot: in *Hum Dil De Chuke Sanam* (1999), Sameer speaks hilariously bad Gujarati, which is attributed to his living abroad, and in *Aiyyaa* (2012), Meenakshi spends time learning Tamil in order to be able to speak more intimately to Surya, the man she is in love with, and watching her learn phrases she can use to seduce him – such as "Please shirtla first buttona pottukada" ("Please keep the first button of your shirt open") – is part of the endearing comedy of that film. In *3 Idiots* (2009), Chatur is from South India so doesn't speak Hindi; when he has to give a speech in Hindi in college, he simply memorizes the words, allowing his rivals to alter his speech with obscenities that he doesn't realize he is saying – again for comedic effect.

Some viewers will notice the increased use of English in contemporary Bollywood movies, which reflects the bilingual nature of many urban Indians.[34] There are even a few songs with English lyrics, such as the title song in *An Evening in Paris* (1967) and "It's the Time to Disco" in *Kal Ho Naa Ho* (2003) – although, in both cases, only the refrains are in English, and the rest of the lyrics are in Hindi. The increased use of English does not mean, however, that newer films are made for an international audience or that they reflect an aping of the west: although brought to India by colonialism, today English is fully an Indian language, and the mix spoken in newer films, sometimes called "Hinglish" – a bilingual, Hindi-English blend – is reflective of how young urban Indians actually speak. Moreover, there were several older films with English titles as well, such as *Mr. and Mrs. 55* (1955), *Guide* (1965), *Love in Tokyo* (1966), and *An Evening in Paris* (1967), and so English is not entirely new in Bollywood.

Indeed, English has been and continues to be a language of the elites, and the unequal access of Indians to English means that it has been the subject of jokes or puns within Bollywood films – the humor of which is too often lost in subtitles. In *Amar Akbar Anthony* (1977), Anthony shouts nonsensically in the middle of a Hindi song: "You see, the whole country of this system is just a position by the hemoglobin in the atmosphere because you are a sophisticated rhetorician intoxicated by the exuberance of your own verbosity!" to which the audience collectively replies, "What?!", poking fun at the fake erudition of India's English-speaking elite. In *Namak Halaal* (1982), when asked whether he knows English, Arjun responds, ridiculously: "I can talk English, I can walk English, because English is a funny language" – again signifying that he in fact knows little English. In the comedy *Andaz Apna Apna* (1994), one of the villains has the tagline: "Sorry, galti se mistake ho gaya hai," which really can't be translated, as "galti se" in Hindi means "by mistake," so it means something like, "Sorry, I made a mistake by mistake"; it is a joke about the lack of intelligence of this film's villains. Films also have fun with cross-lingual puns, such as in *3 Idiots* (2009) when Farhan plays on the homophony between the English word "suffer" and the Hindi word "safar," which means journey, explaining, regarding Raju's commitment to start working hard: "Raju ne train ka dibba badal diya, ab woh Chatur ke saath safar karne nikal pada, Hindi ka safar nahin, Angrezi ka suffer: S.U.F.F. E.R" ("Raju changed his track, now he is beginning to 'safar' alongside Chatur, not Hindi 'safar,' but 'suffer' in English [laughs]").

Another notable feature of Bollywood's language is that since independence, Bollywood film titles, unlike other foreign films (including Indian art films), are rarely translated into English, even when they are released outside India or on Netflix or other international streaming platforms. I am following this convention in this book by using only the original titles and not translating them. The practice of leaving titles in their original language is particularly important because many Bollywood titles are not thematic or metaphoric, in that they do not sum up the main plot of the film or refer to an overarching idea or theme. There are exceptions to this, such as *Purab Aur Paschim* (1970), which means "East and West" and indeed refers to the cultural contrast between Europe and India, *Kati Patang* (1971), which means a cut kite and is used to refer to "a woman untethered to family,"[35] and *Waqt* (1965), or time, which refers to the ravages time can have on a family. However, most titles might be seen as metonymic, referring to a sentiment or sensibility expressed by one of the characters or touched on in one moment in the film, but lacking a summative quality. For instance, *Satyam Shivam Sundaram* (1978) can be translated as "Truth, Religion and Beauty," but the film only tangentially touches on those themes, and is in fact a love story. *Kuch Kuch Hota Hai* (1998) would be translated as "Whatever Happens" and *Hum Dil De Chuke Sanam* (1999) as "I Gave You My Heart," neither of which is particularly specific or tells us much about what the film is about. Thus translating such titles might not be particularly helpful to a non-Hindi-speaking audience.

For most of Bollywood's history, non-Indian audiences were not really considered while films were being made, and even non-Hindi speakers in India would have a basic comprehension of Hindi, so films were rarely subtitled. When films were popular outside of India, such as in the USSR, the Middle East, or Nigeria, they were either dubbed or simply released in the original Hindi. While some VHSs were subtitled, they were inconsistent and of low quality; DVDs were really the first technology that allowed consistent subtitling of Bollywood films, but even these subtitles seemed a bit half-hearted, and there were often mistranslations or skipped dialogues. The quality of English subtitling has improved lately, and on newer DVDs and platforms like Netflix the quality is actually quite good.

The question of realism

The formal traits discussed in this book demonstrate that Bollywood films are, for the most part, not interested in realistic representation.[36] Does that mean, however, that they are not realistic at all? An alternative interpretation might be that Bollywood is interested in representing reality, but not material reality. Thus, the world of Bollywood is the world of dreams, desire, emotion, and fantasy. Bright colors, highs and lows of emotion, and exteriorized drama convey the world as it is felt emotionally rather than what it might look like materially or objectively. That is why Bollywood films are so uninterested in being believable, and why they so commonly use unrealistic plot devices such as excessive coincidence, as will be discussed in Chapter 1.

Melodrama, "a form of drama characterized by sensationalism, emotional intensity, hyperbole, strong action, violence, rhetorical excesses, moral polarities, brutal villainy and its ultimate elimination, and the triumph of good,"[37] represents emotional states and universal truths rather than material realities. Thus even if what occurs on screen is not realistic, the emotional response and the underlying truth might actually be very real. For example, when a truly evil villain faces off against a hero in an epic battle in which the hero necessarily wins, the scene itself is not realistic, but it allows the audience to consider ideas such as fate or poetic justice. Likewise, when lovers express their love for one another in a song-and-dance sequence, it might seem improbable and unrealistic if we are thinking in terms of real time and space. However, that song-and-dance sequence is meant to represent *how love feels*, that sense of being transported, that rush of emotion, and the single-mindedness that comes from love, when the lover cannot think of anything else besides her/his beloved. The sequence is enjoyable to watch precisely because it accesses this level of emotional intensity, not because it could "really" happen.

Sanskrit aesthetic theory identifies several *rasa*, defined as stylized flavors or moods, which are "concerned with moving the spectator through the text in an ordered succession of modes of affect" rather than abiding by Aristotelian "unities of time and place and the dramatic development of narrative"[38] central to many modern texts, and we can see the influence of this on Bollywood. As Tejaswini Ganti writes, "the *Natyashastra* located audience enjoyment in emotional involvement" rather than education or imitation of reality.[39] This corresponds with modern melodrama, which also represents unrealized states, such as dreams, desire, and the unconscious.[40] In Bollywood, we see the importance of dreams when a character falls in love and we jump to a song sequence where she imagines herself with her beloved, even though in real life her love is not (yet) requited. Bollywood also represents joy, sexual desire, aspiration, and other emotional or bodily states. The dreamworld of Bollywood is often visualized via bright colors and hyperbolic settings, a brightness that stands for intensity itself.

Thus, while it is tempting to read Bollywood films as insights into Indian culture, or how Indians think, making a one-to-one association between what we see in these films and what is happening in India would be a mistake. Bollywood films, like operas, Broadway shows, Marvel movies, and the various other unrealistic media we enjoy watching, are expressions of underlying tensions in society but not ethnographic insights into society. So, for instance, we cannot understand the position of women in Indian society by looking at how female characters act or think in Bollywood. Nor should we assume that because we see patriotic themes in some films, Indians are a particularly patriotic people. Just because Bollywood values love as the highest ideal, that does not mean that Indians think love is more important than anything else. The goal of this book is to understand how Bollywood makes meaning *through* its heavily mediated form: its artificiality, its hyperbole, its bright and unrealistic colors, and its constant breaks into song. Only by recognizing and knowing how to interpret these conventions can we then proceed to understanding

Bollywood's relationship to society. Without that, we run the risk of making simplistic sociological judgements about India that impede, rather than encourage, cross-cultural understanding. In addition, we risk losing the pleasurable excesses of Bollywood films and reducing them to their theme or ultimate message.

The fan and the critic

There is a particular challenge in writing an academic book about a subject whose popularity rests on the immense pleasure it gives its millions of viewers. There is a danger of squelching that pleasure in the name of academic analysis.[41] This book is written with that challenge in mind, with the intention of explaining the grammar of Bollywood without losing sight of the pleasure it gives. The discussion here is meant to make the pleasure of Bollywood meaningful within a larger context, rather than to use academic language to apply a rigid analytical frame to that pleasure or, worse, to expose the hidden ideological meanings behind the construction of that pleasure. How can we, this book asks, be *both* fans and critics, both partake of the pleasures offered by a medium and still understand and analyze how it works?

Although the divide between fans and critics is long-standing, it has arguably become more dichotomous in recent decades, as film criticism, both academic and journalistic, finds a certain joy in debunking, revealing to be false, ideologically critiquing or simply dismissing the unique pleasures of Bollywood cinema. But these accusations are often made based on superficial readings that compare Bollywood to other, very different modes of representation rather than seeing how the films work on their own terms. By contrast, Rosie Thomas writes, "what seems to be needed is an analysis which takes seriously both the films and the pleasures they offer."[42] Indeed, understanding how people derive pleasure from the films is central to understanding how they work and what they mean.

Thus, where Bollywood films offer new political imaginaries and awaken new affective engagements, these do not occur in a space apart from pleasure and enjoyment. As choreographer and director Farah Khan said about her film *Main Hoon Na* (2004), "Instead of preaching and … making a really boring film and putting [a] message in, it would be nice to make a complete entertainer which people would watch again and again, and *then* put a message of peace in it."[43] This is very much in the spirit of Bollywood. As viewers, we can find historical value, political meanings, and social messages in Bollywood films, but those must be viewed through the many pleasures of the genre. Otherwise, we might miss precisely the message we are looking for.

Part I

1 Structure

Although Bollywood films vary widely in terms of stories, contexts, and characters across time and across individual films, understanding the basic structure is essential to appreciating how films innovate on that structure. Most Bollywood films operate over a Manichean moral universe of good versus evil. In the most basic plot structure, the moral universe is established, then it is disrupted, and by the end of the film, it is restored. While that basic formula is shared across many films, the qualities attached to each side in the moral universe, the nature of the disruption, and the way it is restored vary widely, thus offering a significant range of possibilities for plots even while using the same basic formula. The moral universe is *always* restored, the hero *always* prevails over the villain, but what that hero represents, the values s/he espouses, and who the villain is changes across films. Recognizing both the consistency of the structure and the way it is subject to variety and repetition across time is the first key to understanding how Bollywood films work and how they make meaning.[1]

Genre

Genre is a word we often use to classify films and works of literature into different kinds (and indeed, the word *genre* comes from the French word for "a kind"), like comedy, romance, horror, and so on. But genres are not only inert categories. They also set the audience's expectations, the parameters for interpretation. In other words, we evaluate works of art differently based on what genre we understand them to be. For instance, it wouldn't make sense for someone to watch a romantic comedy like *Crazy Rich Asians* and say they didn't like it because it wasn't scary enough. Likewise, it would be ridiculous to criticize a Star Wars movie for not being funny. We evaluate films based on the thematic and formal expectations they set up for themselves, and then judge how well they live up to those expectations.

Yet despite this, the term "genre films" – like its print equivalent "genre fiction" and like the adjective "generic" – is often used in a negative sense, reflecting a widely held notion about the difference between "good" and "bad" art against which any study of Bollywood (like any study of science fiction, or chick lit) must contend. Leo Braudy argues that the "prejudice for the unique"[2] that inheres in the critique of genre films comes from European Romanticism's privileging of originality and individual creativity in the evaluation of art. This results in a bias against commercial art, or anything that would have wide appeal, with the implication that anything too popular or too formulaic is not truly art. These views are prevalent in contemporary film criticism, including film reviews and scholarship, which tend to value originality as a positive quality, as opposed to words like "formulaic," "derivative," "stock," and "clichéd," which are always coded as negative. We also see, in film reviews of Bollywood in particular, what Braudy calls the "snide synopsis"[3] – when a film critic or viewer summarizes the plot of a formulaic movie in simplistic and dismissive tones, as if all you need to know about the film can be summed up in two sentences. The snide synopsis reduces the plot to its barest features and suggests that there is little of value in a film whose plot is so simple or predictable.[4]

The disdain of genre films sees genre as restrictive, as putting limitations on individual creativity or the author's originality, and as simply profit-seeking; but we might also see genre as productive, as setting parameters that filmmakers have to abide by while still producing an enjoyable and engaging film. This is, for instance, how we read a sonnet. We do not criticize a sonnet for being too short, or for not varying its meter; instead, we are impressed that a particular poet was able to be so inventive within so restricted a form. The same might apply to Bollywood films; the conventions make films legible but what a particular film does *with* the conventions is what makes it enjoyable and successful.

In this way, saying a Bollywood film is predictable does not take us very far. All Bollywood films are, in the most general sense, predictable: characters do not change or surprise us, and we know there will be a happy ending. But that doesn't mean that all films are the same or that we can't evaluate them in relation to one another. Rather, we need to understand the basic structure on which they operate and evaluate them in relation to that structure. This means reading *for* or *with* genre, rather than against it.[5] Films use common tropes and formulas to build on past films; sometimes, they tell new stories for new times, and other times, they give viewers the comfort of an oft-told tale.[6] Bollywood films offer variations on a theme rather than entirely new themes. Thus we should evaluate films not necessarily for what happens at the end but for how the film gets to that end. Genre films are fundamentally intertextual, meaning that they constantly refer to other films. There is a pleasure in seeing the same kind of film with slight variations. There is pleasure in seeing one star play similar characters or characters with the same name across several films; there is pleasure in watching similar stories again and again.[7]

Accusations that Bollywood films copy or plagiarize stories from other films are in most cases overstated. The use of recognizable formulas leads critics, both in India and abroad, to see Bollywood films as copies of similar Hollywood ones, but Bollywood's form and aesthetics are so distinctive that the differences are often more apparent than any similarities. There are, occasionally, official Bollywood remakes of Hollywood or South Indian films, but most times accusations of plagiarism function as subtle (or not-so-subtle) jabs against

Bollywood's formulaic qualities. The dismissive comments of critics who fixate on Bollywood's lack of originality help cement an overall sense that Bollywood is a derivative genre, unworthy of further analysis, rather than the admittedly more difficult task of looking at how its formulaic qualities actually work.

The moral universe

Film scholar Rosie Thomas defines Bollywood films as operating on an "ideal moral universe,"[8] which is the structure within which good and evil are established and conflicts get resolved. As Thomas writes, this moral universe does not represent any real cultural values, but is part of Bollywood's generic conventions.[9] Most films proceed in the following way: the moral universe is established (usually quite quickly), the moral universe is disrupted (the majority of the film), and then the moral universe is restored (again, very quickly, and right at the end).[10] Put in this way, films might seem frightfully predictable. But in fact, this basic structure allows for a surprising amount of variation.

Establishment of the moral universe

Early on in a film, certain clues will appear that establish its moral center. The moral center can be embodied by one or more characters, or it can be a sensibility. Most commonly, this sensibility is love: when you see a character in love, it is very likely that he or she is the moral center. But other moral values include family, belief in fate, religious faith while simultaneously respecting other religions, "love of one's country, and respect for justice, honesty, and principles."[11] In addition, cinephilia, or passion for films, is also a moral quality. Mothers, or respect for mothers, are almost always coded as good.[12]

Bollywood films are not subtle in their presentation of morality. When a character or sensibility is established as a moral center, the film will convey that centrality in no uncertain terms in the dialogue, through a song, *and*, most likely, through its visual style. Often the morality is underlined each time a character appears, for instance through a reprise of the film's theme song or colorful visuals. Moral characters are often able to do unbelievable things in Bollywood; in *Bobby* (1973), Jack Braganza is an elderly man who spends most of the day drunk, but he can win a physical fight when he needs to. In such cases, ability comes from morality rather than the other way around; Jack Braganza can fight well because he has morality on his side, he is not moral because he is a good fighter.

As viewers, we are given the clues to pick up on the moral universe right from the start. Knowing that love is so valued in Bombay cinema, when we hear a group of friends debating whether love or money is more important early on in *Paying Guest* (1957), and Shanti argues in favor of love, we immediately know that she will be the film's hero. Sometimes, there are competing clues and we have to decide which to value more. Early in *Dilwale Dulhania Le Jayenge* (1995), we are introduced to our hero, Raj, in a dream sequence where

Simran is fantasizing about the man of her dreams. His centrality to Simran's dream suggests that he is the hero. Yet when we first meet the actual Raj, he acts like a goofy, immature child, showing up late to his own graduation and disrespecting his father, suggesting a more questionable morality. This characterization continues as Raj does increasingly reprehensible things, like trick an older man into keeping his convenience store open past its opening hours so that he can buy beer. The immaturity, the deception, and the alcohol-drinking suggest serious character flaws in Raj, even though that early song sequence had presented him as the likely hero. What we gradually discover is that despite being immature, ultimately Raj believes in love and family. The conflict between these two sides of Raj in fact becomes the plot of the film, as Simran's father has to be convinced that this immature man has the qualities that would make him worthy of his daughter. This is an example where although the moral universe is established early on, enough ambiguity about Raj's character is left open to motivate the narrative.

In the many Bollywood films that are love stories, the moral universe is founded upon love. In these films, the hero is the lover, and the disruption to the moral universe occurs when a character, several characters, or another force impedes the lover in attaining her or his beloved, whether family, an accident or death, a rival lover, or something else. Love is tied so deeply to Bollywood morality that it even trumps love of family, love of country, or other important values. Chapter 2 offers a detailed discussion of love in Bollywood.

Fate is also an important signal of the moral universe. If something is fated in a Bollywood film, usually that means it is the moral center. In a love story, the lovers' paths might cross even before they have met or even heard of one another, suggesting that their love is fated. In *Sarfarosh* (1999), Seema's dupatta blows off her body and randomly lands on Ajay, precipitating their meeting and their eventual romance. This sense of fate or divine will is not connected to a particular god or religion; it is fate more in the melodramatic sense, a popularized version of karma, or cosmic justice. This belief in fate is summed up in the protagonist's line in *Om Shanti Om* (2007), when he says: "Kehte hain ki … agar kisi cheez ko dil se chaaho toh poori qayanat use tumse milaane ki koshish mein lag jaati hai" ("It is said that if you want something with your full heart then the entire universe will work to try to make sure you get it"). In *Karz* (1980), fate is defined as the debt (the eponymous *karz*) that Monty, a reincarnation of the murdered Ravi, has to repay to Ravi's mother and to society as a whole. Although he begins as a devoted lover to Tina, once he realizes the extent of this past obligation he pursues its redemption single-mindedly, thus prioritizing his *karz* over his love.

But despite the black-and-white morality that is often established early on, individual films also play with typical heroic traits to tell new kinds of stories. Thus, what counts as good and evil can be different across time and in different films. In *Sarfarosh* (1999), the hero is an Indian police officer who exposes a Pakistani spy, whereas in *Main Hoon Na* (2004), the hero is an army officer saving India from a rogue Indian soldier who hates Pakistan. Both films operate on the same basic formula, but *Main Hoon Na* resignifies what counts as heroism and patriotism to mean peace with Pakistan rather than continuing enmity.

Disruption of the moral universe

Once the moral universe is established, most films show its disruption, which constitutes the film's plot. The nature of the disruption will vary based on what values are associated with the moral universe. If the moral universe is centered around love, then the disruption will be something that impedes that love from flourishing. If the moral universe is centered around family, then the disruption will often take the form of a family separation, what is known as a lost-and-found plot (discussed further below). If the moral universe is centered around love of one's country, then the disruption will be an enemy of the country. The key to understanding a particular Bollywood film is identifying the moral universe and the nature of its disruption.

Often, evil is presented as resolutely evil, with no shades of grey, and like the moral universe, evil is established resolutely and without subtlety. Qualities of Bollywood villainy are the opposite of those of Bollywood heroism: a lack of faith in love, an excessive or lustful sexuality, mistrust or misguided love of country, religious chauvinism, disrespect for elders, especially the mother, and mistreatment of women.[13] Villainy is represented visually and aurally through foreboding music (often recurring), dark lighting, dark-colored costumes, an abundance of "gadgetry ... [and] slick style,"[14] and hyperbolic makeup and facial expressions. Bollywood has some terrible, memorable villains. A Bollywood villain often has all the bad traits one can ever imagine rolled into one character. Perhaps the most famous of these is Gabbar Singh, from *Sholay* (1975), who is so sadistic that he kills children, dismembers his enemies, and shoots his own henchmen just for fun. Another is Mogambo from *Mr. India* (1987), whose catchphrase is "Hail Mogambo, King of India!" accompanied by a Hitleresque salute, and who puts bombs in children's toys and kills his enemies and even his own soldiers by forcing them to jump into a vat of boiling acid.

But even human-like villains have easily recognizable villainous traits. In *An Evening in Paris* (1967), when we find out that Shekhar has gambling debts and is an alcoholic, we immediately know he is the villain. In *Kati Patang* (1971), Kailash demands that his pregnant lover have an abortion, a misogynistic dictate always associated in Bollywood with villainy. In *Seeta Aur Geeta* (1972), when Chachi wishes for the death of her mother-in-law, we know she is the villain; likewise with Ranveer Chopra in *Tamanna* (1997), who leaves his three babies out to die because they are girls, physically and mentally abuses his wife, and is unashamed about having a mistress.

Sometimes villains are exaggerated expressions of larger social or political problems. In *Purab Aur Paschim* (1970), the villain is Onkar, an Indian man alienated from his homeland by having lived in the west too long, who wears leather, is a sexual predator, and ends up hitting his mother and shooting his own grandfather. In *Amar Akbar Anthony* (1977), the separation of the family, which constitutes the disruption in the moral universe, is caused by two factors: the selfish greed of Robert, who represents India's wealthy and uncaring elite, and the failure of Indian secularism, represented by the three brothers going in different directions despite being left by their father at the base of a statue of Gandhi. In *Main Hoon Na* (2014), the disruption of the moral universe takes place when a former commando in the Indian Army tries to disrupt plans for a prisoner exchange between the two historical enemies, India and Pakistan. Likewise, a common trope, especially in films before the 1990s, is that excessive wealth is inherently corrupting, so even when a moral character finds wealth, that wealth can lead him or her to immorality. This happens with Raju in *Guide* (1965) as well as with Kishenlal in *Amar Akbar Anthony* (1977), both of whom are good men who become immoral when they become rich. There are, however, exceptions to these rules: Deepa in *An Evening in Paris* (1967) is the film's hero and is wealthy but remains morally uncorrupted, and Meenakshi in *Aiyyaa* (2012) is obsessed with sensuality but she is nonetheless the film's moral center.

Conventions for representing villainy also change over time. Classic signs of villainy in the 1960s and 1970s included references to hunting, smoking or drinking alcohol, wearing leather, eating meat, gambling, and speaking with an affected English accent. (These are often exaggerated; the villain in *Deewana* [1992] is in one scene surrounded by *dozens* of full whiskey bottles, as if to make sure the audience does not miss the point!) In both *Ram Aur Shyam* (1967) and *Dostana* (1980), the villains Gajinder and Daaga have a stuffed tiger in their dens, and Gajinder also has various stuffed animal heads mounted on his walls. Kamini in *Karz* (1980) and Aarti's stepmother in *Raja Hindustani* (1996) smoke and drink, immediately suggesting their immorality. (Even in this period, however, there were exceptions, such as Raka in *Seeta Aur Geeta* [1972], who is portrayed as a drunk, but a lovable one, in need of a strong romantic partner to nudge him toward the right path.) By contrast, in post-2000s films it is not uncommon to see a film's hero, even a female hero, drinking in a bar or smoking a cigarette. Conversely, in some earlier films like *Kabhi Kabhie* (1976) and *Chandni* (1989), the male hero is presented as somewhat aggressive in his behavior toward the woman he falls in love with, whereas in newer films directors are usually more sensitive about valorizing stalking, aggressiveness, and other forms of male predatory behavior. Understanding who is the hero or heroine requires understanding, at least in part, the dominant conventions of the day.

In the above cases, it is fairly clear who the villain is, but at other times villainy does not reside in one character but is established *through* the disruption in the moral universe. For instance, parents' disapproval of a daughter or son's love interest can turn them into villains even when, in another film, the family might be the moral center. This common formula – the lover versus the patriarch, in which the lover usually wins – often surprises viewers who think that Bollywood always espouses patriarchal values. This conflict will be discussed further in Chapter 2.

There also exist "semi-villains," to use Rosie Thomas's term[15] – characters who think they are acting morally but have lost or been alienated from morality and are thus misguided. A common case of this is a patriarch who *thinks* he has his child's well-being at heart but in fact does not (as in *Dilwale Dulhania Le Jayenge* [1995]), or a lover who gets distracted and begins to privilege other things, like his family, over his beloved (as in *Damini* [1993]). These are not quite villains, as they are "really acting out of a misguided sense of love for [their] family"[16] and thus their "transgressions are forgivable."[17] Unlike the unshakeable evil villains above, these characters have the capacity for change once they see the situation differently and the restoration of the moral universe requires their change of heart rather than their destruction.

Restoration of the moral universe

The criticism of Bollywood's predictability comes from the fact that the vast majority of films have happy endings. It is true that in most films the moral universe is restored by the end. But *how* that restoration happens is not always self-evident. In part, the nature of the restoration depends on the nature of the disruption. If the moral universe centers on the romantic couple whose union is objected to by some person or force, then the film's resolution requires that the couple overcome that force to unite at the end. If the impediment to love is a controlling patriarch, then the resolution will happen when the patriarch changes his mind. More rarely, we have one member of the couple impeding the love plot, and the moral universe is only restored when she realizes that the one she thought she loved is not in fact the one she is supposed to be with, as in *Hum Dil De Chuke Sanam* (1999). In all these cases, the moral universe is restored, but in different ways.

In films where the villain is the embodiment of evil, the restoration of the moral universe requires the villain's capture and imprisonment, as in *Kashmir Ki Kali* (1964), *Sholay* (1975), and *Amar Akbar Anthony* (1977), or, more extremely, his death, as in *Dostana* (1980), *Mr. India* (1987), *Darr* (1993), and *Main Khiladi Tu Anari* (1994). But when the villain is really a semi-villain, the moral universe is restored not via force, but via moral certitude, i.e. the hero's strongly felt belief that fate will ultimately triumph if she stays on the righteous path. In *Hum Dil De Chuke Sanam* (1999), Vanraj never tries to convince Nandini to love him back, even though they are meant for each other; far from it, he actually tries to reunite her with her former lover. It is that devotion to moral truth rather than a self-serving ethics that marks Vanraj out as a hero and thus the correct lover for Nandini, even though for most of the film, she does not realize it. Similarly, in *Dilwale Dulhania Le Jayenge* (1995), although even Simran's mother advises Raj and Simran to elope rather than seek her father's blessing, they refuse, with Raj convinced that he will be able to change the patriarch's mind. Noble action and staying the course are thus presented as a moral compass that will ultimately bring the moral universe to its rightful state.

This is clear in the short fight scene at the end of *Dilwale Dulhania Le Jayenge* (1995); while physical prowess is often an element of (male) heroism in Bollywood, here Raj physically fighting with Kuljeet's henchmen actually marks a lapse in his judgement, as it threatens to distract him from his moral mission to convince the patriarch of his worthiness for Simran. In this case, physical violence is detrimental to his cause, and he has to stop himself before he goes too far. The restraint he exhibits by *not* punching Baldev is what eventually changes Baldev's mind, making his a moral rather than physical victory. In *Bobby* (1973) as well, Raj's parents are so corrupted by money and prejudice that Raj has no choice but to elope, and only by acting as if to commit suicide rather than being swayed by his parents' pressure do Raj and Bobby compel Mr. Nath to change his mind and permit their marriage.

However, in some cases the forces of moral disorder are so strong that staying the course cannot bring about a happy ending. In *Devdas* (1955), the protagonist's self-destruction after not being allowed to marry his true love precludes any possible happy ending. In *Qayamat Se Qayamat Tak* (1988), the patriarchal family is so unyielding that the only "happy" ending involves the couple finding union in their death.

In cinema halls in India, it is standard practice for audience members to simply get up and leave once they know how the moral universe will restore itself, which usually comes 1–5 minutes before the end of the film. Bollywood films rarely have denouements after the moral universe has been restored. In a context in which a certain ending is expected, the pleasure is in the *how* rather than the *what*. Consequently, there is often little closure: the film can end on a kiss or an embrace once the lovers realize they can be together, or on a shot of the reunited family, but rarely moves forward to show, even for one shot or scene, what happens next. In *Guddi* (1971), the film ends at the very moment Navin and Kusum profess their love. In *Dostana* (1980), once the two estranged friends have defeated the villain together and thus redeemed their friendship, the film immediately ends. In *Dil Dhadakne Do* (2015), the union between Kabir and Farah is not even shown on screen; the film ends when Kabir realizes he needs to follow his love and his father realizes he needs to support his son, but the actual romantic reunion is left to our imagination.

Repetition and coincidence

Bollywood films are structured over repetitions and coincidences that serve the establishment and maintenance of the moral universe by tying particular events, characters, occurrences, gestures, lines of dialogue, and musical refrains to fate. Tropes are often repeated across films, "the problems of one generation recur in the next,"[18] and sensing the meaning of these repetitions is key to understanding a particular film's moral universe. As Corey Creekmur writes of *Devdas*, the narrative "is strongly marked by a literally redundant pattern of departures and returns that carry Devdas between his traditional village … and the modern city of Calcutta … a circular action mirrored by the increasingly repetitive activity that embeds Devdas in the cycle of addiction."[19] In a lost-and-found film such as *Amar Akbar Anthony* (1977), the energy of the initial dispersal of the family produces the desire for an ultimate reunion; thus the repetition of tropes – the burial of the toy gun and then its discovery, the blinding of the mother and then her regaining her eyesight, Robert forcing Kishenlal to clean his shoes and then Kishenlal forcing Robert to clean his, and so on – become modes of developing a structure of parallelism that strengthens the overall plot and enhances viewing pleasure.[20] Repetition is also found in *Deewaar* (1975): when the family first comes to Bombay they are homeless and have to sleep under a footbridge. Later, when the boys have grown up and they are both professionally successful, they meet again under that bridge, which now has come to mark the different paths they took in life, with Ravi becoming a policeman and Vijay a criminal. Likewise, the temple is the site of the first divergence between the two brothers and it is at the temple where Vijay asks to meet his mother just before his death. Here, when flashbacks are used, it is less to establish a historical or psychological explanation for a character's actions than to underline the way history repeats itself and to incite the viewer's recognition of patterns across time.

Coincidence is also a common feature of Bollywood films, suggesting that the moral resolution of the film is fated. Coincidences structure plots, making possible reunions, such as in *Karz* (1980), when Monty meets the sister of Ravi, the man of whom he is a reincarnation, working as a maid in a wealthy house. Although she introduces herself as Laxmi, he immediately recognizes her as Ravi's sister Jyoti, and their reunion sets the stage for Monty's revenge on Ravi's murderers. In *Baazigar* (1993), it is the coincidence of Ajay and Priya running into his childhood friend Vicky at a nightclub that foils Ajay's violent plans for revenge. In *Kati Patang* (1971), there is a series of coincidences that structures the film's plot: Madhu leaves a man at the altar to elope with her lover instead; when she discovers her lover is cheating on her, she moves in with a friend at whose house she ends up meeting the very man she was initially arranged to be married to. Later, she meets a dancer at a club who turns out to be the woman her lover was cheating on her with. These coincidences make possible the film's ultimate resolution. In *Seeta Aur Geeta* (1972), the happy ending occurs only because Raka and Geeta's mother inexplicably end up at Seeta's family's house. In *Silsila* (1981), when Amit and Shobha have a car accident, the doctor at the hospital happens to be Chandni's husband, and the policeman who sees Amit and Chandni together turns out to be a relative of Shobha's. In this case, these multiple coincidences suggest a sort of claustrophobia in the social world that increasingly drives Amit, the protagonist, to despair. In *Aradhana* (1969), Vandana coincidentally meets her son – who does not know he is her son – after spending years in jail for murder. Across all these films, coincidence is linked to fate – a sort of divine will that brings separated family members together. Thus in *Aradhana*, although Vandana does not want anyone to tell her son that she is his mother, her friend insists, "Mere hisaab se toh nahin hogi. Lekin agar bhagwan hai, toh ek din woh zaroor jaan jayega ki uske asli maa-baap kaun hai" ("I won't tell him, but if there is a God, then one day he'll surely find out who his real parents are"), suggesting that familial unity is fated – or, as Suraj's adopted mother later articulates it, that "khoon ne khoon ko pehchan liya" ("blood has recognized blood"). And indeed, even without being told the truth, Suraj coincidentally ends up finding old photos and a letter that reveal to him the truth of his parentage. As with many lost-and-found plots, the film ends almost right at the moment when the reunion occurs and all is now right with the world.

In the lost-and-found film *Amar Akbar Anthony* (1977), the members of the separated family constantly run into one another to an extent that is only explicable through the logic of coincidence. Early in the film, the mother is hit by a car and needs a blood transfusion and the three men they find to donate blood happen to be her three biological children, whom she was separated from many years earlier. Throughout the film, the mother, brothers, and eventually the father continue running into one another without knowing they are related: Anthony and the mother attend Akbar's qawwali performance, Anthony gets arrested by Amar, a police officer, Anthony runs into trouble with Kishenlal, his biological father, and so on. These meetings structure the plot of the film, even though there are other threads as well, such as the three brothers' love interests. Besides signaling a larger cosmic order, this constant meeting of the family is fun to watch and builds anticipation for the plot resolution.

At times, the use of repetition and coincidence verges on the ridiculous, with such an abundance of repeated tropes and meetings that the plot seems even more impossible than usual. But impossibility is embraced in Bollywood films. The final song of *Amar Akbar Anthony* sums up this aesthetic in its absurd lyrics: "Unhoni ko honi karke honi ko unhoni, ek jagah peh jama ho teenon: Amar Akbar Anthony" ("Making the impossible possible and the possible impossible is what happens when the three of us get together: Amar, Akbar, and Anthony"). Here the absurdity of the whole plot – and indeed of Bollywood films more generally – is highlighted in the song;[21] by calling attention to the improbability of this scene's ending, which relies on an abundance of impossible coincidences, the song sequence is both a fitting accompaniment to that ending and generates a cinephilic exuberance. The fact that all three actors are looking straight into the camera in this scene underlines the cinephilic pleasure found in Bollywood's absurdity.

Character types

As a feature typical to the genre, Bollywood characters tend to be types rather than realistic individuals. They are not tied to particular historical moments but have a "culture-free appeal," often bearing generic names like "Ravi" or "Raj" that are not identifiable by region. These features make the characters and the obstacles they face seem to transcend time and space.[22] We are rarely given any insight into *why* a character acts the way she does; we rarely get explanations for either heroism or villainy. How a character responds to a situation has more to do with how her type might respond than with individual motivation. For instance, a lover is a character type who is stricken with emotion when s/he first sees her/his beloved. If the lover fails to act in that way, there is something wrong either with the character or with the moral universe. Likewise, a lover's dogged pursuit usually convinces a beloved to reciprocate the lover's love. If that does not happen, then something is wrong and needs to be fixed. Thus part of interpreting a Bollywood film is knowing what the character types are and how they typically act. That is what allows viewers to notice variations on a type as well as disruptions in the moral universe.

In addition, inner psychological conflicts are externalized.[23] A rainstorm might express grief, as with Anjali's sadness in *Kuch Kuch Hota Hai* (1998), just as thunder and lightning might register foreboding. In *Andaz* (1949), a strong wind becomes the externalization of Neena's inner turmoil. This is why visual style (discussed further in Chapter 4) is so important for understanding Bollywood; visuality is more than a means of conveying setting but often expresses inner moods.

Bollywood characters are sometimes stereotypically portrayed, especially villains: the vamp is a typical female villain, just as the wealthy, westernized dandy is a typical male villain. In older films, Christian characters were sometimes associated with immorality.[24] However, sometimes these stereotypes are exposed as false in the films themselves. For instance in *Deewana* (1992), it is the villain, Dhirendra Pratap, who calls the protagonist a "slut," thus associating such stereotyping itself with villainy. In *Bobby* (1973), Jack Braganza begins as a stereotype of a Christian character – often drunk and in disheveled dress – but he turns out to be the film's true hero, thus refusing the stereotype. Indeed, unlike the more respectable high society of Raj's family, Jack Braganza has a firm moral compass: he sees through social hypocrisy and has unwavering principles, and he can recognize Bobby and Raj's love for what it is, true love, whereas the rich Hindu family refuses to. As in *Deewana*, it is Mr. Nath, the villain, who takes one look at Mr. Braganza and assumes he will do anything for money; in these cases, typecasting and stereotyping are themselves represented as negative qualities.

Kinship

After love, the next most important thematic center of the moral universe is the family unit.[25] A family is generally coded as morally good in Bollywood, and so any disruption to that family will have to be restored, with the exception of when the family impedes the more highly valued love plot. As Rosie Thomas writes, within the family, it is the mother who occupies the place of highest moral authority.[26] If something bad happens to the mother, it is coded as *really* bad. Likewise, the absence of a mother can make all other successes unfulfilling, as in *Karz* (1980), in which Monty has wealth and fame but misses "maa ka pyar" ("a mother's love"). Later in *Karz*, the mother is the only character who recognizes her dead son reincarnated in Monty, showing the power of a mother's love and intuition. When others try to convince her that reincarnation is impossible, she refuses to believe them: "Ishwar sab ko dhokha de sakta hai lekin maa ke dil ko nahin!" ("God can deceive everyone but not a mother's heart!") – and, in the end, she is proven right. In *Om Shanti Om* (2007), another reincarnation plot, it is also the mother who recognizes her reincarnated son before anyone else can. In classic Bollywood melodramas, the mother is lifted almost to the position of a goddess; she also represents "Mother India," or the nation-as-mother, an image that circulated during the nationalist movement in India beginning in the late nineteenth century.

However, Bollywood mothers are also fallible. Sometimes, this fallibility is inexplicable and cannot be redeemed, such as Ashok's unkind mother in *Love in Tokyo* (1966) who goes so far as to curse her son's love interest, Asha, or in *Nagina* (1986), when Raju's mother cannot accept his love for Rajni, and so has to die in order for the couple to live happily ever after. Usually, however, a mother's lapse is the consequence of some other, external force that is *causing* her to go astray. In *Amar Akbar Anthony* (1977), Bharati abandons her children, but it is only because she has been made helpless by the greed and mendacity of her husband's wealthy employer. Thus Bharati's flight is a moral failing attributed to excessive wealth and the moral corruption of society at large. In *Deewaar* (1975), the mother chooses one of her sons to go to school while the other has to work, leading to a profound disequilibrium in the familial unit that has significant consequences for both brothers' futures. But this misjudgement is attributed to a fundamentally unjust world in which children must work instead of going to school. The mother's choice of one son over the other engenders a perverse psychosexual dynamic that repeats itself in a range of Bollywood films, as discussed in Chapter 7.

The sibling bond also has an inherent morality that must be restored by the end of a film. In *Amar Akbar Anthony* (1977), the three brothers separated at birth are adopted and raised by fathers from different religions; thus their reunion allegorically signifies the coming together of India's three main religions – Hinduism, Islam, and Christianity – as brothers. In *Karan Arjun* (1995), the reincarnated brothers at first think they are enemies, but only when they unite can they defeat the villain. This is true of *Main Hoon Na* (2014) as well. Both these films make reference to the Hindu epics (in *Main Hoon Na* the brothers are named Ram and Lakshman, two brothers from the *Ramayana*, and Karan and Arjun are close friends from the *Mahabharata*), suggesting that brotherhood is not just a worldly relationship but a spiritually sanctified one as well.

Conversely, a family member who turns her back on the family or willingly refuses to recognize or acknowledge a member of her family is immediately understood to be a villain. In *Pyaasa* (1957), Vijay's brothers pretend not to know him in order to support the false claim that he has died, so they can claim royalties from his successful poetry collection. In *Purab Aur Paschim* (1970), Harnam sells out his freedom fighter brother to British soldiers, resulting in his brother's death, and he travels abroad with the reward money. Later in the same film, London-based Mohan – corrupted by western values – beats up his father-in-law when he comes to bring him home. And in *Umrao Jaan* (1981), Umrao Jaan's mother and brother turn her away when she returns home to reconcile with them because they are ashamed of her profession as a courtesan. All these characters are unquestionably villains.

Orphans (such as Vandana in *Aradhana* [1969], Seeta in *Seeta Aur Geeta* [1972], Lakshmi in *Amar Akbar Anthony* [1977], and Raja in *Raja Hindustani* [1996]) are to be pitied because they lack blood relations, but often are able to form fictive kinship bonds as discussed in the next section, which reintegrate them into a family unit. Two exceptions are Rahul, the villain in *Darr* (1993), whose mother's death led to a lack of socialization that is partly presented as the reason behind his compulsive and violent behavior, and Ajay in *Baazigar* (1993), who was so traumatized by the injustice his father faced that he becomes sociopathic. Both these films' brief forays into psychological explanations for character represent exceptions to Bollywood's typical stock characterization. Conversely, characters who are prejudiced against orphans, such as Meena's parents in *Waqt* (1965), are presented as morally lacking, because they mistake biological isolation for social isolation.

Fictive kinship[27]

Bollywood films often center on the intrinsic morality of the kin relation, but this does not refer only to biological bonds but also adoptive, chosen, and other bonds created and realized through kindness and love among otherwise unrelated people.[28] The adoptive family, like the biological family, is the center of the moral universe, as in *Amar Akbar Anthony* (1977), where the expression of kin relations in language – calling an older woman "Maa" ("mother") or calling a friend "bhai" ("brother") – is presented as productive of kinship; thus, that person must forever be treated like a mother or brother. Sometimes the importance of adopted kin is specifically named; in *Kashmir Ki Kali* (1965), when Champa finds out she is adopted, she tells her father, "Jo bhi ho, jaise bhi ho, mere baba ho" ("Whoever you are, however you are, you are my father"). We see a similar sentiment in *Ram Aur Shyam* (1967); when Shyam discovers he was adopted, he tells his mother, "Agar mujhe kisi aur maa ne janam diya hai, toh apna pyar aur kshama ki chhau mein tum ne hi pala hai, Maa" ("Even if some other mother birthed me, it is you who have raised me in the shade of your love and kindness"). In *Kuch Kuch Hota Hai* (1998), eight-year-old Anjali *wants* her father to marry again after her mother dies; she seeks out an adoptive mother. Likewise, parents who love their adopted children as their own constitute moral centers, as with Nandini in *Kabhi Khushi Kabhie Gham* (2001), whose love for her adopted son Rahul is possibly even stronger than her love for her younger, biological son Rohan.

Calling someone using kin terms is a moral act in Bollywood. In *Aradhana* (1969), the widowed jailer who welcomes Vandana into his home names her his "moonh-boli behen," meaning a sworn sister (lit., a sister in words). In *Guddi* (1971), Navin loans Kundan some money, which Kundan at first refuses, until Navin says, "Main koi gher nahin hoon. Aap mujhe bhai samjhiega" ("I'm no stranger. Consider me your brother"). By forging kinship with Kundan in language, the film establishes Navin as a moral character; the fact that Kusum is overhearing this conversation makes her see him as a worthy potential lover. In *Nagina* (1986), when Raju's mother forbids him from marrying Rajni because she is an orphan, Raju convinces her by saying, "Aap ki mamta ke jhau mein woh anath nahin rahegi" ("She won't remain an orphan if she receives your motherly love"), thus offering fictive kinship as an alternative to orphanhood. In *Deewana* (1992), Raja forms a bond with Ravi's mother after Ravi's death, so that Ravi's mother gets a surrogate son and Raja, who has broken ties with his oppressive father, regains a parent. Even when it turns out Ravi is still alive, thus reuniting the biological mother and son, she nevertheless retains a space in her life for *both* her "sons." In *Raja Hindustani* (1996), Raja describes his relationship with his Chachaji (meaning uncle, but in this case not biologically speaking) as "khoon ka nahin … dil ka hai" ("not of blood, but of the heart"). And in *Tamanna* (1997), when Tamanna is reunited with her biological mother and brother, she still chooses to live with her adopted family; this case is particularly interesting because her adopted family is comprised of a hijra (transgender) woman and her partner, so the queer adoptive family here trumps the heterosexual, biological one.

Conversely, if a character were to disregard fictive or adoptive kinship bonds, or consider them less important than blood bonds, it would call into question her/his morality. In fact, the disowning of an adoptive child is just as bad, and potentially even worse, than the disowning of a blood child, an action common to various evil stepmothers in films such as *Seeta Aur Geeta* (1972) and *Raja Hindustani* (1996). In *Karz* (1980), Monty's adopted father disowns him after he disobeys his orders, saying "Don't call me Daddy. Yaad rakho, tum mere bete nahin ho!" ("Remember, you're not my son!"). In *Kabhi Khushi Kabhie Gham* (2001), Yash initially loves his adopted son, but when Rahul announces he is marrying Anjali, Yash says one of the worst things an adoptive father could ever say in Bollywood: "Aaj tumne yeh sabit kar diya ki tum mere khoon nahin ho" ("Today you have proven that you're not truly of my blood"). In *Kal Ho Naa Ho* (2003), Gia's grandmother treats Gia badly because she was adopted. In *Mom* (2017), Aarti cannot see her stepmother as anything but a stranger, and the film shows how strong the mother's maternal bond is, despite not being biologically related; the moral universe is restored when Aarti realizes that her stepmother is in fact just like a real mother.

The lost-and-found plot

The lost-and-found is a typical plot structure that realizes the moral strength of kinship. The lost-and-found film involves the separation of the family, sometimes due to bad luck and at other times due to some external evil force. In both cases, the breakup of the family is the disruption of the moral universe so that the restoration of the moral universe requires its reunion. Once again, however, the accusation of predictability should be replaced by the more pleasure-inducing question of *how* the reunion comes about. In *Yaadon Ki Baarat* (1973), *Waqt* (1965), and *Amar Akbar Anthony* (1977) – all films about three brothers separated from each other at a young age – part of the pleasure in watching the films is the dramatic irony of watching characters who don't know they are related constantly meeting one another. In *Amar Akbar Anthony*, as discussed above, the members of the disunited family go so far as to call each other by kinship names, referring to each other as "bhai" ("brother"), "maa" ("mother"), and "beta" ("son"), even though they don't know they are related. In India, it is common to use kinship terms to refer to acquaintances and even strangers; in these films, that practice is rendered ironic as the characters are unaware of their blood bond, and the pleasure is in seeing when and how they will finally realize it.[29]

There are other kinds of lost-and-found plots as well. In *Aradhana* (1969), Vandana's fiancé dies before they can be legally married, and so she has to give up their child – conceived out of wedlock – for adoption. Through a series of coincidences, Vandana ends up as the caretaker of her son's fiancée, even though he doesn't know she is his real mother. This film, like the ones mentioned above, drives towards its necessary resolution: we know that eventually the son will recognize his mother and the pleasure of the film comes in watching how that comes about. In *Fanaa* (2006), Zooni is blind when she and Rehaan begin their relationship; thus, when he re-enters her life after she has regained her sight, she does not immediately recognize him even though the viewers know who he is. Here too, their son seems to instinctively know that Rehaan is his father even though they have never met, and asks him permission to call him "Abba" ("father").

While the lost-and-found can be understood as a conservative formula dependent on the self-evident nature of blood bonds, in fact lost-and-found films such as *Amar Akbar Anthony* show two levels of kinship, one determined by blood and another (per)formed in language (i.e. being discursively "related" to an older women by calling her "Maa") and in action (i.e. caring for a person *as if* she were your mother). Blood bonds are certainly important, as articulated in *Amar Akbar Anthony*'s title song, "Khoon khoon hota hai, pani nahin" (roughly translated as "Blood is thicker than water"); but at the same time, the film is replete with language about the *making* of kinship across class and religious lines. For instance, Anthony talks about "making" Amar his brother, Bharati talks about "making" the three men her sons (which would make them brothers), and Anthony talks about "making" the judge his father. We see this in *Waqt* (1965) as well, when Raja discovers that he and Ravi are brothers before anyone else and he tells Ravi that he had a dream that they were brothers and Ravi responds, "Aao, hum ek dusre ko sachmuch bhai samajh ke lipat jaye" ("Come, let's hug as if we were really brothers"), effectively establishing their kinship even before it is validated by knowledge of their bloodline. This abundance of language to describe the forging of kinship in language means that despite the ideal of blood being thicker than water, Bollywood films simultaneously advance an idea of kinship that exceeds blood and biology. This dual level of kinship opens up the possibility that the family unit might include alternative, non-normative, and queer relations (discussed further in Chapter 7).

Lost-and-found plots usually rely on heavy amounts of coincidence. In *Waqt* (1965), the entire plot is structured in quite fantastical ways to get the three brothers, Vijay, Raja, and Ravi, to reunite: Vijay witnesses his boss murdering someone but promises to keep quiet in return for the money he needs for his mother's operation. Meanwhile, the same boss accuses Raja of the murder and Raja hires Ravi as his defense lawyer. In *Seeta Aur Geeta* (1972), the entire plot relies on Seeta finding herself among Geeta's family and vice versa, and the plot is structured over a large number of coincidental meetings.

Lost-and-found plots can also be about lovers lost and found. In *Kati Patang* (1971), Madhu and Kamal are destined for each other even though neither of them realizes it for most of the film. This is not quite a lost-and-found, but still mobilizes the dramatic irony of the audience knowing the lovers are destined for one another while the characters remain in the dark. In *Deewana* (1992), Ravi and Kajal marry, but he is believed to be killed by an evil relative, leaving Kajal to rebuild her life and marry again. When Ravi returns, he does not try to break the new relationship that Kajal has formed, but instead chooses to die since his love cannot be requited. This is a rare case when the lost-and-found *does not* resolve itself even though both the characters and the audience know that Ravi and Kajal are the rightful pair.

The lost-and-found is one of many conventions that structure Bollywood plots, reflecting their reliance on a relatively straightforward moral universe. As we have seen, even while these structures are repeated over and over again, they lend themselves to a surprising amount of variation. Understanding this basic structure and the possibilities for variation is the first step to understanding Bollywood films more generally.

2 Love

Romantic love is so central to Bollywood that it is better characterized as a generic feature than a thematic one. Morality is often associated with love; characters who believe in love are the heroes, and characters who are skeptical or dismissive of love are usually the villains. Bollywood love is conventionally presented as existing outside the rational world. It exerts a force that possesses men and women, that takes control over their minds and bodies, making them single-minded and distracted from all worldly responsibilities. At times, love can lead to the lover's destruction, as the material world is found to be too banal to accommodate true love. The image of the moth attracted to the flame, even though this attraction could ultimately lead to its death, is a powerful motif in Bollywood cinema, along with the valorization of *viraha*, or separation from one's beloved, as a necessary sacrifice for love to be true.[1] The hero is the character who truly understands the power of love. Some post-2000s films play with this convention, featuring characters who begin by scoffing at the idea of an all-consuming, Bollywood love, but then eventually begin to believe in it when it happens to them.

Pyar, ishq, mohabbat, and the English word "love" are all used to talk about love in Bollywood films. Love "happens" to characters, almost as if an external force. The lover can be an *aashiq*, a *premi*, a *dilwala*, a *mehboob/mehbooba*, a *majnun*, a *saajan*, a *sanam*, a *chahnewala*, or even a *deewana* (lit., crazy one). While these words have slightly different connotations, they all suggest that being a lover is an existential state that affects all aspects of life. To be a lover is the paragon of Bollywood heroism and the entire genre is built around this state.

The lover

Chapter 1 discussed how Bollywood films operate on a moral universe that is established, disrupted, and then restored. Very often, the moral universe is centered around love. Thus, the hero is the lover or the believer in love, and the disruption of the moral universe happens when some powerful force, whether it is family, a villain, a rival, or a socio-political issue, does not believe in or impedes the flourishing of love. Finally, the disruption is overcome and the love story can be requited. This is a formula that is commonly used, but because there are so many different possibilities for how a love story might be disrupted, it results in a surprisingly large and diverse number of plots.

The hero is the character who believes in love, even to the point of neglecting his or her other duties. Hindi films present the lover as, in the words of *Andaz Apna Apna* (1994), a "dilwala ladka," as opposed to a "dimaagh-wala ladka" – a young man driven by his heart, rather than by his head. There is something inherently moral about being driven by your heart, even if it means losing your reason. In *Mughal-e-Azam* (1960), Prince Saleem cannot focus on affairs of the state because of his all-consuming love for Anarkali. His father, King Akbar, reprimands him and tries to make him more responsible as a political leader, but Saleem has no interest in politics. The film shows Akbar going to greater and greater lengths to distract Saleem from Anarkali, first imprisoning her and then threatening to execute Saleem for treason, and finally deciding to have Anarkali killed by burying her alive, although he relents at the last minute and exiles her from the kingdom instead. These extreme measures reflect the problem a passionate, all-encompassing love poses from the perspective of the mundane world of politics.

Love distracts from more conventional masculine and patriarchal pursuits. In the first scene of *Kashmir Ki Kali* (1964), Rajeev is given control of his father's textile mill, but uninterested in money, he spontaneously promises to give ₹500,000 to each worker and leaves town, angering his mother, to sing a song about love instead. From this inability to rule in the world of commerce, we know that he is our hero. In the first scene of *Prem Kahani* (1975), we see Rajesh supposedly caught cheating on a test, but when we realize that he was distracted because he was staring at a picture of a woman, we know he is our hero. Set in the midst of the nationalist movement against colonial rule, Rajesh's brother is a nationalist poet and criticizes Rajesh for focusing on love rather than politics; but in fact, Rajesh is the hero precisely because he is a lover. We see this in *Qayamat Se Qayamat Tak* (1988) as well, when early in the film Raj performs a song at his college graduation in which he announces that he doesn't want to make his name as a famous engineer or businessman, but as a lover in the world of the heart ("Dil ki duniya mein apna naam karega"). In *Deewana* (1992), when Raja falls in love, he falls instantly and hard, to the point where it is experienced as an ailment rather than a positive experience. When his friends ask him what is wrong, he replies:

> Apni zindagi khud barbaad kar li maine! Jaante ho, har waqt uski tasveer meri aankhon ke saamne ubharti hai. Aur main tasveer se har waqt kehta hoon ki ja! Chale ja yahan se, peecha mat kar mera! Lekin har baar uska chehra aise ubharta hai mere saamne … Main kya karoon?

> [I have ruined my life! You know, her picture appears in front of my eyes all the time. And I always tell this picture, Go away from here, stop following me! But her face keeps appearing before me … What should I do?]

To this, his friend responds, "Tujhe ishq ho gaya hai, ab toh apni zindagi ko khuda hafiz kehna" ("You are in love, say goodbye to your life"). Although the dialogue might appear to be ironic, it is not intended as such, and Raja ends it by pounding his head violently against a wall, devastated at this new reality. And *Veer-Zaara* (2004) begins with Squadron Leader Veer Pratap Singh, an Air Force commander, undertaking heroic feats like rescuing people stranded on a snowy mountain by being released from a helicopter on a rope. However, when he falls in love with Zaara and she returns to her home in Pakistan, he gives up his position in the Air Force without hesitation in order to follow her there.

Whereas it is often the male hero whose love for his beloved is all-consuming, women are Bollywood lovers too. In *Pyaasa* (1957), Gulabo is passionately in love with Vijay before Vijay reciprocates. In *Lamhe* (1991), Pooja is the ideal lover and she pursues the more indifferent Viren until she can make him realize that he loves her too. In *Fanaa* (2006), Zooni is raised by her parents to value love above all else, and it is she who transforms Rehaan from a hardened soldier into a lover. In *Aiyyaa* (2012), Meenakshi falls in love with Surya at first sight, and her intense attraction to and desire for him leads her to neglect her work and her family. In *Ek Ladki Ko Dekha Toh Aisa Laga* (2019), the female protagonist is established as the lover, and so even when we find out that the object of her love is a woman, she remains the moral center while homophobia becomes the disruption of the moral universe. In *Veer-Zaara* (2004), Zaara asks her mother whether she thinks her husband would sacrifice his life for her, and her mother dismissively answers, "Ek aurat ki mohabbat aur ek mard ki mohabbat mein bahut fark hota hai" ("There's a big difference between men and women's love"), suggesting that women are more passionate than men. But Zaara refuses this distinction, insisting that the only love that is worthy of her is one in which the lover will sacrifice everything for the beloved, regardless of gender. In *Gunday* (2014) as well, Nandita makes it clear that she is a lover with agency rather than the passive object of a man's love, insisting, "Bikram ne mujhe behkaya nahin, apne baaton mein uljhaya nahin. Maine pyar kiya hai usse. Maine manga hai usse uska pyar apne liye" ("Bikram didn't seduce me or sweep me off my feet. *I* fell in love with him, I demanded his love").

Bollywood love should not be conflated with marriage; sometimes marriage is the rightful resolution of a love story, but other times marriage – especially marriage arranged by others – is represented as a socially sanctioned union that cannot contain the intensity of true love. In *Mahal* (1949), Hari Shankar is pressured into an arranged marriage but both he and his wife end up unhappy as he gets increasingly obsessed with another woman's ghost, whom he believes to be his true love. In *Love in Tokyo* (1966), Ashok is engaged to a woman whom he has no interest in; he falls madly in love with Asha and that is presented as true love, even if it requires that he renounce the arrangement with the other woman. In *Prem Kahani* (1975), both Rajesh and Kamini seem to agree that romance is more fun when it is illegitimate; after Rajesh has to hide to not be seen by her father, she flirtatiously asks him, "Aankhmichauni ke baghair, prem kahani kabhi nahin banti, hai na?" ("Without a little hide and seek, there's no love story, right?") And later, Rajesh defends his reluctance to get married by saying, "Yeh chori chori milne ki mazaa jaata rahega ... Shaadi ke baad ... ishq ka poora romance chaupat ho jayega" ("We'll lose the fun of sneaking around. After marriage, all of love's romance will be ruined"). In *Nagina* (1986), Raju rejects his mother's ideas of prestige and domesticity to pursue a woman with more erotic and transgressive appeal. And in *Kuch Kuch Hota Hai* (1998), Rahul marries Tina and they have a child together, but it is clear that Anjali was his true love, and when Tina dies they have an opportunity to unite.

In Bollywood, love is more important than any other ideal, socially accepted ritual, violence, or danger. Veer chooses a lifetime in prison rather than ruin Zaara's reputation by speaking publicly about their love in *Veer-Zaara* (2004). Many characters would rather die than renounce their love. Love can even be more important than religion; or rather, it is presented in many films as the essence of religion itself.

The ideal lover is steadfast in her/his love. Thus even when the villain in *Sholay* (1975) is torturing Basanti by forcing her, at gunpoint, to dance barefoot on shards of broken glass in front of Veeru, her lover, the song she sings signals her persistence: "Jab tak hai jaan, main nachungi" ("As long as I am still alive, I'll continue to dance"). The ideal lover can be so persistent that to today's viewers, his love might seem excessive. In *An Evening in Paris* (1967), Sam drops all his duties to follow Deepa not only around Paris, but to Switzerland and Beirut as well, following the credo that "Jis se pyar karte hain, qayamat tak toh uska peecha karte hain" ("An ideal lover will follow his beloved all the way to doomsday"). In *Paying Guest* (1957), Ramesh is presented as a "saccha premi" ("true lover") even though that means following Shanti around and even occasionally irritating her. Especially in older films when there was less awareness around issues like stalking, the dogged pursuit of one's beloved is presented as inherently moral.

Minor characters can also be ideal lovers, sometimes in ways that put into relief the flaws of the protagonist. Abdul Sattar in *Pyaasa* (1957) is dogged in his pursuit of Juhi, even as Vijay, the protagonist and Abdul's friend, fails to realize that he loves Gulabo. Sardar Makhan Singh, the driver in *An Evening in Paris* (1967), is also an ideal lover, as is Ashok's friend Mahesh in *Love in Tokyo* (1966).

Models of ideal lovers from folk tales and mythology include Heer and Ranjha, protagonists of an epic Punjabi romance, Radha and Krishna from Hindu mythology, and the Persian pairs Shirin and Farhad and Layla and Majnun. The latter couple is a particularly popular reference in Bollywood; Majnun, whose name means "the crazy one," offers a idealization of love premised on the lover's loss of reason. The j-n-n root to his name also appears in the Hindi-Urdu word *junoon*, which means passion but also possession by a jinn, signifying an irrational, out-of-body element to love.

Bollywood lovers are often young and sexually innocent: Prince Saleem in *Mughal-e-Azam* (1960), Champa in *Kashmir Ki Kali* (1964), Bhola in *Padosan* (1968), Raj and Bobby in *Bobby* (1973), Raj and Rashmi in *Qayamat Se*

Love 37

Qayamat Tak (1988), Prem and Suman in *Maine Pyar Kiya* (1989), Viren in *Lamhe* (1991), Prem in *Hum Aapke Hain Koun* (1994), Rahul and Tina in *Kuch Kuch Hota Hai* (1998), and so on. The innocent lover's open and non-jaded view on love makes him or her the perfect paradigm for Bollywood love. Love strengthens character; Ram in *Ram Aur Shyam* (1967) is a weak-willed man until the moment when he falls in love. Love is a means for young people to question the stranglehold of the past over the present; by refusing the pressure of their parents and normative society and expressing their own desires in a social context usually not very receptive to individualism, love is a pathway to new futures.

There are also lovers who have been burned once before but find love again, such as Brijmohan in *Chalti Ka Naam Gaadi* (1958), or lovers whose beloveds have died and who fall in love with someone else, such as Rahul in *Kuch Kuch Hota Hai* (1998). Rarer are older lovers, but there are a few. In *Waqt* (1965), the song "Meri Zohra Jabeen" is sung by Lala Kedarnath to his wife, and the lines explicitly refer to love in old age: "Tu abhi tak hai haseen/ Aur main jawaan" ("You are still beautiful and I am still young"). The elderly Bauji in *Veer-Zaara* (2004) is deeply in love with his wife and so committed to love more generally that he invents an entire tradition for his village in which men and women can publicly proclaim their love. In *Fanaa* (2006), Zooni's parents are deeply in love, talk constantly about love, and instill the value of love into their daughter. Both Raj's father in *Dilwale Dulhania Le Jayenge* (1995) and Rishi's father in *Kabhi Alvida Naa Kehna* (2006) are flirtatious widowers, and Mr. Malhotra and Ms. Braganza and Naina's grandmother and Mr. Chaddha engage in some heavy flirtation in *Kuch Kuch Hota Hai* (1998) and *Kal Ho Naa Ho* (2003), respectively.

Case study: Qayamat Se Qayamat Tak *(1988)*

Qayamat Se Qayamat Tak is a paradigmatic representation of young love. The film broke new ground when it came out in 1988.[2] It launched one future superstar (Aamir Khan had made one prior appearance in films, but only as a child actor) and secured the career of a second, Juhi Chawla; it had a first-time director, a young cinematographer, and new playback singers, Udit Narayan and Alka Yagnik, who brought a young and fresh sound to the film and ended up being the paradigmatic voices for romantic duets in the 1990s and beyond.[3] The story of two young lovers born into patriarchal, warring Rajput families and thus prevented from requiting their love, *Qayamat Se Qayamat Tak* created a new idiom in which to represent young love specifically, and youth and newness more generally. The original title of the film was "Nafrat Ke Waris" ("Inheritors of Hatred"), underlining how the older generation expects young people to inherit their hatreds and feuds, even when the young people simply want to move on. When the feuding families learn about Raj and Rashmi's love, on both sides they are convinced that if only the two lovers knew of their historical enmity, they would end the affair; but in fact, even when they find out, it changes nothing. Against this attempt to stifle young love with inherited hatred, Raj and Rashmi do their best to chart their own course. While this film ends with the lovers' tragic deaths, it sets the stage for a new representation of young love that has lasted until the present day.

Love and destiny

In Bollywood, love is part of one's destiny. This is why so many Bollywood lovers fall in love at first sight, which is less meant to be taken literally, than to emphasize love as part of some larger divine plan, rather than something within individual agency or control.

The idea of love as destined is conveyed in many Bollywood films. The first moment when a lover catches sight of the beloved is often emphasized in films by extradiegetic music, dramatic visuals, or even a song sequence. Sometimes slow motion is used, as in the very brief scene when Raj and Simran pass each other in Leicester Square in *Dilwale Dulhania Le Jayenge* (1995), before they have actually met. In this slowed-down moment of time, the film represents the Simran–Raj pairing as a destined match and thus reaffirms that their union is the center of the moral universe. That way, when various impediments arise to their love, including Raj's own immaturity, Simran's fiancé Kuljeet, and of course Baldev Singh, the patriotic patriarch, we are comforted in knowing that however hard they try, none of these impediments will actually succeed in pulling their union apart.

Sometimes destined love is so powerful that individual choices do little to thwart it. In *Kati Patang* (1971), Madhu leaves her arranged fiancé at the altar to run away with her lover, whom she quickly discovers is only interested in her for her money. Having eloped, however, she is compelled to stay away, and she decides to live with a woman she meets on a train, Poonam. At Poonam's house, she meets a man named Kamal – who, she later discovers, is the very man she had left at the altar, and, it turns out, the one she had been destined to be with. In *Fanaa* (2006), Rehaan renounces his love for Zooni but then finds himself at her doorstep by accident years later, rekindling his feelings and showing that his human action of abandoning her was powerless in the face of a destined love.

Sometimes, a destined love is so powerful it gains almost magical qualities. In *Chandni* (1989), Rohit expresses his love for Chandni by putting up photographs of her all over the walls of his room. When, after a paralyzing accident, he loses faith in their love and turns away from her (discussed in more detail below), the first thing he does is cover up her photographs with white paint, thus attempting to erase her presence from his life. But despite this attempt to actively forget her, the paint gradually fades and chips off, and the images of Chandni's face begin to reappear, as if magically signaling to him that despite his loss of faith, their love is still true (Figure 2.1).

Sometimes the idea of a destined love is innovated on. In *Mahal* (1949), Shankar hears the story of an ill-fated romance that had taken place 40 years earlier in the house he has just moved into, in which a couple had both

Figure 2.1 Chandni's face reappears through the paint on Rohit's wall, suggesting the indestructibility of their love, in *Chandni* (1989).

drowned. The man looked just like Shankar, which his friend dismisses as an "ittefaq" ("coincidence"), but which leads Shankar into a single-minded obsession with Kamini, the woman who died and who has now reappeared as a ghost, increasingly convinced that they were lovers in a past life. Shankar is so preoccupied with Kamini that he acts almost as if in a trance the entire film; he ignores his fiancée, who represents domesticity and the reproduction of the social structure. But in the end it turns out that the "ghost" was actually Asha, the gardener's daughter, who had made up the whole story in order to seduce Shankar. The fact that he falls for it, however, far from being a liability, shows that he is the hero – an ardent believer in love's ability to transcend time and even death – and he continues to call her Kamini rather than Asha. Although the audience understands that the love was not in fact destined in the way he had thought it was, Shankar continues to believe, and as he is sent to be hanged for murder (for which he was framed) at the end of the film, he promises to reunite with Kamini in his next life. In another innovation on destined love, in *Hum Dil De Chuke Sanam* (1999), Nandini is forced by her father to marry Vanraj, even though she is in love with Sameer. Through Sameer's dramatic introduction, his likeable personality, and the flirtatious banter he and Nandini exchange, the film suggests that he is her destined partner, but it isn't until later in the film that we realize, through his single-minded devotion to her, that her husband is actually better for her than her first love. Here love is destined, but the destined lover is not the one immediately perceived as such.

Love as intoxication

In many Bollywood films, love is presented as an overwhelming force over which the lover has little control. This comes in part from conventions for representing love in Urdu poetry, in which love is presented as an intoxication (*nasha*) that alters the lover's state of consciousness, reduces the functioning of reason, and at times makes the lover act in strange or irrational ways. Love is *pagalpan*, madness, and the lover is a *deewana/i*, or mad person.

In *Raja Hindustani* (1996), Aarti and Raja's first kiss takes place during a thunderstorm, an externalized state of intense passion that suggests that their desire for one another is out of their control. They kiss for several seconds, but then immediately afterwards are jolted back to the real world where they both realize they have done something wrong. After the couple makes love in *Aradhana* (1969), Vandana explains the lapse in her judgement by saying, "Hum apne hosh kho baithe" ("We lost our reason"). In *Chandni* (1989), Rohit is so passionately in love with Chandni that he marries her despite his parents' disapproval. Even after they are married, he takes every opportunity to show her how he feels, to almost absurd lengths. At one point he rents a helicopter and fills it with rose petals that he scatters over her as she stands on her terrace. When she calls him mad, he responds, "Hanh, main pagal hoon!" ("Yes, I'm mad!"). Sadly, however, the helicopter crashes and he is left paralyzed. The accident represents the extremes Rohit is willing to go to show how much he loves Chandni – beyond the scope of reason – which makes him a true hero in the world of Bollywood.

In *Veer-Zaara* (2004), as mentioned earlier, Veer quits his job in the Air Force just so he can follow Zaara to Pakistan. His quitting is never shown, suggesting that it was not a rational decision taken with due deliberation but an almost instinctive expression of his love for Zaara. When Veer goes to meet Zaara at the dargah (Muslim shrine) where Zaara's family is gathered along with her fiancé, the song sequence mobilizes the imagery of love as intoxication through the metaphor of the moth attracted to the flame. The lyrics of the qawwali speak to this sense of intoxication, inevitability, and mutual destruction:

> Aaya tere dar par deewana
> Yeh hai tera hi saudayi, yeh hai tera hi shahdayi
> Tere ishq mein hai isse mar jaana
> Aaya tere dar par deewana
> Zindagi haar doon main
> Jaise shama pe marta hai parvana
> Aaya tere dar par deewana
>
> [The lover has come to your door
> He belongs to you
> He wants to die for your love
> The lover has come to your door
> I will lose my life for you
> Just like a moth dies in a flame
> The lover has come to your door.]

As the song plays, Veer stands in the center courtyard of the dargah and holds his arms out in front of him; Zaara walks to him as if in a trance. Again here her actions defy reason, as she knows that this public declaration of their love will prove disastrous for them both. But the film suggests that the force of Veer's presence is so strong that Zaara cannot act in any other way; her instinct leads her toward her lover, which is simultaneously her destruction, like a moth to a flame.

In *Kal Ho Naa Ho* (2003), Naina's love for Aman is so overpowering that she experiences it like a curse, complaining to herself, "Why do I love him? Why!?" In *Aiyyaa* (2012), Meenakshi can smell Surya before he even enters a room, and scent is represented in this film as a heady, intoxicating, even supernatural sensory experience that is entirely bodily and not of this world. This becomes an apt metaphor for love: something beyond reason, of the senses, and to which the lover is drawn as if by instinct.

Madness, obsession, and self-annihilation

At times, intoxication verges on madness, an extreme state of love that takes over the mind and body of the lover to such an extent that his actions can become violent or self-destructive. This is particularly important to note when the lover is male and obsession drives him to stalk his beloved or pursue her with an intensity that looks like harassment. This kind of intensity has its origins in Urdu poetry and the Sufi tradition, in which love is presented as madness and at times destructive to both lover and beloved: love is a fire that destroys that which sustains it. As Francesca Orsini writes about love in Urdu poetry:

> The lover is always facing death, which he feels is a better fate than indifference; he is often wounded, since the beloved's eyes are like arrows, and his loving heart is bleeding. Or the beloved is a hunter and the lover is the captive prey. Madness and banishment are functions of true love, while death for true love is ecstasy.[4]

Sometimes love is represented as a haunting or possession, a fixation that the protagonist cannot shake and that drives him toward madness, as in the ghost story films *Mahal* (1949) and *Nagina* (1986). In both films, the beloved appears to the protagonist as a spectral presence in the form of a song, a brief glimpse, and, in *Nagina*, in the sound of her anklets. In both films, the haunting prohibits the protagonists from living their normal lives, including fulfilling their arranged marriages, as they become increasingly obsessed with the spirit. In *Nagina*, Rajni's mysterious hold on Raju is presented in marked contrast to the much more straightforward role of Vijaya, the bride Raju's mother has chosen for him. We learn that Raju had been sent abroad 15 years earlier because he had been plagued by nightmares; Rajni takes Raju further away from society, normalcy, family (specifically his mother), domesticity, and marriage; he cannot even speak to his mother, and he describes himself as *bechain* – a word often used, especially in Bollywood songs, to describe the condition of the lover – meaning restless or unsettled. He tells his mother:

Main Rajni ke baghair nahin jee sakta … Maine is ghar ki maryada, aap ki jazbaat … ke bare mein bahut socha. Lekin mujhe laga ki agar mere dil ki awaaz ko daba diya, toh ya toh main zinda nahin rahunga, aur agar haan, toh ek laash ki tarah.

[I can't live without Rajni. I've thought a lot about the family's prestige and your feelings, but I realized that if I suppress my heart's desires then either I'll die, or I'll live like a corpse.]

As in many Bollywood films, Raju means this literally; he *needs* Rajni, he cannot live without her, like a drug or intoxicant. These plots literalize the idea of love as madness. Likewise, as ghosts, both women embody the idea of being mysterious, ephemeral, and possibly unattainable, emphasizing the fact that once love becomes madness or intoxication, it rarely ends in the safe domesticity of marriage.

Despite obsessive love being idealized, actual stalking is considered immoral in Bollywood films. There is a fine line – not exactly the line we would draw today, but a line nonetheless – between devotion, even obsession over one's beloved, and stalking, sexual violence, and rape. In *Aradhana* (1969), Shyam tries to rape Vandana and she tries desperately to fend off his advances and defend herself. When her young son comes upon them and tries to defend Vandana, accidentally killing Shyam in the process, it is seen as a justified death. In *Seeta Aur Geeta* (1972), Ranjit tries to rape Seeta and, later, marry her forcibly, and he is resolutely this film's villain. The refrain of one of the songs in *Darr* (1993) is "Tu haan kar, ya na kar, tu hai meri Kiran" ("Whether you say yes or no, you are my Kiran") which is a statement of nonconsensual pursuit, but it is sung by Rahul, the film's villain. Rahul's flaw is his misguided understanding of Bollywood love; he mistakenly believes love means pursuit without reciprocation, even to the point of instilling fear (the titular *darr*) in his beloved. As his father says about him, "Itni chhoti si baat nahin samajhta hai ki ladki haasil karne ke liye, uska dil jeetna zaroori hota hai. Mangetar ka khoon karne se ladki thodi mil jayegi" ("He doesn't realize this simple thing, that to win a woman you need to win her heart, not murder her fiancé"). This film warps the conventions of the Bollywood love plot into its perverse expressions, where the love song becomes a one-sided fantasy that objectifies Kiran's body and where "sacchi mohabbat" ("true love") – which Rahul claims that he has for Kiran – is expressed in stalking and violence. There are many bad lovers across Hindi cinema, but they are all villains; like Rahul in *Darr*, they do not understand love and think that rape or sexual violence is the lover's right. These characters – Shyam in *Aradhana*, Ranjit in *Seeta Aur Geeta*, the step uncle's son in *Deewana* (1992), Rajiv in *Pardes* (1997), among others – are never condoned but always vilified.

But there is also a whole spectrum of obsessive behavior that in our contemporary world would cross the line into harassment, but which is considered moral in Bollywood films. In *Kabhi Kabhie* (1976), Vicky follows his fiancée Pinky even when she tells him not to, and will not leave when she asks him to.

In *Kabhi Haan Kabhi Naa* (1994), Anna clearly tells Sunil that she is not interested and yet he follows her everywhere, hoping to change her mind. In *Dil Se* (1997), Amar pursues Meghna even when she explicitly tells him to stay away from her. In *Deewana* (1992) Raja carves Kajal's name into his arm, just as Rahul does in *Darr* (1993), but in *Deewana* it is supposed to be an act of devotion. Unlike in *Darr*, however, once they are married Raja promises not to touch Kajal without her consent, and holds true to that promise. These forms of obsession characterize lovers as passionate, devout, and single-minded, rather than indifferent or distracted, which are negatively valued in Bollywood.

Seeing obsession as part of a continuum also inhabited by love as destiny and love as intoxication is helpful in understanding why Hindi film represents obsession so constantly. The intention is not to valorize stalking, but to represent love as a state that puts pressure on the rational, the secular, and the material. Bollywood love is constantly exceeding our limits for how we understand "normal" human behavior, compelling us to rethink the conventional hierarchy that values the mind over the heart, and what counts as happiness and success. In doing so, Bollywood presents a love that is extra-social – even if that means it occasionally veers into the domain of the pathological. Because obsessive loves are usually not requited in Bollywood, obsession also suggests a sort of queering of love, as will be discussed further in Chapter 7.

There is precedent in Indian literature for a woman lover being obsessed with a male beloved, as in the story of the medieval saint Mirabai, who was famously obsessed with the Lord Krishna,[5] and there are also female lovers in Bollywood. In *Guddi* (1971), Kusum is obsessed with the Bollywood superstar Dharmendra, and when she learns in school about the non-earthly love Mirabai had for Krishna, she takes it as an inspiration for her love for Dharmendra. She learns, for instance, that Mirabai was married, but her husband was only such in body, not in spirit, as she had committed her spiritual self to the god. Her obsession thus took Mirabai away from bourgeois domesticity. When Kusum tells Navin she cannot marry him because she's in love with someone else, Navin is shocked, but when he hears that it is the movie star Dharmendra whom she has fallen for, he laughs at her innocence. Yet, the possibility that Kusum invokes, of having two lovers at the same time, one in body and one in spirit, speaks to a non-heteronormative imagination of love that actually characterizes many Bollywood love stories.

The fact that the lover is usually male and the beloved female could be interpreted as patriarchal (the man as the pursuer and agent and the woman only as the object), but also lends itself to an alternative reading, because love is so overpowering that it actually *weakens* the lover while the beloved remains strong and elusive. *Dil Se* (1997) exemplifies this sort of obsession. The film will be discussed more fully in Chapter 6, but for now it is important to note that Amar's love affair with Meghna falls largely in line with love as obsession as we have described it here: immediate attraction, love so intense that he loses all perspective on his job, his family, and other aspects of his normal life, and ultimate mutual annihilation. But once again, although he is pursuing her, it is

Amar who is in fact weakened by his pursuit. Meghna, on the other hand, manipulates his obsession to get certain things she needs for the political movement of which she is a part. Thus as the film progresses, we see Amar get weaker and Meghna get stronger, as he gradually departs from the world of reason and she begins to play him like a puppet. Although he seems to be the aggressor, it is she who holds the power, and their mutual death in the final scene could be seen not as his victory but as his ultimate defeat in the face of a fatal love.

Indeed, madness and obsession often lead to death rather than a happy ending – but it is a death that is presented, in Urdu poetry, Sufi cosmology, and in Bollywood, as the heart of true love. There is something impossible about this kind of love, at least within the world of bourgeois domesticity; it is built on the elusiveness of the beloved rather than her openness or availability, and that elusiveness is precisely what attracts the lover and takes him further from the material world. In *Dil Se* (1997), Amar says to Meghna, "Hum donon ke beech mein jo doori hai, yeh mujhe bahut napasand hai … Aur sab se zyada pasand mujhe yeh doori hai, kyunki agar yeh doori na ho, toh tumhare kareeb aane ka bahana na mile" ("The thing I hate most is the distance between us … and the thing I love the most is that distance, because if the distance weren't there, I wouldn't have an excuse to come closer"). This idea that desire is created by the impossibility of requiting the desire makes theirs an impossible love from the outset. By contrast, there is nothing elusive about Preeti, the woman Amar's family wants him to marry; like so many arranged fiancé/es in Bollywood, she is all surface and no mystery. A future with Preeti is instantly legible and practical; Meghna's elusiveness suggests a queer rejection of that heteronormative legibility, and the fact that their union can never be requited suggests an alternative imaginary to reproductive futurity.

If not reproductive futurity, the end of such a love is instead annihilation (*fanaa*). In Sufi cosmology, *fanaa* refers to the annihilation of the self as "necessary … in order to gain eternal life."[6] Since Sufism associates true love with the divine, in love stories the ideal of *fanaa* suggests that the ultimate success of the spiritual quest is actually in the annihilation of the questing subject rather than in marriage and sexual union. This is a love so pure and true that it cannot exist on an earthly plain and thus death is its only possible ending. This kind of love is idealized in many Bollywood love stories. In *Prem Kahani* (1975), true lovers Kamini and Rajesh cannot be together, as she has already married his best friend Dheeraj; the film ends when Kamini shoots Rajesh, both saving her marriage and, ironically, registering their love as not of this world and therefore ideal – a quality Rajesh recognizes when he says, just before dying, "Meri maut ke sivai is prem kahani ka aur koi ant ho hi nahin sakta tha" ("There was no other end for this love story than my death"). *Fanaa* (2006) is a film named after annihilation, in which the couple's love is presented as so powerful that its only inevitable end is death. Although *Fanaa* (discussed further in Chapter 6) can be read as a story about terrorism, seeing the final standoff between Zooni and Rehaan, when each of them has a gun pointing at the other, as representing an ideal of Sufi love complicates that simplistic reading. Indeed, right before shooting him, Zooni says, "I love you, Rehaan, I love you," showing the inextricability of love and death.

Love as crossing borders

Although Bollywood love is not usually allegorical – not usually a metaphor for some larger political scenario – there are some examples when love serves as a powerful force against the myriad borders and walls that humans and societies have put up for themselves. Love crosses class, for instance; thus Vijay and Meena can be in love in *Pyaasa* (1957) even though he is a homeless poet and she is the wife of a wealthy publisher. In *Bobby* (1973), *Bombay* (1995), and *Gadar* (2001), love can cross religious difference. In *Qayamat Se Qayamat Tak* (1988) love can cross entrenched family enmity and rigid ideas about honor. In *Mahal* (1949) and *Om Shanti Om* (2007), love can even transcend death. And in *Veer-Zaara* (2004) love can cross the India–Pakistan border, so when the lovers finally meet again after many years, their lawyer Saamiya says, "Ab khud khuda bhi Zaara ko Veer se alag nahin rakh sakega" ("Now not even God himself can keep Veer and Zaara apart"). This film will be discussed further in Chapter 6.

Separation

Drawn from the Bhakti concept of *viraha*, which refers to an intensely emotional separation from the beloved that intensifies and strengthens love,[7] "leav[ing] the human lover ever longing for complete union with the divine,"[8] the idea that love can get stronger in separation is also a unique quality of love in Bollywood. The valorization of *viraha* counters the more dominant idea of romantic union, found in the classic Bollywood happy ending, and emphasizes an ethos of *unrequited* love that is presented as the height of romance, taking love beyond physical union into the domain of the spiritual.

Perhaps the most famous Bollywood unrequited romance is *Devdas*, a film that was made and remade multiple times (the three most important Hindi versions being released in 1936, 1955, and 2002) and has attained iconic status.[9] Based on a 1917 novel by Bengali writer Saratchandra Chattopadhyay, *Devdas* is the story of a transcendent love that is never requited, at first due to circumstance and later due to the hero's nihilistic behavior. Devdas and Paro have been in love since childhood but his parents refuse their marriage because of her social status. Devastated, Devdas escapes to Calcutta where he misses Paro, but unable to understand the true nature of his love, he turns to alcohol and the more ephemeral pleasures of a famous courtesan, Chandramukhi. Descending deeper into melancholy, Devdas becomes ill and only returns to Paro on his deathbed to see her one final time. Based on a novel, *Devdas* does not follow the plot of most Bollywood melodramas, lacking the restoration of the moral universe at the end, except in the idea of a love that is so true that it remains strong even after death. Separation, in this formula, is a test that makes love stronger.

Viraha has defined love in a range of films. In *Pyaasa* (1957), Gulabo acknowledges her love for Vijay when she hears a local Baul singer performing a song to Lord Krishna in the voice of Krishna's devotee Mirabai. In the music as well as the lyrics, we see the articulation of a sentiment of erotic longing that is founded in – and even strengthened by – separation:

> Kai jugu se hain jaage, mere nain abhage
> Kahin jiya nahin lage bin tore
> Sukh dikhe nahin aage
> Dukh peeche-peeche bhaage
> Jag soona-soona laage bin tore
> Prem sudha, more saanwariya.

> [My hapless eyes have been sleepless for countless years
> Without you, nothing pleases me
> I see no happiness ahead
> Sorrow follows me everywhere
> Without you, the world is lonely
> O my beloved, the nectar of love.]

Although Gulabo and Vijay do unite at the end of the film, the morality of their love is underlined by this representation via the discourse of *viraha*.

Veer and Zaara undergo a long period of separation in *Veer-Zaara* (2004), another test – specifically named as "mohabbat ka imtehan" ("a test of love") – that proves how true their love really is. The purer the love, in Bollywood, the more tests it can withstand, including perpetual separation.

Erotics

Many commentators note the lack of explicit sex, including kissing, in Bollywood films. Although there are occasionally sexually suggestive scenes, such as in *Deewaar* (1975) when Vijay is in bed with Anita, shirtless and smoking a cigarette, and in *Silsila* (1981), when Amit and Chandni are shown undressed in bed together, it is largely true of Bollywood that nudity and sexual contact are not shown on screen. Some critics attribute this to the puritanism or conservatism of Indian society and the strong role of the state censorship body in the industry. While these do affect what is shown, it is also important to note the erotic features that do exist in Bollywood films, even without the explicit representation of sex.

Thus, the role of censorship is important, but not deterministic. The reason for this is that the entire ethos of love in Bollywood, as we have seen, goes beyond a simplistic association of love and romance with reproductive sex or even the physical body. Thus representing sex in its physical form is less interesting to the Bollywood imaginary than representing the erotic as a domain of sensual and even spiritual bliss.

The erotics of the song sequence will be discussed in the next chapter. Songs are certainly one of the places where female desire, flirtation, and sexual contact are represented beyond what is permitted in the primary narrative. However, there are additional narrative tropes that are repeatedly used to intimate sexual contact or even sex. For instance, putting on bangles, especially a man putting bangles on the wrist of his lover, is coded as an act of sexual intimacy, if not a symbol for sex itself. Early in *Mother India* (1957), when Shamu buys bangles for his new bride, Radha, he tries to put them on her wrist while she is working, but she flirtatiously pushes him away, saying, "Chhodo mere haath se. Maa dekh legi. Chhodo na!" ("Let go of my hand, mother will see. Let go!"). Her worry that his mother will see them suggests that putting on bangles in public is a form of intimacy that resembles kissing or other public displays of affection. When she finally relents, we see a medium shot of her face as Shamu puts the bangles on her wrist outside of the frame, suggesting again a private moment of intimacy that cannot be shown (Figure 2.2). Later in the film, after Shamu has abandoned the family, their son Birju tries to please his mother by stealing cotton and exchanging it for a pair of bangles which he then proceeds to put on her wrist; Birju means the act to show his love for his mother, but the stolen bangles actually stand for the transgression of the son playing the role of the father. The sexuality of bangles is repeated in *Kabhi Khushi Kabhie Gham* (2001); Rahul professes his love to Anjali by buying her a set of green bangles

Figure 2.2 Shamu and Radha share a moment of intimacy after he puts a set of bangles on her wrist, in *Mother India* (1957).

that he puts on her wrist in a highly sexualized gesture, even asking, "Chap toh nahin raha?" ("I hope it's not hurting?"), as she winces when the bangles go over her fingers. In *Fanaa* (2006) as well, Rehaan and Zooni's romance is represented visually in a scene where Rehaan puts bangles onto Zooni's wrist. This trope is also the subject of comedy, as in *Andaz Apna Apna* (1994) when the hero, Amar, who is a dreamer and a layabout, fantasizes about opening a bangle shop – a fantasy that has sexual resonances. Sometimes this use of euphemism to represent sex is parodied, as in *Aiyyaa* (2012), when we see the image of a gas pump going suggestively in and out of the canister until finally some gas spurts out as part of Meenakshi's sexual fantasy.

Watching erotic scenes or engaging in flirtatious dialogues also builds erotic energy between characters, even in the absence of physical contact. In *Sangam* (1964), Radha performs a cabaret dance for Sundar in their hotel room and after watching her he loosens his tie, picks her up, and carries her into the bedroom. In *Waqt* (1965), Ravi and Meena share a sexually charged moment on two different sides of a swimming pool changing room wall (Figure 2.3). In *An Evening in Paris* (1967), Deepa and Sam attend a cabaret which arouses them, leading Sam to try to kiss her in the street afterwards. In *Aradhana* (1969), Vandana accidentally spills water on Arun and he has to take off his shirt to have it dried. Later in the film, the two are driven to their first sexual encounter when they overhear an erotic song,

Figure 2.3 Ravi and Meena share an intimate moment on two sides of a changing room wall, in *Waqt* (1965).

"Roop Tera Mastana," sung by a man to his lover in the hotel room next to theirs (Figure 2.4). In *Duplicate* (1998), when Bablu professes his love for Sonia, he does so in a dialogue that, even though it is ostensibly about a dream he had, becomes erotic in its telling. As he relates his dream in a halting way, she becomes increasingly visibly aroused, until the end, when he laughs off the whole conversation as a joke, in an awkward release:

BABLU: Sonia ji, mera ek sapna hai.
SONIA: Accha?
B: Maine ek bahut hi khoobsurat ladki se…
S: Hm?
B: … shaadi kar li hai.
S: Ah!
B: Bilkul aap ki jaisi.
S: [laughs] Kaun?
B: Ehem. Aur suhag raat par … woh dulhan ke kapde pehne hue, mere palang par baithi hai … aur main ahista ahista … uske paas jaata hoon.
S: Phir?
B: Phir main … uska gungat utaarta hoon.
S: [gasps] … Aur …?
B: Aur phir main …
S: Hanh …?
B: … apne haathon se …
S: Go on …
B: … us se …
S: Hahn? … [breathes in]

Figure 2.4 Arun and Vandana overhear an erotic encounter in the next room, leading them to make love for the first time, in *Aradhana* (1969).

B: … vada pao khilata hoon!

S: Huh? Vada pao? … [then laughs]

[BABLU: Sonia ji, I had a dream.

SONIA: Yes?

B: I … married …

S: Hm?

B: … a very beautiful woman …

S: Ah!

B: She was just like you.

S: [laughs] Who?

B: Ehem. And on the wedding night … she was sitting on my bed wearing her bridal clothes … and I … slowly … went up to her …

S: And then?

B: Then I took off her bridal veil …

S: [gasps] And …?

B: And then I …

S: Yes …?

B: … with my own hands …

S: Go on …

B: I …

S: Yes? … [breathes in]

B: … I fed her a sandwich!

S: Huh? A sandwich? … [then laughs]]

Although they both laugh at the joke about the sandwich, the flirtation of the scene infuses their relationship with an erotic energy that changes its nature. In fact, Bablu's joke is both a joke and is not, because he is in fact in love with Sonia. The trope of talking about a dream or telling another person's story is a common way to represent erotic energy and mutual attraction in a supposedly hypothetical way and without depicting actual physical contact.

Conversely, a character not interested in love or sex is often an object of ridicule. At the beginning of *Padosan* (1968), Bhola (whose name means innocent) professes to be uninterested in love, and is pictured reading a religious text that prescribes that "pacchis baras tak aadmi ko brahmcharya ka palan karna chahiye" ("until the age of 25, a man should be celibate"). His uncle makes fun of him for this, saying that a boy of his age should be out having fun and reading the "Premshastras" instead, referring to ancient Indian sex manuals – a comment that embarrasses poor Bhola. Unsurprisingly, Bhola reneges instantly on his vow of celibacy when he meets Bindu, with whom he immediately falls in love.

Love's enemy

The centrality of love to Bollywood morality results in a unique kind of villain, whom we might call a "pyar ka dushman" ("an enemy of love"). Love's enemy is sometimes explicitly named, as in a dialogue in *Mughal-e-Azam* [10] and the song "Tayyab Ali Pyar Ka Dushman" ("Tayyab Ali, Love's Enemy") in *Amar Akbar Anthony* (1977), but even when not named, the character type exists across many films. The enemy of love is a character who cannot recognize the overriding importance of love and thus trivializes it or even impedes it, whether by accident or by design.

Often this is a role played by the lover's family, which is important to note because it is one of the common perceptions of Bollywood films that family is its moral core. It is true that the family is highly valued, but in the majority of cases, romantic love is actually *more* important than family. Thus when a young lover has to choose between her beloved and her family, a choice that is at the heart of many Bollywood plots, the family is almost always the problem, not the love. In *Bobby* (1973), Raj's wealthy father finds Bobby too low-born for Raj and forbids them from marrying, and he is instantly coded as the film's villain. In *Nagina* (1986), when Vijaya's father sends a goon to kill Rajni, blaming her for Raju's disinterest in his daughter, the crime of trying to break up a true love is considered unpardonable. This particular plot is foiled by the snakes that Rajni has in her spell, suggesting that true love has divine justice (the snake is an animal often associated with Lord Shiva) on its side.

In *Qayamat Se Qayamat Tak* (1988), Raj and Rashmi have to contend with not only two feuding patriarchs as fathers, but an entire tradition of Rajput honor that defines masculinity as the refusal to ever concede, and that valorizes violence and even death over losing face. Here, the power of love's enemies is so strong that the lovers have to escape from society altogether for their love to briefly flourish, and in the end, they have to die. However, the film presents their love as so powerful that it will live on even in the afterlife – so the enemies of love are presented as only temporarily victorious.

But this is a rare ending for Bollywood films, most of which end with the lovers defeating love's enemy. In *Dilwale Dulhania Le Jayenge* (1995), Baldev Singh is strongly opposed to Raj and Simran's romance, so much so that upon hearing of it, he immediately arranges Simran's marriage to another man and uproots their family from London back to the Punjab. Although Baldev represents patriarchal authority, once that authority becomes the enemy of love, it actually constitutes the *disruption* in the moral universe. For the moral universe to be restored and the film to end happily, the patriarch must change his mind; the enemy of love must be vanquished.

This is true also of Yash's disapproval of Rahul and Anjali's marriage in *Kabhi Khushi Kabhie Gham* (2001), when he refuses to give his blessing to the couple's plan to marry by criticizing Anjali's low birth (*wajud*). "Kaise soch liya …?" ("How could you think …?") he begins to ask Rahul, outraged that his son would play so fast and loose with the family's honor. But Rahul interrupts him before he can finish the thought: "Socha toh bilkul nahin, sirf pyar kiya" ("I didn't think at all, I just loved"). The struggle is thus presented as between Rahul, the ideal lover, and his father, love's enemy. Yash then proceeds to disown his son. While Rahul misses having his father in his life, it is only when

Yash can admit his mistake and realize that not thinking, just loving is actually a *moral* act that the family can reconcile. Thus it is important to note that while arranged marriage is a practice in India, and serves as a plot device in Bollywood, in many cases the arranged marriage functions as the enemy of love, as the lover is usually in love with someone of her own choosing.

This idea of the enemy of love can be put in the service of different kinds of plots as well, even ones that transgress the dominant heteronormativity of Bollywood romance. For instance, in *Ek Ladki Ko Dekha Toh Aisa Laga* (2019), the first mainstream Bollywood lesbian movie, we see the primal conflict between the lover and the enemy of love put to use in favor of a queer love story. Sweeti's father and brother oppose Sweeti's love for Kuhu because they are homophobic. However, because Sweeti is presented as an ideal lover from the beginning of the film, her father and Babloo become enemies of love, and thus are necessarily on the wrong side of the film's moral universe. By making Babloo the paradigmatic enemy of love, Sweeti's homosexuality must be affirmed in order for the moral universe to be restored and thus this Bollywood formula is repurposed to a progressive end.

Another kind of enemy of love is a character who thinks love is a commodity, something that can be bought and sold. In *Pyaasa* (1957), Meena leaves a financially struggling Vijay to marry a rich man, revealing her cynical valuing of love in terms of money. Vijay ends up finding happiness with Gulabo, who is a prostitute, but one who believes in love. The woman who sells her body but believes in love is thus opposed to the supposedly chaste bourgeois woman who will only marry a wealthy man. In *Mr. and Mrs. 55* (1955), Anita's aunt pays a man to marry Anita in order to fulfil a provision in Anita's late father's will that would give Anita her inheritance only if she were married. Here, the enemy of love is not a stern patriarch, but a feminist who believes love is patriarchal, but in her attempt to secure the inheritance for her niece, she ends up guilty of the same crime: treating marriage as a financial transaction. In *Kashmir Ki Kali* (1964), the villain is Mohan, who tries to blackmail Champa's father with secrets from his past in order to get permission to marry Champa. This is a theme in *Bobby* (1973) as well, in which Raj accuses his father of selling him for his own gain when he tries to force Raj to marry the daughter of a business associate: "Sauda kiya hai aapne. Rupaiye ke liye meri zindagi bech rahe hain aap" ("You've sold me out. You're selling my life in exchange for money"). By contrast, Bobby's father, even though he is an unkempt alcoholic, is the moral center of the film; he believes in love and even sings a song with the refrain, "Pyar mein sauda nahin" ("There is no buying and selling in love"). Parents who try to marry off their children to extend their business interests, like Zaara's father in *Veer-Zaara* (2004), or who accuse lovers of using love as an excuse to gain wealth, as Mr. Nath does in *Bobby*, or who put excessive weight on dowry or other commodity transactions, all tend to be figured as love's enemies. In *Karz* (1980), Kamini is planning on marrying Ravi in order to have him killed and inherit his wealth; this kind of cynical understanding of love immediately conveys that Kamini is a villain. And in *Darr*

(1993), although Rahul tries to be a good lover by promising his beloved all the riches she deserves, he is negatively contrasted with Sunil, Kiran's boyfriend, in particular when he ridicules Sunil's new house by calling it too small.

Losing faith in love

Sometimes it is not an external force that serves as love's enemy but a weakness of character that causes the lover to second-guess or otherwise question the force of his or her love. In *Chalti Ka Naam Gaadi* (1958), Brijmohan says he hates women, but we realize that he is only disillusioned with love because of a broken love affair in the past – a disillusionment that is quickly dissolved when he is reunited with his beloved. In *Chandni* (1989), Rohit loses the use of his legs in an accident and, even though he is deeply in love with Chandni, immediately doubts whether she can love him now. In this case, it is Rohit's faltering in his belief in love that constitutes the disruption of the moral universe. The restoration of the moral universe thus requires nothing more than Rohit realizing how strong his love for Chandni actually is. When that realization occurs, it is so powerful that it can even cure his paralysis. Of course, this is an unrealistic ending. But seeing it not as an attempt to be realistic, but to claim and make the case for the overwhelming power of love explains this hyperbole. In *Kati Patang* (1971), after Kamal is left at the altar, he drowns his sorrows in alcohol, but when he begins to fall in love with Madhu (who happened to be the woman who had left him at the altar, unbeknownst to him), he stops drinking and begins to write poetry again. Likewise, in *Raja Hindustani* (1996), although Raja knows at one level that Aarti's family is trying to manipulate him to divorce their daughter, he too loses faith in love when Aarti's stepmother visits him to inform him (falsely) that Aarti wants a divorce. Rather than going and talking to Aarti, he resolves never to see her again, thus giving up on love. At the same time, he does not actually sign the divorce papers, showing an underlying faith in love simmering just below the surface. But his overall fickleness surrounding love is presented as a weakness. It leads him to undertake a series of destructive actions – like kidnapping his and Aarti's baby – but in the end, the moral universe is restored when Aarti helps him redeem his faith in their love.

Understanding the centrality of love offers a new perspective on a range of plots. For instance, *Damini* (1993) is the story of Damini, a woman who witnesses a servant in her wealthy in-laws' home being raped by her brother-in-law and a group of his friends. She tries to get justice by telling her in-laws, the police, and others what she saw, but her in-laws, fearing the loss of their *izzat* (honor), enact a massive cover-up with the help of their corrupt lawyer, going to extremes like accusing Damini of being mentally ill, locking her up in an insane asylum, and even trying to have her killed. While Damini pleads with her husband Shekhar, who also witnessed the crime, to tell the truth to his family, Shekhar wavers between his love for Damini and his sense of obligation toward protecting his family. Damini is this film's hero for her dogged pursuit of the truth, even in the face of countless obstacles. However, when seen through the perspective of love, the film has a secondary story: Shekhar's loss of faith in love and his subsequent regaining of it. In the dramatic trial scene at the end of the film, the lawyer makes the surprising decision to put Shekhar on the stand and ask him whether he loves Damini. At first, everyone is confused: what does this question have to do with the case? But the lawyer's strategy is precisely to remind Shekhar of his moral compass, which puts love above all else, including family. When Shekhar realizes this, he can testify on Damini's behalf, leading to the restoration of the moral universe.

Love after marriage

Most Bollywood films are about love before marriage, and assumed within this structure is that romance is distinct from marriage – the former erotic, the latter more social. However, there are also several stories about love after marriage.[11] Some of these are happy marriages, as in *Veer-Zaara* (2004), in which the elderly Choudhary Sumer Singh and his wife, Saraswati Kaur, express their love in a song sequence, "Lohri," whose lyrics joke about the frustrations of married life – with Sumer Singh spending too much time drinking and playing cards, and never remembering what his wife asks him to bring home. However, despite these complaints, she still loves him: "Chaaho badlo, ya na badlo, phir bhi mere ho/ Main toh chaahoon jab janam loon, tum hi mere ho" ("Whether you change or not, you're still mine/ I want you to be mine forever") and then he responds: "Heeriye, main har janam hoon, tera hi jogi/ Tu meri thi, tu meri hai, tu meri hogi" ("I'm going to be yours forever, sweetheart/ You were mine, you are mine, you always will be mine"). This song is notable for expressing love between an older couple who still sing about each other in a romantic, if not explicitly erotic, way.

However, most films that focus on post-marriage life represent unhappy marriages. As Rachel Dwyer writes, "Hindi films are ... quite specific about what marriages should not be. Neglect and insensitivity towards the other are condemned above all other errors,"[12] and this becomes a constant theme in Bollywood. In *Andaz* (1949), Neena's marriage to Rajan is spoiled by jealousy and rivalry. In *Sahib Bibi Aur Ghulam* (1962), Choti Bahu's husband spends his nights with a courtesan, leaving her sexually unfulfilled. She is criticized by her traditional in-laws for pining for her husband; her sister-in-law tells her, "Tum jaisi mard ke liye tadapne wali aurat hum ne aaj tak nahin dekhi!" ("I've never seen a woman so attached to her husband!") but that faith in love, even after marriage, is precisely what makes Choti Bahu the film's hero. In *Guide* (1965), Rosie and Marco have a terrible marriage; he neglects her for his work and it is suggested that he has no sexual interest in her. Marco's desire is more satisfied by the erotic statues he finds in caves (he is an archaeologist) and local courtesans than by his wife, something that leads to Rosie's misery; as she tells him, "Bacchon ka sukh nahin, toh kuch toh sukh aane do mere jeevan mein" ("If you can't give me the joy of children, then at least let me have some joy in my life").

In *Kabhi Kabhie* (1976), Amit and Pooja are in love but both end up marrying different people. Amit especially enters his new relationship moody and resentful, and although he loves his wife and their daughter, the marriage itself gives him little fulfilment. In *Silsila* (1981), Amit marries his late brother's girlfriend out of obligation after his brother dies and leaves her pregnant. But their marriage is shot through with discontent on his side. In *Raja Hindustani* (1996), Aarti and Raja elope but then fail to communicate their feelings to each other, leaving room for Aarti's wealthy family to drive a wedge between them.

Like *Silsila, Kabhi Alvida Naa Kehna* (2006) deals explicitly with marital infidelity, centering on two unhappily married couples: Maya and Rishi, and Dev and Rhea. Dev is plagued with a residual bitterness because of an injury that stalled his soccer career, making him dissatisfied with everything, including his marriage. When he and Maya meet, their frustration with their own marriages finds an outlet in love for each other. This film posits love as explicitly opposed to marriage. While marriage is often presented in Bollywood as the logical outcome of a perfect love, here, in order for love to prevail, the two marriages must fail. In this case, even the older generation – Dev's mother and Rishi's father – support their children in getting divorced, thus refusing the conventional patriarchal role of being the enemies of love.

Love these days

In recent years Bollywood films have included characters who are skeptical of the Bollywood ideal of love as all-encompassing and otherworldly. These films present love more realistically, as only one (rather than the dominant) facet of a well-rounded life that includes professional success, meaningful friendships, and potentially multiple partners. A common character in newer Bollywood films is one who initially does not believe in love, but then, once s/he falls in love, changes her/his mind. In these more self-reflexive films, love is no longer taken for granted but discussed, debated, and questioned.

Dil Chahta Hai (2001) was one of the first films to do this explicitly. Of the three friends, Sameer, Akash, and Sid, Sameer especially tries to be a nice guy when it comes to women, but he goes to such an extreme that he ends up getting robbed by a woman he is dating in Goa. The situation is supposed to be funny, but it also shows how young men might be trying to develop new paradigms for love in the twenty-first century. Later, although Sameer strongly objects to his parents' desire to arrange a marriage for him, he ends up falling in love with the woman they choose, reflecting another configuration of the conflict between love and marriage that has been central to Bollywood throughout the decades. Akash handles the new romantic landscape by mocking the idea of love at first sight: early in the film Akash tries to get Shalini, a woman he just met, to dance with him at a club by making a dramatic proposition of love to her in the form of a hyperbolic Bollywood romantic gesture:

Main tum se aur sirf tum se pyar karta hoon. Meri har saans, meri har dhadkhan, mere har pal mein tum ho, aur sirf tum, Shalini. Mujhe yaqeen hai ki main sirf isliye janam hoon, ki tum se pyar kar sakoon. Aur tum sirf isliye, ki ek din meri ban jao. Tum meri ho Shalini!

[I love you and only you. My every breath, my every heartbeat, my every waking moment contains you and only you, Shalini. I know that I was born only to love you, and you so that one day you would become mine. You are mine Shalini!]

After this he winks at his friend. Throughout the film, Akash mocks romantic films and the idea of love. He even sings a song making fun of people who fall in love. But this defensive humor leaves him lonely and unmoored, and it is only when he realizes the importance of his friends and of love that he can become a full person again. And lastly, Sid falls in love with an older divorcée. The three friends signal three different ways of being a lover in the contemporary world, showing that there isn't just one model anymore.[13]

Love Aaj Kal (2009), whose title means "Love These Days," begins with Jai and Meera, twenty-somethings in London who have moved in together. They both have jobs and their relationship is only one aspect of their full and complex lives. They have both agreed that they won't sacrifice their professional ambitions to stay with one another, which they feel reflects the reality of love in the twenty-first century, and indeed they drift apart when Meera moves back to India and Jai stays in London. Meanwhile, Jai befriends Veer Singh Panesar, an older man who criticizes Jai's practical attitude toward love and tells him the story, over the course of the film and picturized in sepia-toned flashbacks, of his love for Harleen Kaur many years ago, which included love at first sight, an all-consuming love, and personal sacrifice. Jai ridicules Veer Singh's story for its outdatedness: "Are you serious? Abhi tak hello how-are-you nahin hua, aur aapne shaadi ka plan bana liya?!" ("You haven't even said hello or how are you, and you've made a plan to get married?!"). However, as time goes on, Jai begins to miss Meera, and he reconsiders his mockery of love, realizing that it might in fact be more important than his job or his convenience. Ultimately, he dramatically catches her at the airport where he expresses his undying love for her.

We see a similar pattern in *I Hate Luv Storys* (2010), whose protagonist works for a Bollywood filmmaker but who finds Bollywood love stories banal and unrealistic, until he meets the woman of his dreams and realizes he is wrong. In *Hum Tum* (2004) as well, Karan disdains the idea of love until he realizes he is in love with Rhea. In all these cases, modern love is initially defined as more practical and realistic for a skeptical younger generation, but in the end, Bollywood love triumphs.

This is not always the case, and more alternative recent films will be discussed in Chapter 8. For instance, *Queen* (2014) begins with preparations for Rani's wedding, but then the day before the wedding the groom cancels, compelling the dejected bride to go on their honeymoon on her own. In the process, she meets new friends and gains her independence, and realizes that marriage might not be the only happy ending for her.

The significance of films like *Love Aaj Kal* and *Queen* can only be understood via an understanding of conventions surrounding love, desire, and romance in Bollywood more generally. These newer films are certainly innovative, but they also carry on a longer tradition of refining and repurposing classic love plots and stock characters such as the lover and the enemy of love, even as they capture changing sensibilities in India and in the world at large.

3   Song and dance

Song-and-dance sequences are central to Bollywood films and can be, for non-Indian audiences, a significant source of misunderstanding. Song sequences break from the primary narrative and offer access to other states of reality, such as desire and fantasy. Thus, they need to be understood as part of the heterogeneous register of Bollywood films, which often includes jarring and seemingly random breaks in style and narrative. Love is the most common emotion conveyed by song-and-dance sequences. Song sequences are also the place where erotics emerge, often unspoken in the primary narrative. For instance, female characters can express their sexual desire in the form of fantasy songs. As Paromita Vohra writes, "Dance ... provide[s] pure pleasure – guilty, disingenuous or simple."[1] Song-and-dance sequences can be sites of hidden communication, especially in wedding scenes, in which the roles of bride and groom are often played by proxies, allowing for multiple meanings to emerge. Whereas from a realist standpoint, song-and-dance sequences make little sense, learning how to read the Bollywood song-and-dance sequence is necessary to assessing its role in a film's meaning, and indeed in the genre at large.

There is an inherent morality associated with song and dance in Bollywood. If a character gets a song, it means he or she is a moral character. Conversely, villains rarely get song-and-dance numbers. Sometimes, this convention can be used to suggest a change of heart; for instance, in *Padosan* (1968), Bhola's uncle is presented for most of the film as selfish and lecherous, but when Guruji tries to convince him to bless Bhola's marriage using lines of song, and the uncle responds also in song, we anticipate that he will have a change of heart, because true villains rarely get to sing, and only a fundamentally moral character would perceive the morality of song.

Some international critics see song sequences as extraneous to Bollywood films since they do not directly serve the advancement of the plot. While it is possible that taking out song sequences will not affect a viewer's understanding of the *story* of a film, this chapter will show how song sequences are absolutely essential to understanding Bollywood. They are the place where the senses are aroused, which is central to how Bollywood works as a genre. Reducing a Bollywood film to its storyline thus eliminates its heart. The importance of music for assessing a film's success is evident in local film reviews such as this one of *Chingari* (1955) from the *Times of India*, which praises the songs even while criticizing the film: "'Chingari' Dull Picture But Has Good Music."[2]

The centrality of music to Bollywood's meaning also distinguishes Bollywood from "musicals" in the way that term is used to describe Broadway theatrical productions. In Broadway, musical pieces constitute narrative and advance the plot and thus are integral to the mode of storytelling. Bollywood might be more similar to early Hollywood musicals, which were also characterized by "a character bursting into song or breaking into dance with inexplicable orchestral accompaniment,"[3] although those musicals' ties to a particular moment in US film history made them a static and temporary, rather than dynamic, genre. In Bollywood, by contrast, the visual style, lyrics, and choreography of song-and-dance sequences continue to transform themselves to reflect new political and aesthetic sensibilities.

Song sequences constitute a part of even films that might seem too serious in theme to warrant them. For instance, *Darr* (1993) is a violent thriller, but it still contains a light-hearted wedding song and a couple of love songs. In the violent revenge film *Gabbar Is Back* (2015), a flashback allows the protagonist to have a love song with his now-deceased wife, whose death he is working to avenge. Music is part of the pleasure of Bollywood cinema, and because song-and-dance sequences already constitute breaks from the primary narrative, it is not seen as strange to have them interspersed with thematically serious topics as well.

Song-and-dance sequences have a particular visual style founded in complex choreography, unique settings, lavish sets and scenery, and bright colors. The visual style of song-and-dance sequences will be discussed more fully in Chapter 4.

Song-and-dance sequences are intensely pleasurable parts of the Bollywood viewing experience. As we will see in this chapter, they are not always contained within the film's story or narrative, and precisely because of that they condense and carry the emotional intensity of popular cinematic experience in generically particular ways. While Bollywood song sequences can and should be understood for all the qualities discussed below, there is also something to be said for their ineffable aspects – a small facial expression, a gesture of tenderness, a particular lyric, a catchy tune – that capture a mood or sensibility that eludes articulation, that makes a listener want to simply listen to or watch a song over and over again. Understanding the role of song-and-dance sequences in Bollywood cinema must also attend to the sheer pleasure offered by the convention.

Playback singing

Bollywood songs are sung by playback singers and lip-synched by the actors. Although in Hollywood lip-synching is seen as a form of inauthenticity, it is a conventional and much-loved practice in post-1940s Bollywood. Until the 2000s, all sound was added post production, and some actors, like Sridevi and Katrina Kaif, who couldn't speak perfect Hindi, had their speaking voices dubbed over by a dialogue reader as well. Thus, in a context in which sound was always slightly misaligned with lip movements, playback singing never felt exceptional or unsettling.

In fact, playback singing adds to the enjoyment of the song-and-dance sequence. It is not necessarily realistic, since the voice of the singer and the voice of the actor do not always match. But the practice of suturing together "the ideal voice with the ideal body" results in what Neepa Majumdar calls "a composite star"[4] who is bigger and more spectacular than the regular star – even superhuman. This practice abides by the philosophy, like many things in Bollywood, that more is better: that the ideal film character is an accretion of many different ideal persons, regardless of whether this composite is realistic or actually humanly possible.

As Neepa Majumdar has detailed, the use of playback singing began in Bollywood in the 1940s; before that, actors would sing their own songs. At first, she writes, audiences were uncomfortable with the disjuncture between the face and the voice, but by the late 1950s, audiences actually found that disjuncture desirable.[5] Playback singing is itself thematized in a number of films. In *Padosan* (1968), Bhola wants to seduce Bindu with a song but has no singing ability, so he has his teacher, Guruji, sing from a hidden spot while he mouths the words. Because Guruji is played by Kishore Kumar, an actor who was also a very successful playback singer, this play on playback is doubly enjoyable. However, when Bindu finds out that Bhola has been lying to her, she is outraged and breaks off their relationship. Thus playback singing is both used, thematized, and suggested to be inauthentic as part of the fun of this comedic film. In *Shamitabh* (2015), a speaking-impaired young man who wants to be a film star uses technology to pass off another man's voice as his own. As the star becomes famous, the man whose voice is being used believes he deserves more of the limelight, insisting that the star is nothing without his voice, and again allegorizing the duality of voice and body that runs throughout most of Bollywood's history.

The fact that these two films from two very different time periods both feature playback as part of their plots demonstrates that the question of what makes a star – the face or the voice? – remains central to Bollywood cinema. While the visual appeal and skilled body of the star often give her center stage, music is arguably the key site of Bollywood's pleasure, without which Bollywood would, quite simply, cease to be Bollywood. Thus despite their visual anonymity, playback singers have succeeded in gaining recognition that competes with, even if it doesn't exceed, the recognition given to stars. When the practice of playback singing was first introduced, singers were not credited. However, as early as the 1950s, playback singers were being advertised alongside stars and featured in film reviews, suggesting that they were celebrities in their own right. A 1954 event celebrating the silver jubilee of the film *Boot Polish* (1954) in Mumbai began "with the playback singers … among them Mohammed Rafi, Asha Bhonsle, Madhubala Jhaveri and Manna Dey, singing the popular songs from the film, accompanied by a [live] orchestra."[6] Indeed, throughout the decades, Bollywood music has been marketed in multiple forms. This has included collections of songs sung by a particular playback singer (i.e. The Best of Mohammed Rafi) and albums containing the music of a particular film (The Songs of *Sholay*), but also collections of songs "acted" by a particular star (The Best of Madhuri Dixit).[7] The idea of listening to a collection of songs that were lip-synched by a favorite star seems counterintuitive, but the ability to collect songs in this way and associate beloved songs with *both* the singer and the star who played the role is part of the flexibility of Bollywood fandom.

There are a handful of actors who have occasionally sung playback for themselves, such as Amitabh Bachchan in "Mere Angane Mein" in *Lawaaris* (1981) and Abhay Deol and Hrithik Roshan in "Señorita" in *Zindagi Na Milegi Dobara* (2011). In these cases, the actors' amateur voices are part of the aesthetic of the songs. There are fewer actors who are actually full-fledged playback singers – the most notable being Kishore Kumar, who acted in the 1940s and 1950s and sang playback for the next several decades. More recently, films include songs that are not lip-synched even if featured in song-and-dance sequences – that is, the actors dance to the song but don't mouth the words. However, even when this occurs, the song sequences continue to be central to the film's marketing and popularity.

Case study: Lata Mangeshkar

As Neepa Majumdar writes, Lata Mangeshkar is iconic for playback singing in Bollywood and was the dominant singer from the 1950s to the 1990s. Her first film was *Mahal* in 1949, for which she wasn't even credited,[8] but the very next year, Mangeshkar was named by the *Times of India* as "Most popular playback songstress."[9] During her most productive period, Mangeshkar was both a shrewd self-marketer and represented an ideal femininity in her high soprano that for many decades represented the pinnacle of the female voice. In addition, her choice to never marry and the white sari she often wears suggest a kind of iconic, saintly presence[10] that is associated with the idealization of love and beauty in Bollywood as a whole. Mangeshkar's songs can be bought on CDs that contain a collection of her songs from different movies and in many ways, she is as much a star as the actors who have, over the decades, mouthed her music. This suggests that although Bollywood is a visual medium, stardom is aural as well.[11]

Mangeshkar's sister, Asha Bhonsle, is also a playback singer, second in the industry only to Mangeshkar herself. In contrast to Mangeshkar, Bhonsle was often requested to perform more erotic or sultry songs, for instance the songs sung by the *tawaif* (courtesan) Umrao Jaan in the film of the same name. This further associated Mangeshkar with a saintly purity and Bhonsle with sexuality and eroticism. In recent decades, as Mangeshkar's monopoly over female playback singing has decreased, other voices have joined the playback scene and the simplistic association of soprano with ideal femininity has been replaced by more diverse female sounds.

Historically, there has been more diversity in male playback singing in part because it was never monopolized by one figure.[12] Ideal male voices have ranged from the melodic voice of Mohammed Rafi, associated with romantic songs, to the zany vocals of Kishore Kumar[13] to the smooth and romantic voice of Udit Narayan and the earthier voices of A.R. Rahman and Vishal Bhardwaj. Each voice, male and female, has its own appeal. However, the filmmaker has no intention of perfectly merging the voice with the image of the actor who is lip-synching; rather, the disjuncture adds a new dimension to the performance and enhances it by adding a new emotional and aesthetic quality. The goal is never to trick the audience into thinking the actor is singing, but rather to heighten the emotional intensity and aural/visual pleasure of the song-and-dance sequence and of the film as a whole by layering the recognizable face with the perfect voice.

Circulation

Song-and-dance sequences are "free-floating"[14] parts of a Bollywood film, meaning that they also circulate on their own, apart from the film with which they are associated. Songs are released prior to the film, and they often generate anticipation for it. Snippets of song-and-dance sequences appear on television and YouTube and as parts of trailers for upcoming films so it is likely that audiences are familiar with both their visual and aural elements before they see the film.

Bollywood songs are immensely popular and circulate in a number of media. In the twentieth century, before and after a film was released, its songs were played on the radio, and if a song became popular, it was replayed for months, years, and even decades. In 2018, the Saregama music label released a popular audio device in the shape of an old-fashioned radio onto which 5,000 old film songs from the 1950s and 1960s are pre-loaded in digital form. Antakshari is a popular game played especially by students, in which each person has to think of a line from a film song that begins with the last letter of the previous person's line and you are out if you cannot think of one. More recently, reality competition shows like *Saregama* and *Indian Idol* feature Bollywood song-and-dance sequences in their competitions, often with playback singers, music directors, and Bollywood actors as the judges. Playback singers hold sold-out concerts in which they feature songs they have sung for various films. Historically, film music sales have comprised a high percentage of all music sales. Songs are played at weddings, nightclubs, and political rallies and can be heard in taxis, rickshaws, and small shops along the streets in both rural and urban India.[15] In the 1990s and 2000s, Bollywood DVD menus allowed viewers to search by scenes as well as by songs, suggesting that part of the enjoyment of owning a film on DVD was being able to watch the song-and-dance sequences independently of the film. Bollywood song sequences can be viewed on YouTube as well, where there are entire channels devoted to various singers, as well as channels for well-known duet pairs such as Udit Narayan and Alka Yagnik, the most famous romantic song playback duo of the 1990s. These songs garner millions of views, with popular songs such as "Swag Se Swagat" from *Tiger Zinda Hai* (2017) viewed 827 million times on YouTube as of early 2020 and "Badri Ki Dulhania" from

Badrinath Ki Dulhania (2017) with 668 million views. Indian music label T-Series is the YouTube channel with the single most subscribers in the world (140 million in early 2020). Songs are also disseminated on blogs and other digital platforms; the website Agents of Ishq has a feature called "Sexy Saturday Songs"[16] in which guest posters curate a list of Bollywood songs with a brief explanation of why they find them sexy, and these features also circulate on social media, with people posting entire song sequences, clips, memes, and gifs from Bollywood song sequences on Facebook, Twitter, and Instagram.

In the process of such widespread circulation, songs gain meanings beyond their original significance in the film. This explains the popularity of Bollywood songs in queer spaces, where their meaning can proliferate beyond the boundaries of Bollywood morality. In nightclubs, for instance, the campy quality of Bollywood song sequences, when performed by same-sex couples or in drag, allows for the circulation of queer desire even if the characters who sang them were cisgender or straight.[17] Ruth Vanita describes how the well-known song "Pyar Kiya Toh Darna Kya" from *Mughal-e-Azam* (1960) became a queer anthem because of its "defiant eroticism," in which "the power of the erotic … is inseparable from the power of art."[18] Rajinder Dudrah describes a scene in a UK Asian gay and lesbian club where images of the "Chaiyya Chaiyya" song sequence from *Dil Se* (1997) are interspersed "with images of the naked torso of Salman Khan," thus "deliberately queer[ing] and displac[ing] the dominant straight aesthetics of the [*Dil Se*] clip to enable new pleasures around gender, sexuality, and the dancing of the body."[19] Free-floating circulation thus allows for songs to gain new meanings across both space and time.

Understanding the song sequence: diegesis

Key terms for understanding song-and-dance sequences are *diegetic* (also known as *intradiegetic*) and *extradiegetic*. These are terms used for all kinds of texts, but they are particularly useful in film studies.

A *diegetic* aspect of a film is something that takes place in the narrative world of the film: a death, a concert, a sidelong glance – any part of the story that takes place in the world of the characters constitutes a diegetic feature of a film. This is mostly what we mean when we talk about what "happens" in a film.

Extradiegetic is often harder to locate for viewers new to the term, although once you understand extradiegetic features you cannot stop seeing them. This refers to all elements that shape the meaning of a film, but which do *not* take place in the narrative world of the text. All narrative art has extradiegetic features; in a novel, these include the table of contents, the chapter breaks, the prologue, and the epigraphs at the beginning of chapters. All these shape how we read and understand a novel, but they are not a part of the story the novel is telling.

In film, extradiegetic features include the soundtrack (any music that is not heard by the characters, which is usually most of the music), camera angles, lighting, editing, titles and credits, and flashbacks. Attending to these features reminds us that directors' and editors' choices have a significant effect on shaping the meaning of a film. While extradiegetic features that are visual are discussed further in Chapter 4, this chapter focuses on the song-and-dance sequence, which is perhaps Bollywood's most obvious and unique extradiegetic feature.

Song-and-dance sequences

Bollywood song sequences seem to straddle the conventional separation between diegetic and extradiegetic, making them difficult to classify. On one hand, the characters often participate in the song, lip-synching the lyrics and dancing to the music, suggesting that songs occur within a film's narrative, in contrast to conventional soundtracks. At the same time, song sequences require extradiegetic music, often take place in a space and time apart from the narrative, include one or multiple costume changes (from the plot to the song sequence and within different parts of the song sequence), and rely on unrealistic shifts in personality or talent (for instance, a shy character throwing off her inhibitions, or a character who cannot sing or dance suddenly being able to). Clearly, then, there is an extradiegetic element to song sequences as well. Identifying the different kinds of song sequences is a first step to understanding their meaning in individual films.

The most straightforward form of the song-and-dance sequence is when it is part of the film's story, such as if characters are watching a performance such as a qawwali or play, or if a character is a singer or dancer who performs onstage within the film, as in the opening songs of *Ram Aur Shyam* (1967) and *Dostana* (1980), or the ghazal in *Sarfarosh* (1999). In *Amar Akbar Anthony* (1977), one of the protagonists is a professional qawwali singer, and the "Parda Hai" song is part of a performance that he sings on stage at which other characters are present. In *Sholay* (1975), the villains are watching a dance performance and thus the "Mehbooba Mehbooba" song can be understood as diegetic. Similarly, in *Rock On!* (2008), the protagonists are in a band, so all the song sequences are stage performances within the film's story. However, unlike in Hollywood, Bollywood films usually make little attempt to realistically incorporate even these types of songs into the diegesis. In *Pyaasa* (1957), Gulabo hears a woman singing a devotional song to the Lord Krishna, but the music follows Gulabo as she leaves the space where the woman is singing and as she ascends several sets of stairs and walks across the roof deck to approach Vijay; by the end of the sequence, the singer is a good distance away, so realistically the music would have begun to fade. In this example, a song that had begun as diegetic becomes extradiegetic by the end.

Another, more rare form of diegetic song sequence is when a character uses song as a form of communication, to convey something to another character. Two notable examples of this are in the reincarnation films *Karz* (1980) and *Om Shanti Om* (2007), both of which involve unsolved murders whose victims were reincarnated in order to expose their killers. In both films, the protagonist uses a song sequence, dramatized like an opera or a Broadway musical, to tell a story (a *daastan*, the Hindi-Urdu word for story used in both films) that is supposed to trigger the murderer's memory of the murder by eliciting a sense of déjà vu. These song sequences tell a story that is also being acted out and performed in a theatrical fashion as part of the film's plot and are enjoyable in part because they are so uncharacteristic for how Bollywood songs usually function.

But more common than either of these types are extradiegetic song sequences. A common type of song sequence is when a song takes place in a character's dream. This could be a character who is watching a performance and dreams she is taking part in it, or it could be her dreaming of singing a love song together with her beloved. Sometimes a dream is signaled by a fade out, clearly indicating that we have a shift to a dream sequence, but more often it is presented without such a fade, and thus it is not immediately clear whether it is a dream or not. The reason for this lack of clear distinction between dreams and reality, as was discussed in the introduction, is that in Bollywood films, dreams occupy a much more central place than in other types of cinema: the very subject of the cinema is dreams, imagination, and desire, and fittingly, the whole aesthetic of the cinema is dreamlike. In *Dil Chahta Hai* (2001), when Sameer and Pooja see themselves in a song sequence of a film they are watching in a theater, they realize they are being shown their own love story in Bollywood style. In *Om Shanti Om* (2007) when Om imagines himself as Bollywood superstar Rishi Kapoor singing in the film *Karz*, it adds a level of intensity to his already cinephilic existence. Thus dream sequences in songs are not meant to be a distinct mode of representation but one continuous with the entire aesthetic and tone of Bollywood as a whole. These, in turn, have an inherent morality attached to them: love songs that take place in dreams usually signal true love, even when that love has not yet been realized in the film's story. Rahul's dream in the thriller *Darr* (1993) is a rare exception, but the aesthetics of the song are exceptional: Kiran is just dancing by herself, objectified by his perverse imagination. The strangeness of this song sequence conveys the unreciprocated – and indeed non-virtuous – nature of Rahul's love, which ultimately turns to obsessive violence.

The love song will be discussed more fully below; but it is important to note here that even when a song sequence is highly unrealistic, when it clearly did not "really" happen within the story, an emotional or erotic trace from the song sequence does erupt into the narrative and affect the characters and even the development of the plot, further complicating any simple separation of diegetic and extradiegetic elements in Bollywood. For instance, when we see a love song set in the Swiss Alps, we are not meant to believe that the characters went on a trip to Switzerland; however, after the love song is over, the lovers are not unaffected by the intensity that was developed in the song sequence. Thus even though the song did not actually occur within the film's diegesis, the nature of the couple's relationship has "really" changed. This afterglow, so to speak, functions as a form of intensification that is as real, in Bollywood, as any plot event or character trait.

Other complex movements across the diegetic divide occur in various films, and the first step in understanding the meaning and function of a particular song sequence is identifying where it lies, diegetically speaking. For instance, both *Darr* (1993) and *Dilwale Dulhania Le Jayenge* (1995) have short musical motifs that recur throughout the films; these occur *both* as part of the sound-track – where they are extradiegetic – *and* are also, at other times, instru-mentalized, hummed, or whistled by the characters within the film, at times even being overheard by other characters, making them seem like part of the films' stories. We have a similar ambivalence in *Deewana* (1992), whose "Payaliya" song begins diegetically, motivated because Ravi is a famous singer and is on stage just about to begin a performance. He starts singing, then the curtain opens and he and Kajal find themselves in front of an audience. But then, the song becomes extradiegetic as the scene moves to a mountaintop location where they complete the love song that had started on stage. So just because a song sequence begins diegetically, in a realistic space within the nar-rative, it does not mean it has to stay that way. In *C.I.D.* (1956), the song "Leke Pehla Pehla Pyar" is played twice; the second time, it shifts through various diegetic registers. First, Rekha is tossing and turning in bed and hears the song in the distance; the song reminds her of Shekhar and so she is attracted to it. This suggests that the song is somehow within the diegesis. She gets out of bed and follows the sound; the music gets louder, but then Rekha seems to be singing the song, suggesting a more conventional extradiegetic song. Then, once again, she hears it being sung as if by someone else and covers her ears to not be reminded. This pattern repeats itself a couple of times, as Rekha both sings the song and hears it sung as if by a ghost.

Extradiegetic song sequences are an intrinsic part of Bollywood films, for which the question of realism simply does not apply. Some song sequences take place under such unrealistic circumstances that they cannot possibly happen within the story; for instance, in *Kashmir Ki Kali* (1964), Rajiv and Champa are escaping from Mohan, the villain, at a local fair, but even as they are running away from him they stop to sing a love song. The vast majority of song-and-dance sequences are used to intensify an emotional state – most often love – rather than advance the story. They should be considered like set-pieces, breaks in the narrative, and almost theatrical in their presentation. In fact, although we use the term melodrama to designate any exaggerated or sensational work of art, the origin of the term, from the Greek *melos*, actually refers to the role of music in a work of art.[20] In this way, Bollywood films are melodramas par excellence.

Lyrics

Most commonly, the melody of a Bollywood song is composed first, and lyri-cists add words only later. Bollywood song lyrics are often penned by poets and use features drawn from India's poetic traditions. Thus, they do not advance a story, but are affectively or sensorially motivated. They present emotions in highly metaphoric ways, using both classical poetic tropes as well as registering the changing nature of language over time. Recognizable tropes are often adapted from the ghazal, a poetic form that came to South Asia from Persia in the twelfth century and continued in popularity through the nineteenth century. As discussed in the previous chapter, one of the most common tropes to represent love in the ghazal is the image of a moth attracted to a flame. This is a metaphor for the intensity of love and the instinctual and even fatal attraction of the lover to the beloved. We see this trope in a wide range of Hindi film songs. In a song about separation in *Ram Aur Shyam* (1967), Shyam sings, "Kal teri bazm se deewana chala jayega/ Shama rahe jayegi parwana chala jayega" ("Tomorrow this lover will go away from your company/ The candle will remain and the moth will disappear"). A line in "Aaya Tere Dar Par" in *Veer-Zaara* (2004) states: "Zindagi haar doon main/ Jaise shama pe marta hai parwana" ("I'll lose my life for you/ Just like a moth dies in a flame").

The paradigmatic romantic couples discussed in the previous chapter – Radha-Krishna, Heer-Ranjha, Layla-Majnun – appear commonly in song lyrics. The comedic song "Main Sitaron Ka Tarana" from *Chalti Ka Naam Gaadi* (1958), in which Munnu is trying to get Renu to pay the money she owes him, contains the lyrics, "Tere liye Majnun ban sakta hoon/ 'Layla Layla' kar sakta hoon/… Lekin pehle de do mera/ Paanch rupaiya bara anna" ("I can become Majnun for you/ I can shout 'Layla, Layla' all day/… But first give me my five rupees and twelve annas"). In "Chal Diya Banda Nawaaz" in *Mr. and Mrs. 55* (1955), Anita dismisses Pritam's professions of love by calling him a "jungle ka Majnun miya," which could be translated as a "roadside Romeo." "Mohe Chhedo Na" from *Lamhe* (1991) is sung from the perspective of a milkmaid flirtatiously telling Krishna to stop teasing her, since Radha is his true love. "Radha Kaise Na Jale" from *Lagaan* (2001) references Krishna's philandering which incites Radha's jealousy, and Bhuvan and Gauri sing these lyrics early on in their love story. In the "Is Deewane Ladke Ko" song in *Sarfarosh* (1999), Ajay jokingly interrupts Seema's profession of love by reciting the lines, "Arz hai, kuch Majnun bane, kuch Ranjha bane, kuch Romeo, kuch Farhad hue/ Is rang roop ki chaahat mein, jaane kitne barbaad hue" ("Whether Majnun, or Ranjha, or Romeo, or Farhad, who knows how many were ruined by love"). These references appear in contemporary film songs as well, such as "Aisi Taisi" in *Shubh Mangal Zyada Saavdhan* (2020). This song references Majnun and Layla but has much more contemporary style and lyrics: "Ho Majnun ka dil London mein tha/ Aur Layla thi Bihar ki/… Badi tez mohabbat jaag gayi/ Peeche ke raaste bhaag gayi/ Arré aag laga gayi/ Gaaon mein poore pyar ki" ("Majnun's heart was in London/ And Layla was from Bihar/ Their love erupted quickly/ It ran out the back door/ The whole village got burnt in this love").

The most famous early lyricists were poets associated with the Progressive Writers' Movement and the Indian People's Theater Association, pan-Indian literary movements that sought to reinvigorate Indian literature with politically progressive values.[21] Sahir Ludhianvi, one of the most well-known Bollywood lyricists, was an Urdu poet whose writings called out social hypocrisy, economic inequality, communalism, and the mistreatment of women. He penned lyrics for a range of films, and one of his most famous poems was turned into the song "Jinhe Naaz Hai" for the film *Pyaasa* (1957), which criticized the hypocrisy of those who claim to love India but turn a blind eye to the mistreatment of women.[22] Ludhianvi's songs that celebrated religious harmony include "Tu Hindu Banega Na Musalman Banega" in the film *Dhool Ka Phool* (1959) and "Allah Tero Naam Ishwar Tero Naam" in *Hum Dono* (1961). As Manishita Dass writes, lyricists of this era did not just infuse Bollywood cinema with a progressive sensibility; they harnessed the utopian impulses of song to imagine a new form of politics mediated through music and poetry.[23]

While these poetic and political influences continue to be evident in Bollywood song lyrics, what has contributed to the popularity of Bollywood music over so many decades has been its flexibility – its ability to balance classical literary and devotional imagery with the changing language-scapes of India. Thus while Urdu poetry was the most common inspiration for the Bollywood love song in the twentieth century, new influences such as hip-hop and new languages such as "Hinglish" (a Hindi-English blend commonly spoken by young people in Indian cities) have resulted in a wide variety of new types of Bollywood lyrics, which keeps Bollywood songs contemporary. The song "Selfie Re" from *Bajrangi Bhai-jaan* (2015) has the refrain "Chal beta selfie le le re" ("Come on son, take a selfie"), and the song "Swag Se Swagat" from *Tiger Zinda Hai* (2017) contains the line, "Swag se karenge sabka swagat" ("We'll welcome everyone with swag"), the poetry resting on the similarity between the English "swag" and the Hindi "swagat" ("welcome").

Recently, several collaborations have also taken place between Bollywood music directors and international artists on both composition and vocals. The title song of the film *Singh is Kinng* (2008) was composed by British-Indian band RDB and American rapper Snoop Dogg features in its video, which begins with the following lyrics:

> Yo, what up this is big Snoop Dogg,
> Represent that Punjabi,
> Aye yo, hit'em with this …
> RDB, DPGC, Akshay and Snoop D-O double G
> Oh yeah, Singh is king, this is the thing,
> Do you know what I mean? Follow me,
> Listen to me for a second, check it
> Singh is the king … check the records.

Likewise, two songs in *Ra.One* (2011), "Chhamak Chalo" and "Criminal," contain vocals sung by international pop star Akon, who sang in both Hindi and English. Akon does not know Hindi, but a behind-the-scenes "Making Of" video released by the film producers shows Akon learning to imitate the sounds of Hindi to an impressive degree of accuracy, so that it is difficult to tell the songs are sung by a non-Hindi speaker.[24]

Case study: Javed Akhtar

Javed Akhtar is an Urdu poet and one of the most well-known and critically respected screenwriters of the 1970s, as part of the duo Salim-Javed who wrote the screenplays of such iconic films as *Andaz* (1971), *Zanjeer* (1973), *Deewaar* (1975), and *Sholay* (1975). After the 1980s he shifted to being a lyricist and has written lyrics for over one hundred films. In a presentation at Temple University in 2011, Akhtar admitted that part of the challenge for lyricists today is to reflect changes in idiom even while continuing to write poetry set to music. Unlike some others of his generation, he sees the increasing use of English and Hinglish in Bollywood not as a threat but as a productive challenge. This openness is evident in the way his lyrics have changed over the decades. He wrote the following verse for the film *Silsila* (1981), his first project as lyricist:

> Meri saanson mein basi khushboo teri
> Yeh tere pyar ki hai jaadugari
> Teri awaaz hai hawaon mein
> Pyar ka rang hai fizaon mein
> Dhadkanon mein tere geet hai mile hue
> Kya kahoon ke sharm se hai lab sile hue.

> [Your fragrance lies in my breath
> This is the magic of your love
> Your voice is in the breeze
> The color of love is in the air
> Your song is caught up with my heartbeats
> What can I say, my lips are sealed with shyness.]

While colloquial language has clearly changed by the time of the film *Rock On!* (2008), about a contemporary rock band, we also see how Akhtar maintains the poetic resonances seen in the earlier verses:

> Meri laundry ka ek bill, ek aadhi padhi novel
> Ek ladki ka phone number, mere kaam ka ek paper
> Mere taash se heart ka king, mera ek chandi ka ring
> Pichhle saat dinon mein maine khoya
> Kabhi khud pe hansa main, aur kabhi khud pe roya.

> [One of my laundry bills, an unfinished novel,
> A girl's phone number, a useful piece of paper
> There was a king of hearts in my deck
> And one of my silver rings
> When I look at what I lost this week
> Sometimes I laugh at myself, sometimes I cry.]

And, even more recently, in the 2019 film *Gully Boy*, about a hip-hop artist in the Dharavi neighborhood of Mumbai, we see further shifts in language, using Hindi slang mixed with a few English words, as well as in style, even as Akhtar continues his attentiveness to the materiality of language. Akhtar wrote this as a poem and then collaborated with rapper Divine for the final track:[25]

> Yeh toh saara 200 takka done hai
> Jitna kala tera man
> Utna kala tera dhan
> Woh tarfa shoot karte bole gun
> Yeh tarfa karte hain chillum
> Wahan pe peti peti dhan
> Yahan pe kheti kheti gandh
> Ek duniya mein do duniya ujala ek andhera
> Ek sethji aur ek chaila
> Kahin toh Motimahal mein koi jee raha hai akela
> Kahin toh local dibbe mein hai rele pe hai rela
> Unki seva inki mewa, haan?
>
> [One thing is for sure
> Your wealth is as impure as your heart
> On one side there are guns
> On the other side drugs
> Here we sleep on trash
> There you lounge on cash
> There are two worlds, light and dark
> Master and slave
> One lives alone in his palace
> The other fights for space
> We're the rats in your race, right?]

Through these three different songs spanning almost 40 years, we can see Akhtar's keen awareness of how language might shift to reflect the sensibility of the film, and indeed of the age. He is one of the many lyricists who are rethinking what the Bollywood song is and how it must accommodate a changing linguistic landscape, even within the parameters of what is called Hindi, but also including Hindustani, Urdu, and Hinglish.

Songs and emotions

Song sequences can convey a range of emotions. The "Nagari Nagari Dwara Dwara" song sequence in *Mother India* (1957) conveys Radha's pain and help-lessness after her husband abandons her and she is left to provide for her children by herself, with lyrics like "Bedardi baalam ne mohe phoonka gham ki aag mein" ("My heartless beloved has thrown me into a fire of sorrow") and "Pal-pal manwa roye chhalke nainon ki gagariya" ("My heart weeps and tears flow down my cheeks"), accompanied by images of her and her sons crying, amidst long shots of a desolate and uncompromising landscape. A few minutes later, the song "Duniya Mein Hum Aaye Hain" is played over a sequence of Radha and her children accepting their fate; the refrain of the song is "Duniya mein hum aaye hain toh jeena hi padega/ Jeevan hai agar zeher toh peena hi padega" ("We've come into this world so now we have to live in it/ If life is poison we'll just have to drink it") and it accompanies images of the three pushing a plough, carrying water, weeding, and working the land. These songs are not celebratory or joyous, but the music still works in the service of intense emotion.

Grief is another emotion often represented through song. In *Mahal* (1949), the "Ghabra Ke Jo Hum" song represents Ranjana's feeling of loss upon realizing that her husband does not love her. In *Seeta Aur Geeta* (1972), the "Haan Ji Haan Maine Sharab Pi" song seems to be a rejection of social norms, with Geeta pretending to be drunk so that Ravi will refuse to marry her, but in fact it is an expression of Geeta's deep pain (*dukh*). In "Neela Aasman," in *Silsila* (1981), Amit and Chandni sing about their lost love; the song is a duet, but they are not together when they are singing it, and the movement between their two locations within the song sequence formally underlines their separation. *Tamanna* (1997) begins with Tiku's mother's death, and Tiku's grief is represented in a background song that is not lip-synched. In *Dil Chahta Hai* (2001), the song "Tanhayee" represents Akash's loneliness after alienating his friends and the woman he loves. In *Om Shanti Om* (2007), "Jag Soona Lage" plays in the background after Om finds out that the woman he loves is already married. Funeral scenes usually have an intense song in the background, but are rarely lip-synched. However, these songs still circulate like other songs and are popular apart from the narrative to which they were originally attached.

Song sequences can also represent intense joy, such as "Koi Kahe" in *Dil Chahta Hai* (2001). Often this is the joy of falling in love, as discussed below, but it can be other kinds of joy, such as the exuberance of youth. This particular song sequence, set in a nightclub, is full of bright colors, flashing strobe lights, and energetic dancing. The lyrics confirm this sense of newness and jubilance: "Hum hain naye, andaz kyon ho purana?" ("We are new, why should our style be old?").

The love song

By far the most common purpose of the song sequence is the expression of love. In a classic love song sequence, two characters fall in love and then the scene switches to another locale and they are singing to each other about their love and dancing in sync. Often, the setting and their costumes change multiple times within the sequence. When the sequence is over, the two characters return to their normal lives. The audience is not meant to think that the pair actually went to the place where the song sequence was shot and actually sang those words. Rather, the sequence functions more like a dream, a break in the narrative where an emotion, in this case love, can be developed and deepened, through a beautiful setting, poetic lyrics, and an often erotically charged dance. It should be seen as an *intensification* of emotion rather than a development of the story. Indeed, such sequences are often remembered as much as the story of the film, especially as they circulate on television and social media.

The song sequence is an apt form to represent love which is, as was discussed in Chapter 2, the central theme of Bollywood cinema precisely for its affective, rather than cerebral quality. Bollywood love cannot be merely stated; it exceeds the social, material, or linguistic domain. The love song, then, is an aestheticization of love, an extension of its emotional core, an intensification of its affective register, and a pleasurable and interactive means to bring the audience closer to its beating heart.

The love song can announce or generate love, either by a character conveying her love in the form of a song, or by convincing a character that she is in fact in love, which she only realizes through the song. We see these various options in two different song sequences in *Mr. and Mrs. 55* (1955). Early in the film, Pritam falls in love with Anita at first sight, and his friend Johny finds him daydreaming while holding her handkerchief. Johny asks Pritam whose handkerchief it is, but he doesn't answer. When Johny repeats, "Gunga ho gaya? Tu bolta kyun nahin?" ("Have you gone mute? Why aren't you responding?"), Pritam responds by breaking into a love song that explains his situation to his friend in a way that mere prose words could not convey: "Dil par hua aisa jaadu/ Tabiyat machal-machal gayi/ Nazrein milin kya kisi se/ Ke halat badal-badal gayi" ("Something magical has happened to my heart/ My health is unsettled/ My eyes have met someone's/ I'm not the same as I once was"). Later in the film, Anita is starting to like Pritam as well, but she realizes the extent of her love only when they are taking a walk and overhear a passing village woman singing the song "Ab Toh Jee Hone Laga," whose lyrics include: "Thandi thandi thand mein dekho pawan chale/ Dheere dheere kaahe man mein jale/ Aaja kahin dur jaaye/ Dekho tere paas aaye/ Gori tere saajana" ("Just feel the cool breeze/ And feel your heart on fire/ Why are you going away?/ Look, your beloved is coming for you"). The implication is that in hearing these suggestive lyrics, Anita is able to recognize her true feelings for Pritam.

In many cases the love song conveys and enhances the intensity of love, whether it is a first love, a sudden realization of love, or a long-standing relationship that suddenly appears as love. The combination of a beautiful location, evocative lyrics, and energetic choreography make the song exceed a simple message, as it engages with the viewer emotionally and libidinally, generating an affective dimension that invites the viewer to participate in the erotic universe of the film. In *Raja Hindustani* (1996), on the eve of Aarti's departure, Raja sings a song in which he foresees a painful separation for both of them: "Har pal meri yaad tumhein tadpayegi/ Main jaagoonga, neend tumhein na aayegi/ Chodke aise haal mein jo tum jaoge/ Sach kehta hoon jaan bahut pachtaoge" ("My memories will always torment you/ I will remain awake and sleep will elude you/ If you leave me in this state/ You will regret it"). It is the very intensity and eroticism of the song that makes Aarti change her mind and leave her family to elope with Raja. In *Sarfarosh* (1999), Ajay and Seema realize they love each other at his birthday party, surrounded by family and friends, and so the love song, "Jo Haal Dil Ka" – where they are able to express their desire for one another and experience each other erotically – takes place in another space and is interspersed with the domestic setting, so it is as if they are experiencing the domestic birthday party and the passionate intensity of their love simultaneously.

There are also comedic songs that play with these conventions, as in the "Main Sitaron Ka Tarana" song that Mannu imagines singing with Renu in *Chalti Ka Naam Gaadi* (1958), which seems like a love song but is actually an excuse for Mannu to ask Renu for the money she owes him for repairing her car. While she sings, in the poetic idiom of the love song, "Josh-e-ulfat ka zamana/ Laage hai kaisa suhaana/ Leke ek angdaai mujh pe/ Dal nazar ban jaa deewana" ("The time of love's passion is wondrous/ Cast your eye on me and you'll go crazy"), he responds, "Manta hoon hai suhana/ Josh-e-ulfat ka zamana/ Lekin pehle de do mera/ Paanch rupaiya bara aana" ("I believe you that the time of love's passion is wondrous/ But first, please give me my five rupees and twelve annas"). As Mannu's practical request for the money she owes him is cleverly deflected through the poetry of the love song, the song casts comic light on Bollywood love.

Some recent Bollywood films poke fun at the conventions of the love song from a more explicitly parodic angle. In *Main Hoon Na* (2004), a film that affectionately parodies a number of Bollywood conventions, every time Ram sees Chandni, he cannot help but bend down on his knees, spread his arms wide, and sing her a love song, mocking the repeated gestures of the love song sequence. At one point, Ram looks from side to side at his two outstretched arms, wondering why they are posed in this way (Figure 3.1). Parodying the idea that the love song is an irrepressible force that is out of the lover's control,

Figure 3.1 Every time he sees Chandni, Ram hears music and his body makes the Bollywood lover's classic gesture, against his own volition, in *Main Hoon Na* (2004).

the film simultaneously utilizes this convention, as it turns out Chandni is Ram's destined love and they end up happily together.

Erotics

Because the song sequence exists outside the film's diegesis, it is often a place where erotic energy can be more directly conveyed than in the main narrative. Although in most cases, there is no kissing on the mouth as part of song sequences, the lack of overt representation of sexuality does not mean the song sequence is devoid of erotics altogether. In fact, the song sequence's representation of a dream state beyond the material world and its lack of realism means that conventions for representing sex and sexuality within the primary narrative can be transgressed. Thus love songs are often intensely erotic, involving physical interaction, facial expressions like looking into each other's eyes, and sensual dancing and lyrics.

There is something about music itself that is signified as erotic. In the snake dance Rosie performs in *Guide* (1965), she becomes almost frenzied as she gets carried away by the dance, suggesting that song and dance have the potential to take people beyond the limits of society or respectability. It is partly because of this transgressive nature of dance that she tells Raju not to tell her husband about the performance. The inherent sensuality of dance is also the reason Rosie's husband does not want her to dance any longer. After she leaves Marco, who is an inconsiderate and cold husband, the first thing Rosie does is buy a pair of anklets – again confirming the relationship between dance and female erotic freedom. Likewise in *Guddi* (1971), when Navin wants to seduce Kusum, he asks her to sing for him, and her agreeing to do so is read by him as a sign of her reciprocated desire. In *Nagina* (1986), when Rajni tries to distract Raju to protect him, she does this by singing a song to seduce him, with the suggestion that she is trying to distract him from his plans through the possibility of a sexual encounter.

Often the song sequence conveys an erotic message that cannot be spoken in the main narrative. In "Hum Tum Ek Kamre Mein Band Ho" ("You and I Are Locked in a Room") in *Bobby* (1973), the love between Raj and Bobby – for the most part presented as an innocent puppy-love given the characters' young ages – is given a sexual subtext as Bobby closes all the doors of the house and they sing about a private, bedroom love. Similarly in *Darr* (1993), Sunil and Kiran sing a song called "Darwaza Band Kar Lo" ("Close the Door"), suggesting erotic intimacy in the privacy of their new house.

The premise of the song "Zara Sa Jhoom Loon Main" in *Dilwale Dulhania Le Jayenge* (1995) is that Simran is drunk and therefore can be more explicit about her sexual desire. The song is comedic in part because Simran pursues Raj, trying to embrace him and making motions to kiss and undress him, and he tries to avoid her until, frustrated, he starts drinking himself and then he too loses his inhibitions, and which point she starts to run away from him. Both the comedy of the song sequence and the locations in a snowy countryside and a

European city offer the chance for the latent erotic energy between Raj and Simran to come to the surface in a way that both signals their love and allows for a glimpse of what is otherwise still a buried passion. On the snowy land-scape, Simran sings about the heat of her body – "Thandi thandi pavan, jalta hai yeh badan" ("The cool breeze sets my body on fire") – conveying her latent sexuality and desire. Again, although the song does not actually "happen" in the story, the heightened emotion and erotics it generates seep into the storyline, so that when Raj and Simran wake up the next morning and he tells her that "kal raat, wahi hua … jo hona chahiye tha" ("last night, what should have happened did happen"), and then quickly assures her that he is joking, their relationship reaches a new intimacy. When the two embrace afterwards, we see the first diegetic stirrings of desire on Simran's part. This marks a moment when the erotic and the romantic come together to construct the groundwork for their burgeoning love story.

In *Aradhana* (1969), there are two song sequences close to each other that build the erotic energy between Vandana and Arun. In the first, they sing "Gun Guna Rahe Hain Bhanvre," a song that uses bees and flowers as suggestive images of fertility. After the song, they go to a temple to exchange garlands under the eyes of god. This seemingly mundane marriage sequence is rendered erotic because it emerges out of and follows the intensely erotic song. Immedi-ately after the temple, there is a scene where they talk about having children together and then, because it starts raining, they go to a guest house where two lovers are having a romantic encounter in the next room. Overhearing their erotically charged banter arouses Arun and Vandana, and the song, "Roop Tera Mastana," whose lyrics are about the intoxication and madness of love, leads them to make love in their room for the first time.

Rain scenes are particularly erotic, due in part to the association of the monsoon season with fertility. Wetness is often an externalized expression of erotics in songs, as in "Mere Khwabon Mein" in *Dilwale Dulhania Le Jayenge* (1995), where Simran's wet body underlines the lyrics' expression of her sexual desire. In *Deewana* (1992), part of the love song "Teri Isi Ada Pe Sanam" takes place in an isolated park in the rain; both the lovers are soaking wet. In *Prem Kahani* (1971), Kamini is married to another man, but is still in love with Rajesh; she stands by the window during a rainstorm, getting completely soaked, as she sings to Rajesh about her unrequited desire for him, her heart beating wildly. Unable to requite her desire, Rajesh quietly closes the win-dows, blocking out the rain and all it implies. Similarly, in *Fanaa* (2006), the "Dekho Na" song in the rain is highly erotic and results in the couple making love for the first time.

Case study: "Suraj Hua Maddham," from Kabhi Khushi Kabhie Gham (2001)

The "Suraj Hua Maddham" song sequence is a paragon for how eroticism can be conveyed in the space of the Bollywood song sequence, without any kissing and very little touching. Visually, the sequence is picturized and choreographed using sharp edges, modern shapes, and bright, monochrome colors, and it builds on the spectacular popularity of the Shah Rukh Khan–Kajol pairing discussed further in Chapter 5. Set against the backdrop of the Egyptian pyramids and other striking desert landscapes, the lyrics focus on images of heat – the setting sun and the shimmering moon – and energy – "Main tehra raha, zameen chalne lagi" ("I stand still as the earth moves around me") – conveying a love that is experienced as a completely overwhelming, natural force. While Anjali's saris are mostly primary colors, Rahul moves between a sheer top and white pants, an all-black ensemble, and brown faux-leather, and the lovers are pictured sometimes apart, using long shots that diminish their bodies in relation to a striking visual landscape, and sometimes together, in medium or close up shots, dancing in unison, looking into each other's eyes, or both facing the same way, with Rahul behind Anjali, stroking or kissing her neck or running his finger along her collarbone (Figure 3.2). Interspersed with these images are visualizations of both their fantasies about the other joining their family. Thus, the erotic and the domestic flow into one another in this song sequence in a way that neither tames the former nor rejects the latter. The relationship between the domestic and the erotic is one of the underlying – though rarely explicitly expressed – themes of Bollywood love stories, and nowhere is this better conveyed than in this love song sequence.

Female sexual desire

Although the narrative arcs of Bollywood films seem to valorize marriage and the heteronormative romance, song sequences are one of the primary sites where we can see alternative sensibilities emerge. Song sequences are not contained within the narrative and therefore can present unexpressed, and even inexpressible, desires.

Figure 3.2 Erotic love amidst dramatic landscapes in "Suraj Hua Maddham," from *Kabhi Khushi Kabhie Gham* (2001).

As we have seen, Bollywood operates as a sort of dreamworld, with desire and the material world not presented as rigidly distinct. The song sequence only intensifies this overlapping between the two states. In addition to song sequences that express love between two people, song sequences can also represent a one-sided or unrequited love. Here the songs tend to be less joyous and more self-reflective. They can also give an erotic vocabulary to female characters who might not have much space in the dialogue of the film to give voice to their erotic desires.

In *Sahib Bibi Aur Ghulam* (1962), Jaba, whose marriage has been arranged to a man who is not the man she is in love with, sings because she cannot speak; the lines "Meri baat rahi mere man mein/ Kuch keh na saki, uljhan mein" ("My words remain within me/ I can't speak in my confusion") metafictionally comment on the fact that as a woman, she can express emotions and feelings through song that there is no space for her to express in words.

This sentiment is paradigmatic for women's agency through song. In *Guddi* (1971), after Kusum meets the actor Dharmendra, she dreams about him in a fantasy song, expressing a devotion that she cannot explain to her family and friends. In *Kabhi Kabhie* (1976), Pooja has a wedding night love song with her true lover, even though the man who is slowly undressing her, garment by garment, is her actual husband; through the song, her fantasy of her former lover becomes part of the sexual experience of her wedding night. In *Qayamat Se Qayamat Tak* (1988), the song "Gazab Ka Hai Din" is an expression of Rashmi's fantasy of her and Raj occupying a world apart from society: "Tum ho akele, hum bhi akele, mazaa aa raha hai" ("You are alone, I'm alone too, we're having fun"). In this song sequence, Raj comes off as relatively immature and Rashmi, though equally young, as a woman who knows what she wants, romantically and perhaps sexually (she lies down to sleep next to him even after he awkwardly tells her not to). In *Lamhe* (1991), Pooja is in love with Viren but her love is not (yet) requited; the "Kabhi Main Kahoon" song is a one-sided fantasy of her love and desire, and in *Hum Dil De Chuke Sanam* (1999), Nandini dreams of her lover in the song "Chand Chupa Badal Mein" even though she is currently in her husband's house.

In *Dilwale Dulhania Le Jayenge* (1995), the first song sequence is "Mere Khwabon Mein" ("In My Dreams") sung by Simran, the film's protagonist. In the scene immediately preceding the song, Simran's mother finds her diary where she is writing about an unseen, as-yet unknown man of her dreams, whom she will know is the right one for her the moment they meet. As she describes this man to her mother, the film cuts to a song sequence in which we see the character, Raj, who will ultimately be the man of Simran's dreams. The fantasy song thus represents her unarticulated sexual and romantic desire. The song sequence is playful, but at the same time the lyrics reflect her sexual maturity. At times Simran is dancing in the rain, suggesting her sensuality, but she is also in control of her own image,[26] as demonstrated in shots where she is looking straight into the camera (Figure 3.3). By contrast, the interspersed scenes of Raj show him acting in various typically macho ways – playing sports,

Figure 3.3 Simran, singing about her dreams in the rain, in *Dilwale Dulhania Le Jayenge* (1995).

trying to outrun an airplane – but when we actually meet Raj, he is notably *not* macho. Thus this song is revealed as Simran's *fantasy* of an ideal masculinity rather than an accurate representation of Raj. Also notably – and this is true of most female desire songs – it is *Simran's* dreams that are being articulated, with Raj a silent participant. This is also true of Priya's fantasy song in *Baazigar* (1993), which is preceded by her lying on her bed and breathing heavily as she fantasizes about the man she has just fallen in love with.

In *Veer-Zaara* (2004), after the two lovers are forcibly separated, Zaara cannot stop thinking about Veer and her disquiet is represented in the song "Main Yahan Hoon." As the song plays, Veer appears to Zaara as a ghost or fantasy and she sees his figure everywhere she looks. They embrace, and Veer's ghost partially undresses her as they lie down together, with him on top of her (Figure 3.4). Within the story, Veer is not physically present, so this erotic song

Figure 3.4 Zaara fantasizes about Veer in "Main Yahan Hoon," from *Veer-Zaara* (2004).

sequence takes place entirely in Zaara's imagination and reveals her sexual agency. In *Dil Se* (1997), Preeti has a fantasy song as she is preparing for her wedding to Amar, when she imagines him as a shirtless boatman and the choreography foregrounds his physical body, unmistakably asserting her erotic fantasy.[27] And in *Aiyyaa* (2012), a film that is much more frank in its representation of female desire and sexuality, the song "Dreamum Wakeupum" represents Meenakshi's desire for Surya. All these song sequences allow for the articulation of women's desires outside of the primary narrative.

Prohibited desire

In addition to depicting love and desire, song sequences can also express parallel, repressed, or at times contradictory sentiments that cannot be contained within the plot, whether because the characters are not allowed to love each other, or because of the need to keep films "family friendly." This is one of the more interesting usages of the song sequence because it allows alternative and queer desires to exist within what may seem like heteronormative or prudish plots.

At times, highly erotic dance sequences can happen through clever plot moves. For instance, the song "Kate Nahin Katate" in *Mr. India* (1987) has Seema dancing in the rain in a soaking wet sari in moves that resemble passionate embraces. But the twist is that Mr. India has the power of invisibility, and so while most of the song is choreographed with them in various stages of embrace, she is dancing with an invisible man, so their physical contact is intimated but not actually shown. This allows their desire to be represented without crossing any boundaries of propriety.[28]

Through various reconfigurations of expectations, songs can serve as sites where couples who are not supposed to love each other can do so. For instance, there is a convention in wedding song sequences in which the song is performed not by the bride and groom, but by their proxies. This can lead to interesting arrangements. For instance, in "Mehndi Lagake Rakhna," the engagement song in *Dilwale Dulhania Le Jayenge* (1995), Raj sings the groom's role and thus can express his love for Simran, the bride, even though their love is secret. Many of this song's lyrics have a double meaning, so that the invocation of hiding one's face behind a veil, which on the surface level refers to modesty, also refers to the dissimulation, the hiding of the bride's true intentions. Likewise, the line "Lene tujhe o gori/ Aayenge tere sajana," ("Your lover is coming to take you away, o beautiful one"), which is a line typical of an Indian wedding song, here has a double meaning because "your lover" refers not to the groom but to her real lover, Raj.

In the wedding song "Yeh Ladka Hai Allah," in *Kabhi Khushi Kabhie Gham* (2001), Anjali and Rahul both sing and dance as proxies for the bride and groom, and thus as they perform those roles, are able to express their love for each other. Likewise, in "Aaya Tere Dar Par," the qawwali in *Veer-Zaara* (2004) that is supposed to be a celebration of Zaara and Raza's upcoming marriage, Zaara's real lover, Veer, shows up at the dargah (shrine) where it is being performed, resignifying the lyrics of intense eroticism – "Aaya tere dar par deewana/ Tere ishq mein isse mar jaana" ("This lover has come to your door/ He wants to die for your love") – with a meaning that goes beyond – and ultimately ruptures – the marriage plot.

Case study: "Rang Barse," from Silsila (1981)

"Rang Barse" is a classic example of a song sequence that allows for the representation of prohibited desire. In *Silsila*, Amit and Chandni are in love, but after Amit's brother dies in an airplane accident, he feels obliged to marry Shobha, his late brother's fiancée, who is also carrying his brother's child. This sense of obligation makes Amit depressed, and he never falls out of love with Chandni. Eventually, she gets married as well but they continue their affair. The occasion for "Rang Barse" is the Hindu holiday of Holi, a spring festival and a day on which, traditionally, boundaries can be transgressed and social hierarchies can be temporarily upturned. In addition, men often drink bhang on Holi, a dairy-based drink laced with hashish. Holi's associations with transgression are exploited in this song sequence, as Amit uses the occasion to celebrate with Chandni, his true love. Amit sings to Chandni using suggestive lyrics about springtime and fertility – "Rang barse, bheege chunarwali, rang barse!" ("The colors rain on the veiled young woman") – even though there are others present. At first everyone is enjoying the song but as Amit gets more drunk he becomes less subtle in his address to Chandni, eyes locked only with hers and moving physically closer, to such an extent that both Shobha and Chandni's husband start to get uncomfortable. In this case, the erotic engagement of the song sequence is so intense that it spills over into the diegesis and intimates to Shobha and Chandni's husband that their spouses are being unfaithful.

In *Prem Kahani* (1971), former lovers Kamini and Rajesh share a love song, even though Kamini is married to Rajesh's best friend Dheeraj. The song plays while all three of them are in the room, but it is picturized almost exclusively showing Rajesh and Kamini, alternating close-ups of the two of them and thus allowing them to convey their transgressive love. The freedom of the song sequence from abiding by filmic realism also means that conflicting love plots can be picturized within one song. In the title song of *Kuch Kuch Hota Hai* (1998), Rahul and Tina love each other, but Anjali loves Rahul, unbeknownst to him. They all manage to express their love in a single song, each using the lyrics to support her or his own love story. The song becomes a visual expression of the love triangle.

Although it is rarer than the heterosexual love song, duets can also be sung by two men, suggesting a potential queer subtext, a topic that will be covered in more depth in Chapter 7. Sometimes it is two men both singing about their love for a woman. For instance, in *Chandni* (1989), Rohit and Lalit sing "Tu Mujhe Suna" together as they narrate their love stories to each other. The audience knows that they are in love with the same woman, but the men don't know it yet. The fact that it is a love triangle rather than two couples potentially queers the scene. This queering of the love story can also happen through a proxy situation as described above, such as in "Didi Tera Dewar" from *Hum Aapke Hain Koun* (1994), in which a woman plays the role of the groom in a pre-wedding song, so that the latent erotics of the song sequence is between two women rather than the heterosexual couple.

In this way, song sequences can either intensify or subvert normative ideas within the film's plot. Even if the plot suggests a neat progression from love to marriage, the song-and-dance sequences, because of their extradiegetic and excessive quality, suggest myriad alternative possibilities. Because of the importance of song-and-dance sequences and the fact that they are often watched on their own, apart from the narrative in which they were originally embedded, these alternative meanings are just as important as what happens in the story.

Lust and the item number

While usually song sequences portray positive emotions like love or joy, or elicit empathy by representing sadness or grief, one negative emotion represented by the song sequence can be lust, which is usually distinguished from the more tender and erotic qualities of love, romance, and desire. Lust is often conveyed in item number sequences, which are dances that feature a female dancer as the "item" dancer, who often appears only for a cameo in the particular song sequence rather than as a character in the film. Often the dancer is surrounded by a male audience in a setting of ill-repute, such as a dance bar or a brothel. In such sequences, the choreography is often overtly sexual and the eyes of the men are leery and objectify the female dancer.

However, in many cases the objectifying male gaze is questioned even while it is being solicited.[29] In the "Kajra Re" item song in *Bunty Aur Babli* (2005), the actor Aishwarya Rai plays with the familiar dance-bar setting in which her body is the object of the male gaze by coolly rejecting the men attempting to woo her (Figure 3.5).[30] Likewise, both Madhuri Dixit's dance to "Choli Ke Peeche Kya Hai" in *Khalnayak* (1993) and Priyanka Chopra's to "Asalaam-e-Ishqum" in *Gunday* (2014) (which are not technically item numbers since both actors play characters in the film), where they perform, scantily clad, in front of a crowd of men, turn out to be deliberate attempts to seduce and thus distract the men; as we later discover, both women are cops working on a case.

Elsewhere as well, the item number as a site of female objectification is commented upon within the moral universe of the film itself, as the men in the scene are usually associated with immorality, and so rather than condoning the objectification, the film is implicitly criticizing it. This occurs in "Meri Raaton Ki Neendein Udade" in *Sarfarosh* (1999), in which the villain Gulfam and his criminal associates are watching women dance for their entertainment, and in *Sholay*'s (1975) item number "Mehbooba Mehbooba," which features Helen, a well-known item dancer in the 1960s and 1970s, who is performing for the den of villains led by Gabbar Singh. Gabbar's men are so fixated on the dance, intoxicated by lust, that the film's heroes, Jai and Veeru, use this opportunity to

Figure 3.5 The item dancer is not impressed with the men who try to objectify her, in *Bunty Aur Babli* (2005).

attack their encampment (Figure 3.6). Part of Jai and Veeru's heroism here is that *they* do not get seduced by the vamp but remain fixated on their mission to enact justice against the villain. The suggestion here is that lust is a weakness that heroes can exploit.

Another scene in *Sholay* thematizes the item number from another direction. The villain Gabbar Singh kidnaps both Basanti and Veeru, and once he realizes they are romantically involved, decides to torture them both simultaneously by forcing Basanti to dance in front of him and his men while Veeru is tied up in such a way that he is forced to watch. In doing so, Gabbar mobilizes the objectification inherent in the item song as a means to make Veeru suffer. But far from capitulating to this attempt at humiliation, Basanti's ensuing dance resists objectification in a number of ways. In the refrain, "Jab tak hai jaan,

Figure 3.6 Gabbar Singh (second to the left) is so fixated on the dance that he does not notice the arrival of our heroes to his camp, in *Sholay* (1975).

main nachungi" ("While I have life, I will dance"), she announces her agency over her own body. This is replicated in her unflinching gaze; rather than acting coy or ashamed, she stares back at Gabbar Singh as she dances, clearly disconcerting him. Likewise, the camera refuses to frame her in the traditional perspective of an item song, using exaggerated high and low angles and multiple spinning shots to create a disorienting effect that replicates *her* perspective, as she spins around in the blinding hot sun, rather than – as is conventionally assumed – that of the men who are watching her. Even as Basanti tires, she keeps dancing, asserting her body as a site of resistance rather than humiliation. Consequently, as the song continues, Gabbar's face registers increasing frustration rather than triumph, as the conventional power dynamics of the item song have been turned on their head and Basanti's dancing body refuses to be the consumable object of his gaze.

Thus, while lust might be seen as the limit case of the Bollywood song sequence, there are cases in which countervailing dynamics are enabled even within the supposedly objectifying item number. In all these cases, song sequences make meaning by resignifying expectations established in earlier films. In this way, song-and-dance sequences are not only essential to how Bollywood engages its audience, but might be seen as the very heart of the cinema. Understanding the different elements of the song sequence, how it functions diegetically, and how it is innovated on is essential for understanding this long-misunderstood aspect of the Bollywood film.

4 Visual style

In Bollywood's visual style, more is generally better. Bollywood films have a unique look, often unabashedly embracing artifice rather than attempting to be realistic.[1] Elaborate sets, theatrical lighting, tableaux, and bright colors dominate. It is an aesthetic of overstatement and excess[2] – an aesthetic in which, much like Broadway or a drag performance, outrageousness is favored over subtlety. The illusion of realism is also broken by filmic techniques such as rapid zooms and pans and repeated cross-cutting, and characters often look directly into the camera. At times, Bollywood's theatrical visual style substitutes for psychological interiority. At other times, these visual effects intensify an emotion or mental state, like italicizing or highlighting a word on a page. And lastly, Bollywood's colorful and anti-realist visual style adds to Bollywood's cinephilic quality, more of which will be discussed in Chapter 5.

Many scholars trace Bollywood's unique visual style to the Parsi theater, a hybrid European and Indian form of drama popular in India in the late nineteenth and early twentieth centuries.[3] The frontal view, theatrical staging, and overall "structure of excess,"[4] in addition to a thematic focus on love, characterized the Parsi theater and can be seen as a prototype of Bollywood. However, few contemporary viewers know much about or have access to the Parsi theater, and so today, most of these visual qualities are associated primarily with Bollywood rather than with any predecessor.

Bollywood visuality extends beyond the films themselves. Images from films were historically circulated in the form of newspaper advertisements, handbills, booklets that included song lyrics, publicity brochures, souvenir booklets, lobby cards, hand-painted posters, and hoardings, which eventually became television commercials and production house websites.[5]

Morality and visual style

In Chapter 1 we saw how a Bollywood film's moral universe is established early on. The moral universe is conveyed primarily visually. Generally, beautiful, colorful, and well-lit visuals are associated with heroes, and dark lighting and low or otherwise disorienting angles are used for villains. A bright, well-lit artificial set full of family members and friends anticipates a requited romance, whereas a remote location, far from society, as in the secluded mansion in *Mahal* (1949), represents a story at the edge of social sanction where morality might not be so clear-cut.

The visual introduction of a character is one of the primary ways a film conveys morality. One technique often used is delaying the introduction of a character by, for instance, showing her back before showing her face, as with the introduction of the title character in *Chandni* (1989), played by Sridevi, or by another character calling out to her, then showing her with hair covering her face for a few seconds, until finally – a good five seconds later – dramatically brushing her hair away, as with Kajol's Simran in *Dilwale Dulhania Le Jayenge* (1995). In *Raja Hindustani* (1996), the hero Raja, played by Aamir Khan, is introduced first by his feet sticking out a car window where he is sleeping inside, then a shot of him kicking open the car door is repeated three times, and only then does he sit up to reveal his face. In *Kal Ho Naa Ho* (2003), Aman, played by Shah Rukh Khan, is first shown from the back and then the top of his head before his face is finally revealed. Since in all these cases the audience is well aware of who the hero is and which actor he or she is being played by, these dramatic, hyperbolic visual markers of heroism serve to enhance the anticipation of seeing the star and, ultimately, the pleasure of seeing her. They also serve to further link visuality with morality.

Conversely, low angles or otherwise strange and disorienting angles are often used to represent villains; for instance the rapist Shyam in *Aradhana* (1969) is represented through low angles to emphasize his villainy. A wide angle that underlines the emptiness of the Naths' massive entry hall, with Raj dwarfed at the center, suggests loneliness and alienation in *Bobby* (1973), which becomes a critique of the family's wealth, moral corruption, and lack of love toward their son. Vicky is also shot from a low angle in *Baazigar* (1993) when he gains control of the Chopra company, and Bollywood's most paradigmatic villain, Gabbar Singh from *Sholay* (1975), is constantly shot in low angles, especially in the scenes in his desert den.

Visuality is tied to morality in other ways as well. The explicitly nationalist film *Purab Aur Paschim* (1970) begins under colonial rule and in black and white, and the whole film switches to color at the moment of independence, suggesting a straightforward connection between bright colors and morality. In short, visual style is not merely the vehicle for the transmission of meaning but actually contributes to meaning.

Color

Color film was not popularized in India until the 1960s, even though the first color film was produced in 1937.[6] The use of color enhances the visuality of Bollywood and allows it to express its hyperbolic aesthetics even more intensely and directly. As Rachel Dwyer and Divia Patel write, color film allowed filmmakers to "shift ... from texture and light constrast to the use of colour co-ordination" as part of the visual appeal of the cinema.[7] Early filmmakers experimented with color first in individual song sequences within a film, such as "Chaudvin Ka Chand" in the film by the same name (1961) and "Pyar Kiya Toh Darna Kya" from *Mughal-e-Azam* (1960).[8] Beginning in the 1950s, bright Eastmancolor gave new vibrancy to Bollywood visuals, setting new standards for the visual appeal of sets, song locations, and costumes.[9] Color film also encouraged filmmakers to shoot in foreign locations, "as colour film encouraged the use of landscape as spectacle."[10]

Color is linked with morality. Bright colors usually signify a moral universe and the possibility of love and sexuality. As Clare Wilkinson-Weber records, color and especially "color combinations" are central to defining a star's look. Within films, celebrations such as weddings and the Hindu holiday of Holi, when friends and loved ones are smeared with brightly colored powder in an enjoyment of springtime, are always full of color and are thus moral occasions. Conversely, Bollywood widows are often dressed in white, signifying their distance from joy and eroticism. This is emphasized in the Holi scene in *Sholay* (1975), when the young widow Radha stands apart from the colorful celebration in her white sari, marking her as outside the domestic sphere and highlighting the sense of loss and powerlessness that motivates that film's vigilante plot. Likewise, when the bandits attack the village in the midst of their Holi celebration, they symbolically desecrate all the moral associations that color has in the Bollywood universe.

The sensuous quality of color in Bollywood is allegorized in *Aiyyaa* (2012), in which Meenakshi's attraction to Surya is mediated by the smell of paint that follows him everywhere. When she enters his studio she picks up his brushes soaked in blue paint in order to smell them and runs her fingers through the brush basin, which is shot as if from the bottom of the basin, so the water clouds up in a visually striking way. Meenakshi's heightened sense of the erotic is here directly associated with a deep and vibrant color palette.

Costumes

Elaborate, colorful, and stylish costumes are an essential part of Bollywood's visual repertoire. For Bollywood's first several decades, women's costumes received more attention, not only as a part of the female hero's overall glamor, but also as a site of intense pleasure and identification. As with many other aspects of Bollywood's visual style, costumes can be over the top in a number of ways. Conventionally, bright colors are an important part of especially women's aesthetics in India, but Bollywood costume designers tend to take that to another level by adorning stars in bright, multi-colored saris or salwar kameezes, often with gold or other shiny embroidery.

As discussed in Chapter 1, sartorial conventions change over time, and so it is important to know the conventions for the period in which a film is made and set before making assumptions about what a character's costume means. In the 1950s, wearing a miniskirt might suggest immorality, but that is not the case in the 2000s. It is common for female characters in contemporary films to dress at times in Indian clothes and at other times in western clothes, and that should not be read as a sign of so-called westernization but as a facet of contemporary reality – just like the fact that many contemporary protagonists switch from Hindi to English and back. That bilingual and bi-sartorial reality is part of the contemporary Indian landscape that many newer films are representing.

In addition, the traditional–western binary does not account for the malleability and semiotic multiplicity of Bollywood clothing. The sari, for instance, is worn in Bollywood by mothers, widows, and grandmothers, but is also a sensual or erotic garment. As Clare Wilkinson-Weber writes, the sari's "erotic potential emerges from its essential character as a sinuous wrapping of the body that continuously hints at unwrapping."[11] This is evident in the various fabrics used for the sari as well as the different drapes accentuating different parts of a star's body. Likewise, the veil also "figures … in cinematic courtesans' erotic performances. They dance with it, covering and uncovering their faces, teasing viewers with it, sometimes flinging it off, and sometimes entering with faces fully covered."[12] The song "Parda Hai" in *Amar Akbar Anthony* (1977) plays with the erotics of the veil, as Akbar's love interest Salma enters the auditorium with her face covered, under the watchful eye of her conservative father, and Akbar flirtatiously sings to her, "Pardanashin ko beparda na kar doon toh Akbar mera naam nahin hai" ("If I can't unveil the face under the veil then my name isn't Akbar").

Changing fashion trends and India's multi-layered modernity means that although it is tempting to read symbolic meanings into costumes, such readings do not always generate accurate analysis. As Clare Wilkinson-Weber writes,

> a costume is deliberately engineered to be simultaneously depth and surface: depth in its heightened salience, or how it signifies mood, personhood, and status in ways more deliberative and purposeful than in real life; surface in the choices and treatments of fabric, color, and embellishment that turn dress into spectacle.

Even in Bollywood's early decades, there were multiple meanings of clothes such as the sari or the salwar kameez; thus, neither should be interpreted simply as a sign of virtue or respectability. In *Guide* (1965), Rosie wears saris but, coming from a family of temple dancers, she does not fit into conventional bourgeois morality. The viewer is asked to pick up on multiple signs of Rosie's transgressive nature – including the anklets she wears when she dances – but in this case, her saris are not part of that repertoire. Throughout Bollywood, therefore, clothes should equally be understood as visual markers – of beauty, desire, and identification – and as allegorical indications of a larger political or socio-cultural meaning.

Costumes and costume changes constitute one of the many pleasurable aspects of Bollywood films, especially seeing a star in multiple outfits and in multiple types of outfits over the course of a film or even in one individual song sequence. As Clare Wilkinson-Weber argues, these multiple, temporally "compressed" re-presentations of the self offer a fantasy space in which epic transformation is envisioned within a short space of narrative time. These changes have multiple possible meanings: "as a marker of passing time, as a clue to inner states, or as an indicator that the characters are enjoying the imaginary pleasures of embodying different kinds of people."[13] Sometimes costume changes are thematized in the film, as in the "Zara Sa Jhoom Loon Main" song sequence in *Dilwale Dulhania Le Jayenge* (1995), when Simran sees a dress she likes in a store window and brandishes a rock, and then in the next scene is pictured wearing the dress. Of course, this is all within the fantasy space of the song, so we are not meant to believe that she stole the dress. But this scene nevertheless demonstrates how costumes operate similarly to song sequences and other aspects of Bollywood's visual style, inciting characters' and viewers' desire.

Case study: An Evening in Paris (1967)

The pleasure and affective exuberance of costumes are evident in *An Evening in Paris*, a film in which the glamorous style icon Sharmila Tagore is shown in a range of costumes, including a cosmopolitan hybrid sari with a sleeveless blouse (Figure 4.1), a colorful ghagra-choli (Figure 4.2), a sequined cabaret number (Figure 4.3), and a bright blue, one-piece bathing suit (Figure 4.4).

The range and multiplicity of the kinds of costumes and their constant shifting intensify the star's already glamorous image. Moreover, they offer multiple sites of identification across a range of both regional and cosmopolitan markers, which enhance this film's own seamless image of Indian cosmopolitanism in Europe.

Each decade witnessed costume trends and trendsetters. In the 1940s and 1950s the saris were fashionable, elegant,[14] and covered most of the body,

Figure 4.1 Sharmila Tagore in a glamorous sari with a sleeveless blouse, in fashion in the 1960s, in *An Evening in Paris* (1967).

Figure 4.2 Sharmila Tagore dresses up as a poor woman in order to meet a man who doesn't just want her for her money, in *An Evening in Paris* (1967).

Figure 4.3 In a double role in *An Evening in Paris* (1967), Sharmila Tagore also plays Suzy, a cabaret dancer.

while in the next few decades we saw "shorter, tighter blouses, a hint of skin, and bold makeup"[15] for women and brighter colors to capitalize on the wider use of color film. In 1968 superstar Mumtaz made a splash with her unique sari drape in *Brahmachari* (Figure 4.5). And polka dots came into fashion as the 16-year-old first-timer Dimple Kapadia radically changed fashion trends in 1973 in

Figure 4.4 Deepa enjoying the water in *An Evening in Paris* (1967).

Figure 4.5 Mumtaz's iconic sari drape in *Brahmachari* (1968).

her first film *Bobby* (Figure 4.6). These massively popular styles were copied by shirtmakers and tailors at the request of their clients around India.[16]

In the 1980s we saw brighter, neon colors and designs, including chiffon saris, sequins, and permed hair. Superstar Madhuri Dixit was well known for her purple sari in *Hum Aapke Hain Koun* (1994) with its big, bright jeweled embroidery (Figure 4.7). Briefly in the late 1990s, in the wake of India's

Figure 4.6 Dimple Kapadia's look in *Bobby* (1973) sparked new fashion trends.

Figure 4.7 Madhuri Dixit and her iconic jeweled sari in *Hum Aapke Hain Koun* (1994).

economic liberalization, we saw more branding in costumes, as with the Gap product placements in *Kuch Kuch Hota Hai* (1998). In the early 2000s, leather pants and club wear became more popular, as in the "Koi Kahe" song in *Dil Chahta Hai* (2001). Yet this film also marked a turn, visible in some newer

films, toward more realist costuming, meaning not only that "the main characters are dressed like regular people who are part of the Bombay club and
party scene,"[17] but also that rather than fully changing outfits throughout the
film as had been done earlier, a *Dil Chahta Hai* character "does not wear a new
dress every day but rewears, recombines, and revitalizes clothing items in each
succeeding scene," much like people do in real life.[18]

Historically, men's costumes have been given less attention, although Dev
Anand was known as a style icon (Figure 4.8), and stars like Rishi Kapoor and
Amitabh Bachchan have often been dressed in over-the-top costumes, as in
Karz (1980), in which Kapoor wore a metallic sequined jumpsuit for the song
"Om Shanti Om" and when Bachchan wore a full tuxedo and bowler hat and
sported a pointed umbrella for the goofy "My Name is Anthony Gonsalves"
song in *Amar Akbar Anthony* (1977) and a high-collared trench coat in *Kabhi
Kabhie* (1976) (Figure 4.9). However, in recent years this has changed and
costume designers have gotten more innovative with male costumes and have
developed more suggestive and hyperbolic looks for male stars, as with
Munna's tapori look in *Rangeela* (1995), with the top buttons of his shirt open
(Figure 4.10), Akash's club outfit and leather pants in *Dil Chahta Hai* (2001),
and Sam's fur-collared white coat over a neon orange sweater in *Kabhi Alvida
Naa Kehna* (2006). Matching costumes for couples have been used throughout

Figure 4.8 With his bouffant and cravat, Dev Anand was a male style icon of the 1960s,
here in *Guide* (1965).

Figure 4.9 Amitabh Bachchan in *Kabhi Kabhie* (1976).

Figure 4.10 A new, male, street aesthetic in *Rangeela* (1995).

the decades, as in the "Mera Dil Hai Tera" song in *An Evening in Paris* (1967) and "Jo Haal Dil Ka" in *Sarfarosh* (1999). In the "Koi Ladki Mujhe Kal Raat" song in *Seeta Aur Geeta* (1972), Ravi's tie and handkerchief are the same bright orange as Geeta's outfit, offering a striking complementary visual appeal. This also is seen in the neon colors and matching or complementary costumes of

Bunty Aur Babli (2005), which underscore that film's playful and fun aesthetic. In the "Mere Haath Mein" song sequence in *Fanaa* (2006), the two stars' costumes are color-coordinated with each other and with the visual landscape.

Locations

Bollywood love songs often take place in locations drastically different from the primary settings of the films. Beginning in the 1960s,[19] this often meant European locations, such as the tulip-covered Dutch field in "Dekha Ek Khwaab" in *Silsila* (1981) or the Scottish countryside in the title song of *Kuch Kuch Hota Hai* (1998), but most commonly in Switzerland.[20] Visually, Switzerland represents the polar opposite of most Indian landscapes, with its meadows, snowy mountains, and vast empty spaces. These landscapes provide a beauty and lushness to visually represent the intensity of the couple's romance or merely to elicit pleasure. A location that looks absolutely unlike anything else in the film, or anything in the viewer's own life, is the visual equivalent of representing love as sublime, as a state that transports the lovers away from the mundane world. The snowy landscapes or lakes of Kashmir were a common domestic location in the 1960s and 1970s, similarly because they offered an unrecognizable wintry landscape that was in marked contrast to most of India's arid or tropical settings.

Song sequences often take place in desolate locations, signifying not only distance but also isolation, something that for the most part only exists in fantasy because most real contexts in India are full of people. A love song in a space far away from society conveys love as something fantastical and extrasocial. For instance, when Kusum and Navin have their first love song in *Guddi* (1971), it takes place in a cave, whose otherworldliness signals the trueness of their love. In *Aradhana* (1969), a dramatic mountainous landscape is the perfect space for Arun and Vandana to declare their love (Figure 4.11).

Foreign locations are still used in the 1990s and beyond, but many filmmakers have moved beyond the recognizable landscapes of Switzerland. The "Suraj Hua Maddham" song from *Kabhi Khushi Kabhie Gham* (2001) was shot in Egypt, and "Guzarish" from *Ghajini* (2008) in Namibia. Part of *Dil Chahta Hai* (2001) is set in Sydney, Australia, but the innovation of the "Tanhayee" ("Loneliness") song is to take a populated urban landscape as the backdrop for Akash's loneliness and alienation. The song is picturized with Akash moving through the anonymous city, or standing still with urban life whizzing past him, looking out over the water, or sitting alone at a crowded cafe. In the song sequence's long shots, Akash's body is dwarfed in relation to a vast and alienating landscape. *Kaho Naa Pyaar Hai* (2000) takes place in New Zealand, *Dil Dhadakne Do* (2015) on a cruise ship touring the Mediterranean Sea, and *Kuch Kuch Hota Hai* (1998) and *Albela* (2001), among others, were shot in Mauritius. Another use of an urban location is the "Pretty Woman" song from *Kal Ho Naa Ho* (2003), shot in Queens, New York.

Figure 4.11 Arun and Vandana declare their love in front of a dramatic, mountainous landscape in *Aradhana* (1969).

There has also been a trend of setting songs in visually striking parts of India that might not be immediately recognizable to Indian audiences. The well-known "Chaiyya Chaiyya" song from *Dil Se* (1997) is set on a train supposedly in India's Northeast (although it was actually shot in the southern state of Tamil Nadu). In this film, placelessness – not being able to identify exactly where a scene is set – is part of how that song functions in the overall narrative. This song sequence represents Amar's fantasy; he has just laid eyes on Meghna and immediately fallen in love with her, and her perceived exoticism, because he cannot place her through the conventional markers of identity in India, generates this placeless fantasy. Locations are used to represent fantasies in other films as well, for instance in the first rendition of "Ghar Aaja Pardesi" in *Dilwale Dulhania Le Jayenge* (1995), in which Baldev's fantasy of a green Punjab is overlain with the more depressing reality of his life in grey London. *Dil Se* (1997) and *3 Idiots* (2009) have scenes set at the visually striking Pangong Lake in Ladakh, whose dramatic scenery and turquoise water comprise another surreal and striking landscape (Figure 4.12). *Highway* (2014) is set in desolate landscapes outside of Delhi and we see the depressing but also freeing aestheticization of highways from the perspective of a young woman trapped by her patriarchal family. The climax of that film is also set in a dramatic mountain village.

Whether in India or abroad, when films are shot in real, outdoor locations, it is common for background crowds not to be erased nor made to look realistic as they would be in other cinematic genres. Frames often contain passers-by gathered in crowds around the shooting, clearly staring at the actors and enjoying the spectacle of the production. In *Chandni* (1989), a song sequence that takes place at Delhi's India Gate has a whole crowd of people watching the

Figure 4.12 The striking landscape of Pangong Lake is a fitting backdrop for the inventive choreography of "Satrangi Re" in *Dil Se* (1997).

film shoot in the background, and no attempt is made by the director to either get rid of them or make them look like they have a reason within the story. In "Tu Mujhe Suna" in the same film, which takes place in a European city, onlookers in the background are clearly watching the shooting and some people even turn their heads toward the camera to see what is going on. In *Deewana* (1992) we see this in both scenes that take place in public locations: one at Juhu beach and a second at the Gateway of India. In *An Evening in Paris* (1967) we see similar crowds gathered in the background, even in the scenes set in outdoor locations in Paris. Like so many other aspects of Bollywood's visual style, this break in realism poses no threat to the film and might in fact be a source of cinephilic enjoyment.

The pervasive use of multiple locations, despite the significant expense required to move the cast and crew, indicates the importance not only of unique locations but of movement among different locations, which heightens the visual appeal of the Bollywood film.

Sets and the role of artifice

Bollywood sets are meant not to look realistic but to celebrate theatricality, color, and surface pleasures. The courtyard of Mamaji's house in *Padosan* (1968), for instance, is clearly a painted set, with the tree in the background decorated not with leaves but with brightly colored paper in pink, yellow, and red. *Padosan* is a comedy and so revels in the absurd and the unbelievable; the visual style is marshalled to this thematic. But even films like *Dilwale Dulhania Le Jayenge* (1995) use painted sets that make no attempt to hide their two-dimensionality, as in the brightly-painted set of the family mansion. An even more blatant disregard of realism is in the unrealistic set that is supposed to represent the real Delhi neighborhood of Chandni Chowk in *Kabhi Khushi Kabhie Gham* (2001). While the old Mughal neighborhood is structured around narrow and congested streets and alleys, the wide opulence of this Chandni Chowk is clearly staged and theatrical.

Houses are often vast and unrealistically opulent, from Gopal's bungalow in *Sangam* (1964) to Viren's family manor in *Lamhe* (1991) to the Durbar haveli in *Hum Dil De Chuke Sanam* (1999) and the Raichand mansion in *Kabhi Khushi Kabhie Gham* (2001).[21] These are not meant to be realistic dwellings but to represent excess. Their hyperbolic quality adds to the pleasure and awe elicited by the films. In earlier films in which excessive wealth tended to be inherently amoral, this opulence sometimes signified the hollowness of character; thus in *Bobby* (1973) when Raj's body is dwarfed in relation to the grandeur of his family's house, it is part of the film's critique of his rich and thoughtless parents (Figure 4.13). In *Nagina* (1986) we see a similar representation of a wealthy family's house as repressive of youth and romance. In newer films, this is less the case; there is less embarrassment and criticism of excessive wealth now, so images of grandeur are more for the enjoyment of excess itself.

Opulent sets are most evident in period pieces set in Mughal India; films like *Mughal-e-Azam* (1960), *Jodhaa Akbar* (2008), and *Bajirao Mastani* (2015) lavishly try to recreate the grandeur of the Mughal and other royal courts.[22] The set for the song "Pyar Kiya Toh Darna Kya" in *Mughal-e-Azam* cost ₹1,500,000 (over $20,000, a substantial sum in 1960) and was built over two years, with imported glass for the shiny decor (Figure 4.14).[23] Likewise, Sanjay Leela Bhansali,

Figure 4.13 The long shot captures Raj's alienation in a wealthy house that lacks familial love, in *Bobby* (1973).

Figure 4.14 The extravagant palace set in *Mughal-e-Azam* (1960).

the director of *Bajirao Mastani*, is reported to have spent years planning and designing the opulent sets of that film, sparing no expense, including spending over ₹100,000 ($2,000) on just the fan in Kashibai's room and an equivalent on her pillow covers.[24]

The unashamed artificiality of sets and locations is sometimes thematized within the story, as in *Guide* (1965) where "Kya Se Kya Ho Gaya," a song sequence performed on a stage among exceptionally artificial-looking sets, is an attempt to expose the falsity of love. We also see this in films whose stories take place on Bollywood sets, which offer yet another level of cinephilic enjoyment of artificiality. In *Om Shanti Om* (2007), Om invites Shanti on a date on a film set where he demonstrates the power of mechanical beauty as he pulls down a cardboard cut-out of a moon and sits in a car pretending to drive while a screen projects a moving background behind him. Om, a Bollywood superfan, enjoys the artificial aesthetics of Bollywood sets as a form of beauty on their own rather than as fake substitutes for the real thing.

Not all sets are artificial-looking, especially in newer films. As Ranjani Mazumdar writes, one of the unique aspects of *Dil Chahta Hai* (2001) is its use of interiors rather than outdoor spaces, represented "through angular shots that convey an almost modernist and minimalist framing,"[25] and its use of a modern, blue color palette rather than the bright reds and yellows of conventional Bollywood. Newer films are set in more realistic public locations as well, such as coffee shops, restaurants, nightclubs, and more modest homes, as in *Love Aaj Kal* (2009), *Ae Dil Hai Mushkil* (2016), and many other recent films featuring young protagonists. Likewise, new kinds of social films set in small towns, such as *Toilet: Ek Prem Katha* (2017), or urban settings, such as *Gully Boy* (2019), are also more realistic in their settings, usually with the exception of the song sequences.

Case study: **Devdas (2002)**

When Sanjay Leela Bhansali's *Devdas* was released in 2002, it was the most expensive Indian film ever made, costing more than $11 million. The sets were epically grand;[26] Devdas's house is palatial, with a full-size fountain out front and lavish furniture and drapery inside; Paro's house is also surrounded by stained glass windows and has an opulent interior. Apparently, Bhansali used over 12,000 pieces of stained glass for the inside of Paro's room.[27] The camera emphasizes the grandeur of these spaces with sweeping shots and few cuts. In the first scene of the film, Devdas's mother receives a letter announcing Devdas's return to India after a long absence, and the camera follows her as she moves joyfully through the various rooms of the house, relaying the news to the rest of the family, in an extended continuous shot that lasts a full minute and a half and emphasizes the palatial dimensions of the house.

Devdas's costumes were based on nineteenth-century designs but made more opulent and lavish. The costume designers used traditional Bengali fabrics and updated them using contemporary styles.[28] Chandramukhi, the courtesan, wore especially lavish and intricately woven costumes, made of brocade and silk – one of which weighed 65lbs (Figure 4.15).

Devdas generated a new aesthetic of opulent excess that became standard in the years following, especially for period pieces. However, the director's decision to go lavish on this film also garnered some controversy since the film is based on a novel, and has several earlier Hindi versions – especially the ones from 1936 and 1955, which were well-loved on their own terms and were noticeably more stripped down in their aesthetics. Critics argued that making both Paro's and Devdas's families wealthy weakened the tragic element of the original novel for the sake of visual appeal. While it is true that the 2002 adaptation is less faithful to the novel than the previous two, Corey Creekmur argues that it might be better read as a cinephilic homage rather than simply a

Figure 4.15 Chandramukhi's costumes were just some of the extravagant designs on the set of *Devdas* (2002).

remake.[29] Indeed, this new *Devdas* is as much about the spectacle as it is about the tragic romance of Devdas and Paro.

Gestures and expressions

Bollywood acting operates on repeated gestures that often substitute for complex interiorized representations. Although this practice has somewhat diminished over the last few decades, there is a repertoire of gestures – throwing one's head back in grief, running toward each other with outstretched arms, looking into each other's eyes, wiping away tears, enacting a "breast pulse"[30] (the rhythmic pulsating of the chest, mimicking a heartbeat), tapping one another fondly on the side of the nose – that continue to be widely used. As in Parsi theater, these gestures signify a register of emotion outside of language.[31] They are hyperbolic in many cases, but that is meant as a way to "extend and intensify"[32] meaning rather than to be taken as original or unique indicators of a personality in each case.

Crying abounds in Bollywood, most often for grief but also for happiness. Fake tears – or "glycerin tears," named after the substance that makes artificial tears – have become somewhat of a joke in the industry and among audiences today, mocking the melodramatic propensity of Bollywood characters for tears and the unconvincing acting and the fakeness of Bollywood cinema more generally. Conversely, some actors are known and respected for crying real tears when they perform; in a 2013 interview Sonam Kapoor proudly claimed that "I can never cry with the help of glycerine. Whenever I cry on screen, I cry naturally."[33] However, the debate over the veracity of tears misses the point; tears in Bollywood are not meant to express genuine emotion, but are meant, as in many melodramatic modes, to engage the audience on a bodily level so that they too are moved to tears. Like laughter, fear, or other heavy-handed emotions, tears work to open the text up to involve the audience in ways that refuse the illusion of much realist cinema, which is meant to be watched with a more distanced, or detached, gaze.[34]

There are also widely used gestures that have a more specific cultural significance. One is a hand brought up to the forehead in greeting – a South Asian Muslim greeting known as *aadab arz*. Another is the act of putting on or wiping off sindoor, an externalized way to represent love and romantic union or the death and loss of a husband, respectively. Applying sindoor suggests a symbolic marriage even without a marriage ceremony, as in the elopement scene in *Qayamat Se Qayamat Tak* (1988).[35] Conversely, the smudging of sindoor could be a bad omen. In *Sangam* (1964), Radha's friend Sakina accidentally smears some blood on Radha's forehead, foreshadowing an unhappy marriage for Radha. In *Amar Akbar Anthony* (1977), we see various symbolic meanings of sindoor, first when Bharati falls and her sindoor smudges, signifying the breakup of the family, and second when, many years later, her son finds her long-lost husband and offers her sindoor as a way of telling her the news. Unable to believe that her husband is still alive, Bharati understands the turn of events upon seeing the sindoor, which speaks for itself, as it were, to convey her extant marriage. The conventional gesture of putting sindoor in the parting of a woman's hair is also parodied in more recent films; in *Om Shanti Om* (2007), the actor Sandy must recite a monologue about the importance of sindoor for an Indian woman, but she cannot get through the scene without laughing because the sentiment feels so old-fashioned.

Because Bollywood dance sequences are replicated in school performances, stage shows, and especially weddings, Bollywood gestures circulate far beyond the cinema hall. It is common for friends of the bride or groom to put on a dance show at a wedding in which they copy the gestures of a favorite song sequence. Actors perform stage and awards shows, often replicating dance gestures they are known for; on a recent episode of *My Next Guest with David Letterman*, Shah Rukh Khan taught Letterman how to perform his characteristic gesture of his arms outstretched to his sides (Figure 4.16).

Bollywood's queer possibilities will be discussed in more detail in Chapter 7, but it is important to note the importance of what Kareem Khubchandani calls "diva gestures"[36] in queer appropriations of Bollywood dance. These "effeminate gestures," Khubchandani finds, are ways for gay men to enact modes of becoming through the transgression of "gender propriety." Gestures are thus important not only for the meaning and pleasure of the films themselves but also as they circulate and are resignified beyond the cinema hall.[37]

Facial expressions are also part of Bollywood's visual style. Some of these come from classical Indian dance, which has a repertoire of facial expressions that have been incorporated into Bollywood dance sequences, such as lifting an eyebrow, biting one's lip,[38] a half-smile, and a seductive open mouth. *Abhinaya* is the term for the art of expression in ancient Indian aesthetic theory, which inspires Bollywood's repertoire.

Figure 4.16 Arms outstretched to the sides: this is one of superstar Shah Rukh Khan's signature gestures – here in *Kal Ho Naa Ho* (2003).

Case study: Sridevi

Possibly the most expressive Bollywood actor ever, Sridevi (1963–2018) was known for her range of facial expressions, which included "naughty, funny, sober, intense, [and] sexy."[39] Screenwriter and lyricist Javed Akhtar called Sridevi "the first heroine who had no qualms in expressing herself fully through her body,"[40] which included piercing stares as in *Nagina* (1986) (Figure 4.17) and uniquely comical and quizzical expressions as in the "Hawa Hawai" song in *Mr. India* (1981) (Figure 4.18). "Hawa Hawai," choreographed by Saroj Khan (who is discussed in more detail later in this chapter), was one of Sridevi's most famous dances, enhanced by "her trademark trick-stumbles, eye rolls, [and] a cross-eyed moment halfway through the song."[41]

The range of expressions not only makes Sridevi a versatile actor, but, across so many films, renders her body the site of intense affective engagement which exceeds the meaning of any given text and makes possible queer or otherwise transgressive forms of identification. As Kareem Khubchandani writes about *Nagina*, "this film and particularly Sridevi's climactic performance of 'Main Teri Dushman' ... have become camp classics," not only because of the skill of the dance but her "piercing stares, unbroken eye contact, unwieldy ground rolls, whipping turns, and sudden darts."[42] These intense gestures and expressions offer the possibility for multiple sites of identification in the circulation of her image.

The tableau and the fourth wall

Another unique Bollywood visual formation is the tableau, a term that refers to a still group of figures who, in their arrangement, signify a meaning outside

Figure 4.17 Sridevi as the reincarnation of a female snake in *Nagina* (1986).

Figure 4.18 One of actor Sridevi's goofy expressions in the song "Hawa Hawai" in *Mr. India* (1987).

themselves. As Sangita Gopal argues, "The tableau performs such an important function in the melodrama – it consolidates the moral order that the action will fulfill."[43] The tableau is a common arrangement of figures in Bollywood, but it does not conform to normative film standards because the figures are not arranged in a believable way and the illusion of there being no camera is dispensed with. As M. Madhava Prasad writes, the tableau offers up the text as "the bearer of a message" rather than as a site for interpretation.[44] Sometimes, this positioning affects the plot, as in *Mahal* (1949), when Hari Shankar and Kamini are both facing the camera at the frontal plane, leaving the opportunity for Ranjana to stand behind them and eavesdrop on their conversation. But most often, the tableau registers the underlying tensions of the plot spatially. In *Sangam* (1964), there is a high angle tableau with Sundar and Gopal on either side of Radha, who is crouching down. The high angle allows the viewer to see the inequality of the different relations within this love triangle, with Sundar and Gopal the true (but impossible) lovers and Radha the sacrificial victim between them (Figure 4.19). Rachel Dwyer describes the tableau in *Silsila* (1981), when Amit's wife and mistress "stand back to back as if they are to commence a duel,"[45] each staking their claim on Amit.

Case study: Deewaar (1975)

Deewaar is a film that uses tableaux often. There is a tableau of the two brothers walking down separate paths, signifying the separation that marks their respective futures. We also have the image of them standing back to back under the bridge where they grew up, again spatially representing the divide between them. The image of the two brothers at their father's funeral also marks the distance between them, which has, by this point in the film, become irresolvable. All these tableaux are metaphoric, underscoring the idea of the *deewaar*, or wall, between the two

Figure 4.19 The tableau renders the love triangle in spatial form, in *Sangam* (1964).

brothers that gives the film its title. In addition, they reflect outward, referring to the separation between law and justice that characterizes many films of the 1970s.[46]

In Figure 4.20, the presentation and the arrangement of bodies is more theatrical than cinematic; the three characters are facing the camera and they are fanned out in order to be simultaneously visible. The cinematic illusion that the viewer is a secret witness to a real scene is discarded here for a more iconic presentation of the conflict between the characters. This frontal address, even though part of a scene with narrative content, is extended such that it asks to be interpreted also as still image, as tableau. In this tableau we see externalized the primary narrative conflict of *Deewaar* (1975), the conflict between two brothers, on opposite sides of the law, centered around the problematic figure of the mother, whose love and special sanction both brothers crave. The mother as the centerpiece of this tableau crystallizes the multiple conflicts between the two brothers (social, political, economic) into a familial one[47] that is thus legible within the larger Bollywood moral universe. Little interpretation is involved as the conceit is presented to us as visual surface.

Case study: Amar Akbar Anthony (1977)

In Bollywood, spatial positioning within the frame can offer not only con-densed accounts of a film's themes but simultaneously an aspiration for its

Figure 4.20 The mother stands at the crux of the familial conflict in *Deewaar* (1975).

resolution. We see this in an image from *Amar Akbar Anthony* of the three protagonists simultaneously donating blood to a woman who happens to be their biological mother, from whom they were separated many years earlier (Figure 4.21).

The three men are brothers by birth, unbeknownst to them since they were
separated in childhood. Moreover, they have each been adopted by men from
India's three main religions; thus Amar was raised Hindu, Akbar Muslim, and
Anthony Catholic. In this tableau image, we can see both their "real" biological connection to one another as a family bound by blood, as well as their
religious difference, glimpsed in the windows behind each of the beds, where a
Hindu temple, a mosque, and a church are depicted, respectively. Given that it
is unlikely that three religious structures would be visible from three windows
of one room in this way, realism is here sacrificed for the larger project to
represent, using an iconic still image, unity–in–difference across India's religions.

Sometimes, a character will appear to look directly into the camera, breaking
the "fourth wall" that is considered essential to the illusion of the cinema and
further recalling the stage. Bollywood directors have few qualms about this
kind of direct address.[48] In *Chalti Ka Naam Gaadi* (1958), during the song
sequence in which Mannu announces his love for Renu, the actor Kishore
Kumar looks straight into the camera (Figure 4.22). In *Love in Tokyo* (1966),
when Ashok and Asha are looking into each other's eyes, the camera takes the
place of each one of them, so they appear to be looking straight into the

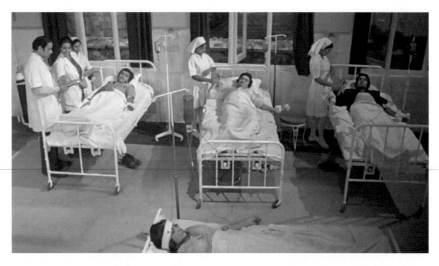

Figure 4.21 The three brothers, separated as young boys, donate blood to a woman whom they later discover is their mother, in *Amar Akbar Anthony* (1977).

Figure 4.22 Breaking the fourth wall in *Chalti Ka Naam Gaadi* (1958).

camera. And in *Dilwale Dulhania Le Jayenge* (1995), Simran looks straight into the camera during the song "Mere Khwabon Mein," affirming her desire to control her own destiny.

None of these presentations, which break cinematic conventions, is seen as problematic, because Bollywood generally puts little purchase in realism as an aesthetic value. Both the frontal address of the tableau and the character's direct gaze into the camera are meaningful because they rupture the conventional distance between narrative and audience, inviting the spectator to partake in the scene in an embodied way that disrupts the filmic illusion.[49] The tableau thus offers an opening where the audience becomes part of the filmic world. Moreover, there is an element of cinephilia in this presentation because the star is positioned in relation to the spectator in a way that feels like a direct address, intensifying the viewer's enjoyment of the star.[50]

Angles, zooms, and pans

The repeated use of heavy-handed editing techniques such as dramatic or disorienting high and low angles, zooms and pans reflects in part a cinema that externalizes character interiority, so a character's emotions are presented visually and the meaning of a scene is conveyed formally as well as through dialogue. It also reflects a cinema that does not seek to hide its filminess – that does not feel the need to buy into the cinematic illusion so central to realistic and parallel cinema.

The unrealistic opulence of space, discussed above, is often reinforced through dramatic angles and pans. In *Raja Hindustani* (1996), the second shot of the film is a high angle shot that emphasizes how rich and soulless the Sehgal family is. Vast space is similarly resignified in *Kabhi Khushi Kabhie Gham* (2001): at first, the camera celebrates the grandeur of the Raichand house through swooping crane shots and pans that highlight its sheer opulence, but in the scene when Yash disowns his son for choosing the wrong lover, that vastness is instantly resignified, via a high angle long shot, as a space of loneliness and coldness (Figure 4.23).

In *Deewaar* (1975), when Vijay witnesses the death of a coolie who had refused to pay the required portion of his salary to the local gangster, the

Figure 4.23 The opulence of the Raichand mansion suddenly becomes lonely and alienating when Rahul is disowned by his father for marrying his true love, in *Kabhi Khushi Kabhie Gham* (2001).

camera rapidly zooms in on his face from a long shot to a close up. As a substitute for access into Vijay's psychology, the rapid zoom underlines the significance of this moment for Vijay, as it is the first time he understands the nature of injustice. Later in the same film, we see a similar zooming pattern when Ravi finally confronts Vijay about his criminal dealings in front of their mother; the repeated, rapid zooms mark the new way the family sees one another after this revelation.

In *Love in Tokyo* (1966), when Pran realizes that Ashok and Asha are a couple, there are multiple quick zooms on his face to show his discomposure. In *Deewana* (1992), when Kajal finds out that her beloved Ravi is in fact alive, after having mourned his death for years, we see a sequence of rapid cuts: first a zoom-in shot of her face is repeated three times, and then her face is shown from a number of different angles in 12 rapid cuts that all occur within five seconds. Here zooms and cuts replace any dialogue or facial expression that Kajal might otherwise have used to show her discomposure at Ravi's reappearance. In *Nagina* (1986), when Raju's voice echoes around the ruined fort, the bouncing of his voice is shown using a series of rapid zoom outs. Zoom in/ zoom out patterns might also represent internal debate. In *Purab aur Paschim* (1970) when Mohan meets his young son and wife whom he had abandoned for an English woman, the camera first repeatedly zooms in and out on Mohan's face, and then we see four rapid zoom ins, representing Mohan's ambivalence about taking his son into his arms.

At times, these camera movements do not correspond with the experience of the characters, and thus are particularly disorienting. For instance, in the helicopter chase scene at the end of *Love in Tokyo* (1966), the multiple zooms don't correspond with the helicopter's movement and thus contribute to the overall disorienting effect of the scene as a whole. In these cases, the angles, zooms, and pans do not replicate particular perspectives but emphasize drama or disorientation more generally.

Editing

Cuts are perhaps the most subtle form of extradiegetic signification. The shot-countershot is an editing technique used in most narrative filmmaking, often in service of a realistic presentation of a conversation or interaction between two characters; in Bollywood, however, a rapid repeated shot-countershot pattern is a common way of showing a conflict or intense battle of wills. We see this when Dilip and Neena meet after several years in *Andaz* (1949) and in the epic meeting of Swami and Rajni, enemies from a previous birth, in *Nagina* (1986). In the final scene of *Dilwale Dulhania Le Jayenge* (1995) when Raj has boarded the departing train and is waiting for Baldev's permission for Simran to go with him, there are six shot-countershots in a row, with almost the exact same framing of both men's faces, showing the battle of wills between Raj and Baldev. This is repeated three more times after Baldev grips Simran's arm to stop her from boarding the train, and then another four times, and then finally another nine times, ending only when Baldev releases Simran's hand, allowing her to board the train. The visual effect is to underscore both characters' stubbornness, but more specifically underlines the way Raj's unflinching determination to marry Simran only with her father's approval is precisely what convinces Baldev of his morality.

In realistic filmmaking, the shot-countershot technique generally subscribes to the 180-degree rule, which requires that the camera appears to be a third "person" in the room, showing one character from the front right and the other from the front left. In most realistic cinema, this rule is never broken; doing so is considered jarring. In Bollywood, the 180-degree rule is sometimes used, and at other times it is broken. In the shot-countershot sequence in *Dilwale Dulhania Le Jayenge* (1995) discussed above, midway through the conflict between Raj and Baldev, the camera suddenly switches to shooting the two men from a different angle, this time allowing Simran to enter the frame and reminding the viewer that this moral battle between the two men involves her as well. The jarring nature of the break might be interpreted to reflect the importance of her positionality at this moment. In *Baazigar* (1993), the 180-degree rule is broken to represent Vijay's disequilibrium when he realizes his revenge plans are beginning to fail. Similarly, in *Silsila* (1981), when former lovers Amit and Chandni meet in a sari shop and he asks to meet her again privately, the break in the 180-degree rule reflects his profound disturbance at seeing her when they are both married to another people but still in love with each other. This coupled with the multiple mirror shots highlights the disorientation and transgressive quality of adulterous love.

Another edit widely used, especially in early Bollywood, is to replace a sexual image – even as tame as a kiss – with a veil, a curtain, or a proxy image. While this is in part to skirt the censors, the result is, like so many other conventions, a unique visual aesthetic of its own. In *Sangam* (1964), the love song between Radha and Gopal is preceded by multiple shots of flowering trees, and similarly in *Purab Aur Paschim* (1970), when Bharat consents to marry Preity, we see a series of shots of flowers. In these cases, the reason is both censorship and metaphor – the flowers signifying fertility, beauty, and abundance. In *Aradhana* (1969) when Vandana and Arun make love for the first time, the camera moves away from them and onto an image of a roaring fire. And in *Dostana* (1980), Vijay and Sheetal's kiss is partially obscured by flowers in the foreground of the frame, leaving the kiss suggested but not actually visible.

Montage

Montage is sparsely used in Bollywood. In *Purab Aur Paschim* (1970), when Bharat takes Preity to India to show her the sites, the various monuments of India's historical heritage are collected into a tourist-montage that conveys India's greatness to an alienated Preity. Another usage is in older films to avoid having to narrate or show sex or violence. In *Mother India* (1957), there is a montage of three scenes that underline Radha's helplessness: the first of her mother-in-law's death, the second in which she has to spend her scant money feeding a group of Brahmins as part of the funeral ritual, and a third of her delivering her baby with the sound of her older sons banging on the door outside to be let in the room. These powerful images of death, injustice, and then birth visually highlight the cycle of life without having to show gruesome images of death or childbirth. In *Guide* (1965), there is a montage in which Rosie conveys to her mother that her husband Marco is impotent; we never hear her say those words, but we see her crying while lying awake next to her snoring husband in bed, and then the film cuts to her dancing when her husband walks in and tells her to stop, and a final cut to her saying to her mother, "Ab main tumhein kaise bataun Maa, bas itna samajh lo, is ghar mein kabhi bacchi nahin ho sakti" ("How can I tell you this, Maa? Just understand this, a child can never come into this house.") The montage allows us to access the meaning of Rosie's sexual dissatisfaction without her ever having to articulate it explicitly.

Another use of montage is in the context of loss, caused by either a lover's betrayal or their actual death. Such montages recollect images of the couple or family together, often repeating scenes or images that have already been shown in the film and thus intensifying the sense of pain and loss. We see this in *Chandni* (1989), when Rohit finally realizes he has to return to Chandni after selfishly abandoning her; images of her flash before his eyes along with the sound of her voice and laughter. This montage represents the deluge of memories that affect him when he allows himself to remember his beloved.

Choreography and picturization

Choreography is a central part of the song-and-dance sequence. Choreography can be very simple, as in a love song where the two characters are singing to each other in a relatively sparse setting. For instance, in "Bole Re Papihara" in *Guddi* (1971), Kusum sings a song to Navin in the small space of a cave, and the choreography is nothing more than the two of them moving around each other in the enclosed space. Alternatively, choreography can be very complex, with intricate dance moves and a large cast of backup dancers. Where there is complex choreography it adds to the spectacular, theatrical quality of the song-and-dance sequence, where each song can feel like a Broadway production. And indeed, these song sequences are expertly and thoroughly choreographed, rehearsed, costumed, and staged. Then they are painstakingly picturized and filmed with specific angles and edits to support and accentuate the choreography.[51] For particularly grand dances, we sometimes see bird's eye shots that look directly down at the action. These highlight the symmetry of the choreography and present the kinetic form as a geometric pattern, as in "Sajan Ji Ghar Aaye" in *Kuch Kuch Hota Hai* (1998) (Figure 4.24), "Silsila Yeh Chahat Ka" in *Devdas* (2002), and "Des Rangila" in *Fanaa* (2006).

Bollywood dance reflects a hybrid of classical Indian, contemporary Indian, and western or global dance moves and styles. This hybridity has always existed, and early films were often criticized by dance purists for Bollywoodizing

Figure 4.24 A song-and-dance sequence seen through a bird's eye shot that highlights the symmetry of the dance, in *Kuch Kuch Hota Hai* (1998).

classical Indian dance forms such as Bharatnatyam and Kathak. Thus, the increasing use of western dance moves should not be read simplistically as reflecting the recent westernization of Bollywood. In *Pyaasa* (1957) and *Kabhi Khushi Kabhie Gham* (2001) we see waltzes alongside Indian dances like bhangra, and in *Gully Boy* (2019) we see moves taken from hip-hop dance.

Many female stars, especially of Bollywood's early decades, were trained in classical dance, including superstars Waheeda Rehman, Vyjayanthimala,[52] Hema Malini,[53] and Madhuri Dixit. In some instances, films starred in by these women featured characters who were also dancers, as in *Guide* (1965), *Teesri Kasam* (1966), and *Devdas* (2002).[54] Where films include classical styles of dance, Shruti Ghosh notes that "the dancers mostly perform in a rectangular or a circular space, decorated with pillars and arches having statues of Gods in the background to simulate temple courtyards or royal courtrooms where traditionally the classical dances were performed."[55] Likewise, costumes "are derivative of the traditional Bharatnatyam and Kathak attire and so are the dance movements."[56] The visual appeal of classical dance adapted into a shorter and more accessible format was one of the particularly enjoyable aspects of early Bollywood.

For most of the twentieth century, male stars were typically not trained in dance and often did not dance, with some exceptions such as Shammi Kapoor, Rishi Kapoor, Mithun Chakraborty, and Govinda.[57] As Shruti Ghosh notes, Shammi Kapoor's "quintessential … style" was marked by "ecstatic head movements, jumps and leaps, [and] comical facial expressions" that made his films very popular and that distinguished him from his fellow-actor brothers, who tended to be more restrained.[58] Dancing expectations for male stars have changed in the last several decades, a topic that is discussed further in Chapter 8.

Bollywood choreography is highly stylized and elaborate, reflecting the importance placed on not only lyrics and melody, but also the visual aesthetics of song sequences. There are three primary kinds of choreography; realistic choreographies that have the characters singing in seemingly real locales and interacting with the local scenery, outdoor fantasy dance sequences often in visually dramatic landscapes, and dance sequences on a stage or in front of a real or imagined audience. But even in the first case, where the appearance might be more realistic, the moves are carefully choreographed. For instance, in *Mr. and Mrs. 55* (1955), Pritam and Anita come across village women hanging saris out to dry and use that as a setting for a flirtatious song of hide-and-seek behind and among the hanging clothes. In a memorable scene in *Sholay* (1975), after Veeru has been kidnapped by the villain Gabbar Singh, he forces Veeru's lover, Basanti, to dance for him, warning her that if she stops dancing, he will shoot Veeru. Despite the harsh outdoor setting, Basanti moves across the limited space, up onto a large boulder, and mixes her dance steps with gestures of love and of beseeching. When one of Gabbar's henchmen smashes a bottle at her bare feet, she leaves bloody footprints as she dances and when she gets a shard in her foot, she dances on one foot until she is able to pull it out. Here limited space allows for particularly dramatic and skilled choreography. And in a scene of a kite battle in *Hum Dil De Chuke Sanam* (1999), the choreographer transforms the pushes and pulls on the kite strings into a dance, as the two competitors move forward and backwards trying to control their kites, and the onlookers become background dancers.

Songs shot in dramatic outdoor scenery are also meticulously choreographed. We often see conventional gestures like lovers running toward each other with arms outstretched – often accompanied by the crescendoing opening bars of a song – but the choreography is highly stylized nonetheless. The editing usually alternates between close ups of the lovers' faces and longer shots that emphasize the dramatic scenery, and even distant shots in which the two lovers appear as specks on a dramatic horizon.

Staged performances – even if not on a diegetic stage – are often accompanied by backup dancers who enhance the intensity of the dance. Often they have matching or complementary costumes to the star and the result is a spectacular stage-show-like performance that often has no diegetic justification, but significant energy and visual impact.

Mujra dancing – a popular dance form from the Mughal era – is common in courtesan films, some of which have become iconic in Bollywood cinema, such as *Mughal-e-Azam* (1960), *Pakeezah* (1972), and *Umrao Jaan* (1981). These use elements from kathak dance such as "*chakkars* (pirouettes) and *tatkaars* (footwork)"[59] and enhance them with camera angles and edits that heighten their aesthetic quality (Figure 4.25). A more modern version of a mujra is found in the "Kajra Re" song of *Bunty Aur Babli* (2005).

Case study: Saroj Khan

Saroj Khan (1948–2020) was the most well-known Bollywood choreographer of the 1980s, having worked on thousands of films and having choreographed some of the most well-known dance sequences in Bollywood, including "Hawa

Figure 4.25 Complex footwork and gestures distinguish the mujra performance "In Aankhon Ki Masti," in *Umrao Jaan* (1981).

Hawai" from *Mr. India* (1987) and "Ek Do Teen" from *Tezaab* (1988). Born to a Hindu family who migrated to India after Partition, she began as a child actor and worked as an assistant choreographer for many years before achieving success on her own. Even as a child, she was known for memorizing and being able to imitate a star's dance moves and expressions down to every detail.[60] She was associated in particular with expressive superstar Sridevi, discussed above, and then with Madhuri Dixit, both known for their skilled dancing. Today, in an era of reality television competitions, the most well-known choreographers have achieved celebrity status;[61] Saroj Khan, for instance, was a judge on several reality dance shows, including *Nach Baliye* and *Nachle Ve with Saroj Khan*.

Saroj Khan was credited with professionalizing choreography and with achieving the mix of classical and contemporary aesthetics that has grown to define Bollywood dance. She understood not only dance but how to incorporate dance into the cinematic medium.[62] Likewise, in working closely with female stars on the minute movements and gestures of their bodies, she epitomized the corporeality of Hindi cinema that is always verging on the transgressive and the homoerotic.[63] As Usha Iyer writes, Khan's "production numbers may be read as intimate dialogues between choreographer and the dancing heroine, who had conceived and rehearsed the moves over days, figuring out which steps worked best, what fabric most effectively accentuated their undulating bodies, or what kind of bodice would show off their heaving chests to greatest advantage."[64] Khan imagined the dance moves after hearing the song, but before even knowing the storyline of the film, thus offering dance, like the song sequence more generally, as excessive of narrative or plot.[65] It was supposedly because of her that Filmfare added a choreography award to its roster in 1989, which she won that year for "Ek Do Teen."[66] As Paromita Vohra writes, Khan imbued classical dance styles "with a contemporary, open sexiness never before seen in dances by heroines. The sexuality of her dances was very bodily, very frank and not dependent on a hero's touch alone." Her mode of teaching dance – making the movements and expressions herself and having the star repeat them until she gets them right – offered a new intimacy between the choreographer and the star, "asserting," Vohra continues, "that the body of the dancing heroine contained also the body of the choreographer."[67]

Kitsch and visual style

As we will discuss further in the next chapter, Bollywood films are remarkably self-aware about their own use of conventions, and at times this becomes full-on parody. In the "Woh Ladki Hai Kahan" song in *Dil Chahta Hai* (2001), we see a parody of earlier Bollywood conventions for hairstyle, costumes, and other song and style aesthetics. Costumes in this song include tuxedos, pomade-slicked hair, pencil moustaches, and dramatic up-dos in the 1950s, polka dots, hoop earrings, bell bottoms, and men's scarves in the 1970s, and perms, sleeveless blouses, and chiffon saris in the 1980s. This song sequence also parodies extravagant sets and Alpine backgrounds, while simultaneously drawing from their hyperbolic aesthetics to make what ends up being itself a spectacular song sequence. We see a similar parodic overuse of period costumes in *Om Shanti Om* (2007), whose first half is set in the late 1970s and early 1980s. *Om Shanti Om* also parodies other aspects of Bollywood's visual style, including repeated gestures, stylized acting, rapid zooms and pans, the tableau, and artificial sets. In *3 Idiots* (2009), Raju's family is poor, but the film has fun with that representation by showing scenes of his house in the conventions of 1950s Bollywood films, shot in black and white (the actual film is, of course, in color) and with melodramatic gestures resonant of an earlier age. These films serve as continuations of and developments on Bollywood visual style, homages to earlier styles, as well as affectionate parodies, all rolled into one.

Kitsch is defined as art considered to be in poor taste but appreciated ironically; the term only partially applies in the Bollywood context. Bollywood's aesthetic is over-the-top, but for the most part, it is meant to be enjoyed on its own terms, rather than through an ironic lens. However, especially since 2000, we have seen some films moving toward kitschy and self-parodic visual styles that take Bollywood's hyperbolic visuality to ironic extremes. In *Gunday* (2014), for example, the fight scenes include not only slow motion, which is fairly common in Bollywood fight scenes, but *extended* slow motion to the point of absurdity. There is no reason for this in terms of the plot; it is almost as if the film is building a new aesthetic at the extremes of the classic style.

Recently, Bollywood aesthetic-as-kitsch has circulated in prints and other objects in Mumbai, Delhi, and other Indian cities. Shops like vintage poster shops, the Kulture Shop, and online venues sell a range of items with Bollywood images, such as vintage posters, coasters, pillowcases, and laptop and iPhone covers. These display funny lines from well-known films, film posters, and images of popular actors. These types of industries are trying to turn Bollywood visuality into something cool and commodifiable, like kitsch industries elsewhere.

Case study: Karan Johar

Karan Johar is a contemporary director whose unique visual style is grounded in Bollywood's campy extremes. Beginning his career as an assistant director and minor character in *Dilwale Dulhania Le Jayenge* (1995), Johar went on to direct some of the most successful and iconic films of the 1990s and beyond. His early films in particular are characterized by an over-the-top aesthetic. As one film scholar writes, "If Hindi films are notoriously long, the 'KJo' [Karan Johar] film is even longer; if the relation of Hindi cinema to reality is weak, the 'KJo' film intensifies this artifice; if Hindi cinema is star-driven, the 'KJo' film is star crazy."[68] Johar's directorial debut was *Kuch Kuch Hota Hai* (1998), whose look was completely different from anything that had come before, with a visually striking and unrealistic college campus setting and a new kind of aesthetic that was capitalist-friendly and "cool." *Kabhi Khushi Kabhie Gham* (2001) was Johar's second film, featuring not only the much-loved Shah Rukh Khan–Kajol romantic pairing, but those actors playing Rahul and Anjali, the same names they had in *Kuch Kuch Hota Hai*. Johar's third film, *Kabhi Alvida Naa Kehna* (2006), also starred Shah Rukh Khan, and his fourth film, *My Name is Khan* (2010), brought back the Khan–Kajol pairing. This persistent return to the same pairing makes Johar's work an exemplar of the kind of Bollywood cinephilia discussed in the next chapter.

Kabhi Khushi Kabhie Gham (2001) in particular has a look that makes it unique even in Johar's oeuvre. It has an epic feel, utilizing many swooping crane shots, long shots, and high angles, emphasizing the grand settings and its unabashedly melodramatic storyline. The film's thin plot suggests that the film asks to be read as a celebration of Bollywood *as* aesthetic rather than simply as story or plot. Everything about the film is over-the-top: the sets are even more magnificent than in most films, the conflict more dramatized, the characters less interiorized, the costumes more lavish, the dance scenes more populated, with dozens of backup dancers, and numerous overhead and high angle shots to emphasize the size and splendor of the Raichand mansion. Instead of one song establishing the romantic interest between Rahul and Anjali, Johar gives us two, a mere five minutes apart. Every scene is extended beyond its necessary length: for instance, when Rahul returns home, the reunion with his mother is extended in not only dramatic, but *overdramatic* fashion, as if to draw attention to its own hyperbole. The whole film is similar: sacrificing the movement of plot, every scene or emotion is extended beyond its purpose in the story, as if to draw attention to extendedness itself. The sets are completely unrealistic, from the Raichand mansion, which is supposed to be in Delhi but is in fact a country manor in Buckinghamshire, England (Figure 4.26) to the sanitized Chandni Chowk set discussed above. But these fake settings should not be seen as failures of Johar's cinematic vision but rather central to his aesthetic.

This aesthetic of excess, in which more is always better, is furthered by the fact that so many of Johar's films are multi-starrers. There is a visual element to this form of cinephilia: the sheer enjoyment of seeing so many stars on screen at the same time. *Kabhi Khushi Kabhie Gham* (2001) stars three generations of stars, Amitabh and Jaya Bachchan, Shah Rukh Khan and Kajol, and the then-relatively new stars Kareena Kapoor and Hrithik Roshan. *Kabhi Alvida Naa Kehna* (2006) stars the four top stars of the time, Shah Rukh Khan, Rani Mukerji, Preity Zinta, and Abhishek Bachchan, in addition to stalwarts Amitabh Bachchan and Kirron Kher. *Kabhi Khushi Kabhie Gham* in particular grafts all of these aesthetic elements onto a conventional Bollywood plot about the battle between love and family, and indeed, in an absurd upending of the cliché, the parts are larger than the sum; the film is as invested in the accumulation of these various elements as it is in telling its story.

Thus, narrative complexity is not the point of Johar's films. Rather, it is lushness and expansiveness; together, his oeuvre constitutes a sort of campy homage to Bollywood aesthetics. In *Kabhi Khushi Kabhie Gham* (2001), Yash is a patriarch from another kind of film, and thus although he tries to protest against his son's choice of life partner, he waves his arms a bit and cannot get very far: the entire film is on the side of color and love, and Yash is sort of a sad lost cause; his principles are unable to compete with the overwhelming impact of Bollywood visual style.

Figure 4.26 The Raichand mansion in *Kabhi Khushi Kabhie Gham* (2001), where Rahul arrives by helicopter.

5   Cinephilia

Bollywood is an intrinsically cinephilic genre. This is evident in a number of ways. For one, by basking in the artifice of filmmaking, many Bollywood films tell a particular story but also celebrate filmmaking itself. Films are also intertextual, meaning that they constantly refer to other films. This is in part because it is expected that audiences have seen other films and the pleasure in watching each film comes from the way it innovates on the Bollywood formula rather than from its originality. In more recent films we have seen an express turn to parody, poking fun at Bollywood conventions even while utilizing them. I call these *affectionate parodies* because they are not meant to be disparaging but to generate additional film-viewing pleasure by reflexively calling attention to the cinema's own formulaic features. Karan Johar and Farah Khan are notable filmmakers in this regard, but this kind of overt cinephilia is an aspect of many contemporary films.

Within film studies, cinephilia is defined as a passionate engagement with film characterized by "spectatorial pleasure, fetish, intertextual citation, cinephilic collection, nostalgia, and memory." This "pleasure … is accidental and contingent and … ruptures with the film's linear narrative."[1] In Bollywood, cinephilia is so prevalent that it can be understood as a generic feature of Bollywood itself: the soliciting of pleasure by a film's very filminess – but with a populist, rather than theoretical or critical, inflection. This shift is required, I argue, in the context of a popular cinema, where theoretical or intellectual consideration of film's materiality must account for the sensuous, erotic, or emotional engagement with film, through its populist pleasures. Cinephilia then must be displaced from its association with high theory and considered as it appears in cinema halls, among hooting or catcalling audiences, in the legitimate and transgressive circulation of songs, in the non-ironic reception of its avowedly non-realistic visual style, and the hyperbolic image of the star and her passionate, even obsessed, fans.

Because Bollywood has such a large cultural presence in India, the adjective *filmi* is often used to describe something excessively romantic or over-the-top; Urban Dictionary defines filmi as "Hinglish slang referring to anything that seems like it could be from a Bollywood movie."[2] This term is commonly used in regular conversation, and also appears in films themselves. In *Guddi* (1971), when Kusum refuses to tell Navin whom she is in love with in a melodramatic announcement, Navin retorts, "Chod aise filmi dialogue!" ("Enough with your filmi dialogues!"). In *Deewana* (1992), when Kajal's mother worries that Kajal's marriage to Ravi won't work because of differences in their class status, her husband tells her, "Arré, tu badi purani filmon ki dialogue bolti hai!" ("Hey, you're just speaking a dialogue from an old film!"). And in *3 Idiots* (2009) when Rancho tells Pia what real love should feel like – "ki hawaein chalne lagi, slow motion mein dupatta udne laga hai …" ("as if a breeze started blowing, as if your dupatta started flying in slow motion …"), she responds, "Aise sirf filmon mein hota hai, real life mein nahin" ("That only happens in films, not in real life"), and then later, when she does fall in love with Rancho, the silly song they sing together, "Zoobi Doobi," describes love as "jaise filmon mein hota hai" ("just like it happens in films"). Conversely, when a parent wants to crush his child's dreams, he accuses him of being too filmi; in *3 Idiots* when Farhan tells his father he wants to be a photographer rather than an engineer, his father sarcastically responds, "Film dekhkar aye ho?!" ("Did you watch a film before coming here?!").

The pervasiveness of Bollywood across Indian society makes it a vehicle often used to convey information. This was evident in a recent public service announcement made by the Indian Police Foundation in response to the Covid-19 pandemic.[3] The video explains what Covid-19 is, describes its symptoms and how it is spread, and instructs the police on how to handle the nationwide lockdown, but it does so using the voices of Bollywood's most famous fictional policemen, Vijay from *Zanjeer* (1973), played by Amitabh Bachchan, Chulbul Pandey from *Dabangg* (2010) played by Salman Khan, and Abha Mathur from *Jai Gangaajal* (2016) played by Priyanka Chopra (Figure 5.1). In addition, the characters also quote well-known and easily recognizable lines from other Bollywood

Figure 5.1 A frame from the Indian Police Foundation's video on how to stop the spread of Covid-19, narrated by three well-known Bollywood police. © Indian Police Foundation.

films such as *Kabhi Kabhie* (1976) and *Don* (1978), as they inform viewers about how to control the spread of the virus. Cinephilia thus becomes part of the form of even this serious message.

Cinephilia and the star

Bollywood is a celebration of stardom. The biggest stars often play characters who are at the center of the moral universe, and stars themselves occupy a significant presence in Indian life. There are opportunities to see stars outside of films, at awards shows broadcast on television, on billboards, advertisements, and magazine covers. Televised Bollywood awards shows are even more dramatic than their equivalents elsewhere, with stars performing songs with a whole backup crew, and making dramatic entrances, as on one occasion during a stage tribute to noted Bollywood director Yash Chopra, when Shah Rukh Khan descended onto the stage on the back of a replica of a white horse as it was lowered on pulleys from the ceiling. These forms of off-screen stardom intensify the cinephilia and pleasure of the films themselves. Additionally, the star is an important generic feature of Bollywood cinema – specifically, the charismatic star that is its moral center. Stars carry a trace from one film to the other whereby audiences watch each film both for its story but also to see the recognizable attributes of a favorite star. Bollywood stars often break the rule of "impersonation," a "norm … [which] states that in playing any character, the 'real' personality of the actor should disappear into the part or, conversely, that if the range of the actor is limited to parts consonant with his or her personality then this constitutes 'poor' acting."[4] Rather, Bollywood films are enjoyable precisely because the actor never fully disappears into the role.

Filmmakers play up and capitalize on the star persona in a number of ways. Nirupa Roy was cast as the mother in several films in the 1970s and 1980s,[5] including *Ram Aur Shyam* (1967), *Deewaar* (1975), *Amar Akbar Anthony* (1977), *Mard* (1985), and *Lal Badshah* (1999),[6] and with each new appearance brought a trace of her earlier roles from the previous ones. Often, stars whose pairings are particularly successful in one film will be cast as romantic couples in additional films. Raj Kapoor and Nargis were paired opposite each other in *Andaz* (1949), *Barsaat* (1949), *Awaara* (1951), *Anhonee* (1952), and *Shri 420* (1955), among others. After *Baazigar* (1993) and *Dilwale Dulhania Le Jayenge* (1995) made Shah Rukh Khan and Kajol a popular romantic pair, they acted opposite one another again in *Kuch Kuch Hota Hai* (1998), *Kabhi Khushi Kabhie Gham* (2001), *My Name is Khan* (2010), and *Dilwale* (2015). Recurring pairs generate cinephilic pleasure that exceeds any particular storyline. In *Chalti Ka Naam Gaadi* (1958), the three brothers are played by three real-life brothers, Ashok Kumar, Kishore Kumar, and Anoop Kumar, adding another level of enjoyment to the already comedic caper. In *Andaz Apna Apna* (1994), the two stars, Raveena Tandon and Karishma Kapoor, play characters named Raveena and Karishma, respectively; this becomes a source of humor later on when it is discovered that the two women had switched names to deceive their suitors, so Raveena Tandon is really playing Karishma and Karishma Kapoor is playing Raveena.

Another convention is for stars to play roles with the same name across several films, as Raj Kapoor did with Raj in the 1950s, Amitabh Bachchan with Vijay and Amit in the 1970s, and Shah Rukh Khan with Rahul and Raj. Although all the Vijays are not meant to be the same character, having the same name links the various films and roles in playful extradiegetic ways. Actors such as Pran and Prem Chopra were known for playing primarily villains, and they both at times played villains who bore their real names: Pran in *Love in Tokyo* (1966) and Prem Chopra in *Bobby* (1973). Having an actor known for villainous roles often dictates how an audience will understand a scene; *Kati Patang* (1971), for instance, begins with a wedding in which the bride is upset because she is not marrying the man she loves. While love is usually valued in Bombay cinema, when we discover her lover is played by Prem Chopra, we immediately doubt the trueness of their love, and indeed, we quickly learn that he had wanted to marry her only for her money.

Billu Barber (2009) is a film about a movie star who visits a small town to shoot a film. The star, Sahir Khan, is played by Shah Rukh Khan and the film is as much about the real Shah Rukh as it is about the fictional Sahir. So, when Sahir comes to the village, he is greeted with a huge display of posters of all his previous films – which in this case are also Shah Rukh Khan's previous films (Figure 5.2). The film shows an extended scene in which Sahir Khan enters the village and is greeted by fans – and the extended length of the scene has little other purpose than to intensify the cinephilia and the stardom of Shah Rukh Khan, even in a film that is ostensibly about a fictional star.

Fandom

When a Bollywood film is popular, it gains a massive and passionate fan following. *Sholay* (1975) "was the longest running film in Indian cinema until [*Dilwale*

Figure 5.2 In *Billu Barber* (2009), the fictional star Sahir Khan, played by Shah Rukh Khan, is greeted in the village with a display of posters from many of his past films, which are in fact real posters of past Shah Rukh Khan films.

Dulhania Le Jayenge] broke its record in 2001,"[7] running for 286 weeks straight in one Mumbai theater. Records of its dialogue were released after its success, so that, as one critic writes, "watching *Sholay* in the theatre had become a little like a Karaoke experience. The entire audience would be mouthing the dialogue with the characters. Some had even memorized the sound effects, down to the last flipped-coin sound."[8] *Dilwale Dulhania Le Jayenge* (1995) ran for a whopping 23 years continuously at the Maratha Mandir cinema in Mumbai, a run that finally ended in 2018.[9] Repeat viewings of successful films are common, even, at times, to excess; Bollywood superstar Dharmendra claims to have watched the film *Dil-lagi* (1949) more than 30 times,[10] and India's most famous modern artist M.F. Husain claims to have watched *Hum Aapke Hain Koun* (1994) 85 times.[11] Clothing from films sparks nationwide trends, so that, in the 1970s, "a shirt worn by Rajesh Khanna in a film releasing on a Friday would be duplicated and ready for sale by the following Monday."[12] Lines from individual films have also become famous, such as "Tera kya hoga Kaliya" ("What will happen to you, Kaliya?") from *Sholay* and "Mogambo khush hua" ("Mogambo is happy") from *Mr. India* (1987), which often circulate apart from the films, especially today in internet memes.

Bollywood stars have huge fan followings, with some fandom bordering on obsession. A *Times of India* article from 1950 records that "Police intervened and escorted popular film, stage and radio artistes as they walked out of the Excelsior Theatre, Bombay, on Sunday morning after staging one of the most successful shows of the season in aid of refugees," after which they were mobbed when "a thousand people crowded the approaches to the theatre to have a glimpse of their favourite stars."[13] When Amitabh Bachchan was seriously injured on the set of his film *Coolie* in 1982, there were vigils outside the hospital where he was being treated and many devoted fans prayed and even went on pilgrimages for his recovery.[14] To this day, Amitabh Bachchan, possibly Bollywood's biggest ever star, emerges from his house in the Juhu neighborhood of Mumbai most Sundays to greet fans with a wave; fans crowd around the security fence surrounding his house for several hours, hoping to catch a glimpse of him. Shah Rukh Khan's house, Mannat, is similarly always surrounded by fans who take selfies at the front gate.

There are also well-established fan clubs, both in-person and online. While fan clubs are most popular in South India,[15] where they are often linked to mainstream politics, there are many fan clubs around India. Many online fan clubs cater to Indians living abroad as well.[16] Two important documentaries on India's fan cultures include *Being Bhaijaan* (2014) on fan cultures around superstar Salman Khan and *For the Love of a Man* (2015) on the massive fan following of Tamil superstar Rajinikanth and its political mobilization. Film gossip magazines like *Filmfare* and *Stardust* are also extremely popular, with the latter published in both Hindi and English.

When fans appear as characters in Bollywood films, they are mostly always moral centers. Fandom is arguably second only to love as a moral virtue; in *Karz* (1980), the term "fan" is used interchangeably with words for lover such as *deewana* and *aashiq*.

There are several films about cinema, stars, and fans, which both represent Bollywood's intense fan culture and also are themselves celebrations of cinephilia. In some of these films, actors play themselves or stars just like them and the protagonist (played by another star but appearing as a regular person) is a fan. In *Guddi* (1971), teenage girls sit around and discuss their favorite movie stars: Kusum is a fan of Dharmendra and won't even listen to her friends who prefer Jeetendra or Rajesh Khanna (all three big stars of the 1970s). The fact that the young women skip class to go watch films suggests a transgressive element to cinephilia as well – a quality that cannot be contained within bourgeois rules and respectability. In fact, Kusum rejects a marriage offer and pledges to marry the movie star Dharmendra in a spiritual sense, much like Mirabai, a sixteenth-century mystic poet, abandoned her earthly life, including her husband, to devote her life to the Lord Krishna. Much of *Guddi*'s story takes place on film sets as Kusum and Mamaji watch Dharmendra – who is playing himself – shoot various scenes. These scenes revel in the materiality of cinema. At one point, Navin opens a bathroom door which leads nowhere, as it is just a painted set. In another moment Guddi realizes a scene is being played by a stunt double rather than the actor. Later, after watching a scene being shot, Mamaji praises Dharmendra's singing and Dharmendra has to remind him that he was only mouthing a song that had been recorded by a playback singer. In a cameo, superstar Rajesh Khanna has to do several takes of a scene, first because he walks too close to the camera and second because he forgets a line. When actor Pran, known for playing villains, gives Dharmendra his watch, Kusum warns him not to take it because "zaroor kuch matlab hoga" ("he must have some evil intention"), leading Dharmendra to laugh at her: "Is liye ki yeh filmon mein villain ka role karte hain?! Asal zindagi mein yeh aadmi … hamesha dusron ke bhale mein lage rehte hain" ("Why, just because he plays villains in movies?! In real life this man is always looking out for others"). Such moments highlight the pleasure of the cinema, and showing the materiality of film production imbues the film with cinephilia. However, unlike most Bollywood films, *Guddi* ends up being a warning about the dangers of cinephilia. As the film proceeds, Kusum's family gradually teach her, with Dharmendra's help, not to be seduced by the lights and glamour of film sets and to focus on real, attainable love instead.[17] In this way, despite its cinephilia, this film is more an exception than a rule.

Case study: **Main Madhuri Dixit Banna Chahti Hoon (2003)**

The film *Main Madhuri Dixit Banna Chahti Hoon*'s title translates to "I Want to Be Madhuri Dixit," referring to the massively popular Bollywood superstar Madhuri Dixit who was prominent from the 1980s to the early 2000s. The film tells the story of Chutki, a small-town young woman who loves to dance and who is affectionately known as "hamare gaon ki Madhuri Dixit" ("our town's Madhuri Dixit") because of her resemblance to the star. In a classic cinephilic scene, the townspeople are watching the 2002 film *Devdas* (in which

Madhuri Dixit played a central role) on a projector when the reel runs out and they have to wait for the next one to arrive. As the audience gets restless, Chutki begins to perform a medley of Madhuri Dixit's popular song-and-dance sequences in front of changing painted backdrops, including "Ek Do Teen" from *Tezaab* (1988) and "Maar Daala" from *Devdas* (2002). The audience erupts in cheers. The visual style of this scene, with its sparse setting in a village hall, foregrounds the contrast between the sumptuous aesthetics of a film like *Devdas* – which, when it was released, was the highest-budget Bollywood film ever made – and the relative simplicity of far-flung cinema halls where Bollywood is most often enjoyed. But rather than a critique, the film celebrates small-town fandom, and Chutki's ambitions signal the importance of desire and fandom for young women around India. The fact that she goes to Mumbai to realize her dreams suggests the promise of futurity embedded in Bollywood.

Indeed, Chutki is presented as the moral center of the film *because* she is such an earnest fan. While watching *Devdas* with the townspeople, she waits eagerly for Madhuri Dixit to come on screen, which doesn't happen until about halfway through the film. When Madhuri finally appears, Chutki is entranced and refuses to leave her seat even when the reel runs out and everyone else is asking for a refund, insisting, "Main toh nahin jaungi. Main poori phillum dekhungi" ("I'm not going. I want to see the rest of the movie!"). Her mother tells her to stop embarrassing the family, or else what will people say, to which Chutki responds, "Nahin hota hai na, mujhse, Maa! Jab gaane sunti hoon na, pata nahin kuch … hone lagta hai, kuch … aisa kuch currentsa daudne lagta hai, badan mein" ("I can't help it! When I hear the music I … I don't know … something happens in me … some current starts to run through my body"). Fan obsession is here likened to obsession in love: a bodily experience that takes you out of the world so that you can no longer act according to normal protocols or conventions. In fact, like Kusum's romantic obsession with Dharmendra in *Guddi* (1971) discussed above, Chutki's focus on her filmic career is so intense that she refuses to get married; the fact that marriage and fandom are presented as opposed suggests something inherently queer about fan obsession. Conversely, her parents insist on getting her married, implying that marriage will tame her obsession.

When Chutki and Raja arrive in Mumbai, they single-mindedly pursue Chutki's dreams of becoming a Bollywood heroine. She gets hired as a junior artiste, but it is not enough for her: it is as if there is something magical about being a film's hero that motivates her, as she and Raja are willing to spend all their money on an agent and reject smaller roles, irrationally holding out for the big break. Finally Chutki gets a hero role but it ends up being a low-budget film that flops at the box office. She returns, dejected, to her hometown, but then, in a surprise twist, she discovers that the film is a success after all, and they move back to Mumbai, this time actually married out of love, not only convenience – but, notably, a love based in Raja's complete and utter commitment to Chutki's Bollywood career. The film shows the struggles of joining the industry as an outsider, while it also celebrates fandom and cinephilia as moral centers.

Aiyyaa (2012) is another film that celebrates cinephilia: the film opens with Meenakshi lip-synching and dancing to Madhuri Dixit's part in "Kehdo Ke Tum," a song from the film *Tezaab* (1988) and then to Sridevi's role in a song from *Chaalbaaz* (1989). Later Meenakshi fantasizes about her and Surya acting out the wet sari song sequence from *Mr. India* (1987). Her bedroom is covered with pictures of male film stars like Aamir Khan, Shah Rukh Khan, and Salman Khan. When her fiancé tells her that he prefers "old fashioned" films because in those days, "na koi makeup, na koi glossy designer kapde [pehnte the] … aur … zyada naach-gaane bhi nahin hua karte the" ("they didn't wear makeup or glossy designer clothes, and they didn't sing and dance very much"), Meenakshi is horrified by his taste and it is clear that she cannot marry this man because it is precisely those aspects of Bollywood that she adores. In addition to these direct references to cinema culture, *Aiyyaa* is unique for being filled with so much laughter and joy – erotic, familial, visual, sensorial – that it represents, in its very excess, the kind of exuberance that epitomizes Bollywood cinephilia.

Shamitabh (2015) is a film about superfan Disham, a young boy in rural Maharashtra, who is speaking impaired, but still wants to be a film star. He is obsessed with films; he can think about nothing except films, so when his teacher asks the class who Gandhi was, Disham writes on his paper "Ben Kingsley," referring to the actor who played Gandhi in Richard Attenborough's 1983 film, and when asked what Gandhi contributed to India – the correct answer being *azadi* or independence – Disham writes "an Oscar," referring to Attenborough's *Gandhi* winning the Best Picture Academy Award that year. Early in the film, a song titled "Ishq-e-Fillum," or "Film Is Love" is devoted entirely to Disham's fandom:

> Ishq-e-fillum, junoon-e-fillum
> Hai dard fillum, davaa hai fillum
> Dua hai fillum
> Jumma jumma jahaaz fillum
> Hansi khushi ka hai raaz fillum
> Hai naaz e hai
> Jeena nahin, jeena, fillum bina bina
> Khuda ka bhi kehna hai, fillum hai na hai na
> Salaam-e-fillum.

> [Film is love, film is passion
> Film is both pain and cure
> Film is a blessing
> Film is the way to fly every Friday
> Film is the secret to laughter and joy
> Film is pride
> I don't want to live without film
> Even God says, thank God for film
> I salute you, film.]

Andaz Apna Apna's (1994) opening sequence features Amar daydreaming about coming to the rescue of Bollywood superstar Juhi Chawla (playing herself), whose car has broken down. He takes her to her film shoot and there meets Govinda (another star, also playing himself). The jokes abound: Govinda tells Amar (played by superstar Aamir Khan), "Tum itne khoobsurat naujawan ho, filmon mein try kyon nahin karte?" ("You're so handsome, why don't you try acting in films?") and Chawla is humming a song from another film she starred in, *Darr* (1993), and when she gets startled, she says, "Mujhe laga hai ki Shah Rukh Khan aa gaya" ("I thought that Shah Rukh Khan was here!"), referring to the fact that Khan had played a stalker and she his victim in *Darr*.

Fan (2016) is a film about fandom that takes a different direction, referencing the wild popularity of Bollywood superstar Shah Rukh Khan but also revealing the dark side of fandom. The film shows how fandom can turn into obsession, but also how stardom is ironically reliant on that very obsession. Shah Rukh Khan plays a double role as both Aryan Khanna, the Bollywood superstar, and Gaurav, his fan. Khan's face was transformed using makeup, prosthetics, and digital alteration to play Gaurav, adding to the sense of uncanny proximity between star and fan. Gaurav is obsessed with Aryan Khanna to the point of physically assaulting anyone who says anything bad about him. But Aryan is repulsed by this overeager fan. When Aryan confronts Gaurav, Gaurav reminds the star of how often he says, "Main jo bhi ho, jahan bhi ho, jis makam pe bhi ho, apne fans ki wajah se. Agar mere fans nahin, toh main kuch nahin" ("Whoever I am, wherever I am, it's all because of my fans. If I didn't have my fans, I'd be nothing"), a line that stars often repeat at awards shows and beyond. But Gaurav takes this line literally, modifying it to justify his stalkerish obsession with Khanna: "Gaurav hai, toh Aryan hai. Gaurav nahin, toh Aryan kuch bhi nahin" ("Aryan exists because of Gaurav. If there were no Gaurav, Aryan would be nothing"). This darker story about fandom complicates Bollywood morality, as the audience expects to support the fan but his turn to violence suggests that even cinephilia can be taken too far. At the same time, Shah Rukh Khan's double role makes watching the film a cinephilic experience, as the viewer gets to enjoy the technological feat of seeing him twice – albeit a bit different – within the same frame (Figure 5.3).

Fandom in Bollywood also unleashes transgressive energies that can, at times, be read as queer. In the examples given above from *Guddi* (1971) and *Main Madhuri Dixit Banna Chahti Hoon* (2003), we see cinephilia explicitly contrasted with marriage. Cinephilia is thus presented as a quality that cannot be contained by the heteronormative structures of heterosexual romance. This is true in *Aiyyaa* (2012) as well, in which Meenakshi is so absurdly filmi that her family laments that she has no marriage prospects. Cinephilia is presented as romantic both in the sense of desiring love rather than an arranged marriage, and, even more intensely, of wanting to be carried away by passion or excess, and unable to live within the social structures of the real world.

Fandom also offers possibilities for queer embodiment in the circulation of Bollywood images, costumes, gestures, and dance moves in nightclubs, drag

Figure 5.3 Superstar Aryan Khanna faces off with Gaurav, his devoted fan, in *Fan* (2016), with Shah Rukh Khan playing both roles.

performances, and the intimate spaces in front of a mirror.[18] Female stars like Sridevi and Madhuri Dixit are often centerpieces of queer dance, and beefy male superstars like Salman Khan also cultivate queer fan followings. India's primary gay magazine, *Bombay Dost*, often includes articles and discussions on the queer resonances of Bollywood. In a well-known incident, *Bombay Dost* founder Ashok Row Kavi wrote an article called "Saif Sex" about the suggestive homosociality between actors Akshay Kumar and Saif Ali Khan in one of the songs in the film *Main Khiladi Tu Anari* (1994);[19] while Khan was insulted, Akshay Kumar took it as a compliment, and even stated, after being voted "the ultimate gay fantasy" in a viewer poll in *Bombay Dost*, "It feels really nice to be a gay fantasy."[20] Parmesh Shahani describes how in gay bars in the early 2000s, men looking for hookups would rarely give their real names, instead "call[ing themselves] either 'Rahul' or 'Raj'" after the most common screen names of superstar Shah Rukh Khan.[21] These examples further confirm cinephilia's transgressive potential.

Double roles, twin plots, and cameos

Double roles, twin plots, and cameos are widespread cinephilic features in Bollywood. The double role, besides its plot function, allows the viewer to see more of the star and thus adds to the pleasure of the film. There are various kinds of double roles. In *Lamhe* (1991), Sridevi plays the roles of Pallavi, who dies in childbirth, and then, 18 years later, her daughter Pooja. Similarly, in *Aradhana* (1969), Rajesh Khanna plays Arun Varma, a fighter pilot who dies in a plane crash and then, two decades later, he plays Suraj, his son. In *Main Khiladi Tu Anari* (1994) and *Om Shanti Om* (2007), Shilpa Shetty and Deepika Padukone play double roles that allow the second character to masquerade as the first one in order to solve a crime. In *An Evening in Paris* (1967), Sharmila Tagore plays Deepa, a wealthy heiress, and Suzy, a cabaret dancer – who, it turns out, is Deepa's long lost twin sister. Here the twin plot has little bearing on the film, suggesting that it is a means of intensifying cinephilia rather than a political or social allegory. In *Paying Guest* (1957), Dev Anand plays Ramesh, who then dresses up as the elderly Mirza Sahib in order to rent a room in Shanti's father's house. This is not a double role in the traditional sense, since the character Ramesh is in disguise within the narrative, but it still offers the pleasure of cinephilia, culminating in a funny scene in which Mirza Sahib pretends to fight Ramesh at Shanti's request; Mirza Sahib enters his room, fake-shouts at Ramesh and pretends to threaten him if he doesn't leave. He then fake-hits him with a stick, actually punching a pillow and banging some cupboard doors, which Shanti hears from outside, thinking a real fight is taking place. Then he changes his outfit and emerges as the wounded Ramesh; this happens several times before Mirza Sahib announces his victory, claiming that Ramesh has escaped through the window. Similarly but with a twist, in *Baazigar* (1993) Shah Rukh Khan plays Ajay and Vicky who we think are two different people until right before intermission, when it is revealed that Ajay is disguising himself as Vicky in order to enact revenge on the Chopra family for the death of his father. In *Duplicate* (1998), Shah Rukh Khan plays the double role of the naïve Bablu and the street-smart criminal Manu. This was particularly pleasurable in 1998 because of the rising stardom of Shah Rukh Khan at that time. Brand new to superstardom, and referencing his own background of beginning in villainous films and then gradually transitioning to being a hero, this double role becomes a metacommentary on Khan's own cinematic career up to that point. In *Kaho Naa Pyaar Hai* (2000), Hrithik Roshan plays Rohit, who is killed by corrupt government officials when he witnesses an illegal transaction. When Sonia, mourning his death, goes to New Zealand on holiday, she meets Raj, who looks strikingly like the dead Rohit, and is also played by Hrithik Roshan. Across films, there is no single formula for double roles, but in every case it enhances the pleasure of film viewing by giving the audience more of the star than is humanly possible.

Twin plots have been quite popular in Bollywood as well. *Ram Aur Shyam* (1967) featured superstar Dilip Kumar in the double role of twin brothers separated at birth, who had developed two radically different personalities; the opening credits specifically announced: "Dilip Kumar, in his first dual role." This film merges cinephilia with the lost-and-found plot; in one scene relatively early in the film, Shyam eats in a restaurant and then leaves and Ram enters and sits in the same seat, confusing the waiter. However, the brothers do not actually meet until the very end, and the enjoyment of that resolution is intensified by the fact that the audience finally gets to see Dilip Kumar twice in the same frame. *Seeta Aur Geeta* (1972) featured superstar Hema Malini in a double role, playing twin sisters separated at birth and brought together when they are mistaken for each other. Geeta is the stronger and more gutsy sister and Seeta is terribly mistreated by her family; here the trope of twins suggests a split in ideal femininity between strength and submission, which is resolved in favor of strength when Geeta saves her sister's life. *Kaminey* (2009) allegorizes a grim urban futurity with a pair of twins – both played by Shahid Kapoor – who are on divergent paths and struggle to survive within a warped moral universe. And *Dhoom 3* (2013) has a surprise twin plot that worked diegetically but also exploited cinephilia.

Star cameos are another common cinephilic feature of Bollywood. Dharmendra plays himself in a significant role in *Guddi* (1971), but Ashok Kumar, Amitabh Bachchan, Rajesh Khanna, Pran, and several other actors also appear for surprising and at times humorous cameos in that film, much of which takes place on a film set. Aamir Khan makes a cameo in an early scene in *Damini* (1993), Kajol makes a cameo in *Duplicate* (1998), as does Tabu in a song sequence in *Main Hoon Na* (2004). *Veere di Wedding* (2018) includes a cameo of the film's own star, Kareena Kapoor, in a wedding video. These various guest appearances serve different purposes. Some have no bearing on the plot but are just pure cinephilia, as in *Damini*, in which Aamir Khan plays no part in the rest of the film. In *Duplicate*, which stars Shah Rukh Khan, having Kajol in particular appear in a cameo is a nod to *Dilwale Dulhania Le Jayenge* (1995), Shah Rukh Khan and Kajol's most successful film together and the one that launched them as a popular Bollywood couple. The pleasure is not only in seeing Kajol but in seeing her and Shah Rukh Khan together; this cinephilia only enhances the already-existing enjoyment of seeing Shah Rukh Khan's double role in that film.

Two notable song sequences in Bollywood have featured multiple stars performing together. The "John Jani Janardhan" song sequence in *Naseeb* (1981) takes place at a dinner party whose invitees are famous Bollywood stars, and well-known actors such as Raj Kapoor, Shammi Kapoor, Dharmendra, Rajesh Khanna, Sharmila Tagore, and Waheeda Rehman appear as themselves, signing autographs for the party guests. Johnny is singing the song, and by the end all the stars are dancing together enjoying the music, in a scene of cinephilic pleasure that has little to do with the plot of the film. In "Deewanagi" in *Om Shanti Om* (2007), Farah Khan goes even further, featuring 30 Bollywood stars from different generations who all appear in a single song sequence. Many of the stars perform dance moves associated with their past films, including Govinda, and Kajol and Shah Rukh Khan playfully tap each other's noses in a move from *Kuch Kuch Hota Hai* (1998). This film, as will be discussed below, is cinephilic from beginning to end, and so "Deewanagi" both serves that theme while also being intensely pleasurable on its own (Figure 5.4).

Film titles

As discussed in the Introduction, Bollywood film titles rarely identify a theme of the film or offer a summary of its story, but work metonymically, naming a line spoken in the film, characterizing an affective sensibility the film invokes, or referring to another film. Thus, at first glance, many titles may seem somewhat random. For instance, the title of the film *C.I.D.* (1956) refers to the Criminal Investigation Department, which is just one of the institutions involved in the detective story, but not even the primary one. *Padosan* (1968)

Figure 5.4 Multiple stars had cameos in the "Deewanagi" song sequence in *Om Shanti Om* (2007). Pictured here: Sanjay Dutt, Saif Ali Khan, and Salman Khan, along with the film's star, Shah Rukh Khan.

simply means female neighbor, which refers to Bindu, the woman the protagonist Bhola falls in love with, who lives next door. More recent films take this convention even further, with titles like *Deewana* (crazy), *Kuch Kuch Hota Hai* (something happens), or *Hum Dil De Chuke Sanam* (I gave you my heart), which are so generic they could refer to almost any love story. Another fairly common practice which furthers this disjuncture between title and theme is to name films after a line from a song in an earlier film. This is rarely meant as an active reference to the other film, but is a playful reference to the Bollywood genre itself. Examples include *Zindagi Na Milegi Dobara*, a 2011 film whose title comes from a lyric in "Rock On," the title song of the 2008 film by the same name. The title of *Meri Pyaari Bindu* (2017) comes from a line in the "Mere Bhole Balam" song in *Padosan* (1968). The title of *Ae Dil Hai Mushkil* (2016) comes from the song by the same name from *C.I.D.* (1956). *All Is Well* (2015) comes from a song in the film *3 Idiots* (2009); *Jab Tak Hai Jaan* (2012) is the title of a song in *Sholay* (1975); *Dum Maro Dum* (2011) was a song in the film *Hare Rama Hare Krishna* (1971); *Kambakkht Ishq* (2009) came from a line in the film *Pyar Tune Kya Kiya* (2001); *Bachna Ae Haseeno*'s (2008) title is from a song by the same name in *Hum Kisise Kum Naheen* (1977), and *Ramaiyya Vastavaya* (2013) was named after a song from *Shri 420* (1955). The examples of this abound.

Most of the time, these references have little meaning in terms of the content or theme of the film and are simply expressions of cinephilia, although there are exceptions. *Om Shanti Om*'s (2007) title comes from a line in a song in the film *Karz* (1980); like *Karz, Om Shanti Om* is also about reincarnation and the films have several plot pieces in common. Thus, in this case, the title can be understood as a deliberate homage to the earlier film. Similarly, *Ek Ladki Ko Dekha Toh Aisa Laga*'s (2019) title comes from the well-known song of the same name, from the 1994 film *1942: A Love Story*. Here the title is put to particularly clever use, as "Ek Ladki Ko Dekha Toh Aisa Laga" is a love song about the experience the protagonist has when he sees his beloved ("ek ladki," or a girl) for the first time. But in the 2019 film, which is Bollywood's first film with an openly homosexual love story (see Chapter 7 for more on queer Bollywood), this title is resignified to refer to a *female* protagonist, who also feels a certain way when she sees *her* beloved, who is also female ("the girl"). This literalizes what Ruth Vanita identifies as a larger trend in Bollywood love songs, whose lyrics are often "ungendered"[22] and thus open to sexual ambiguity.

Other kinds of cinephilic film titles include films named after past famous Bollywood protagonists, such as the film *Jai Veeru* (2009), which refers to the two protagonists of the 1975 film *Sholay* (1975). *Gabbar Is Back* (2015) also refers to *Sholay*, whose villain is named Gabbar Singh. There are also films named after Bollywood film conventions, such as *Break Ke Baad* (2010), or "After the Break," referring to the portion of a Bollywood film that follows the interval, or *Phata Poster Nikhla Hero* (2013), whose title means "Out of the Poster Came the Hero," which refers to Bollywood film posters. Recently we have also seen film titles named after the particular sounds of Bollywood cinema, such as *Dishoom* (2016) and *Dishkiyaoon* (2014). "Dishoom" refers to the hyperbolic sounds of a Bollywood fight scene, and "dishkiyaoon" refers to the specific artificial sound of a bullet (both are similar to the English "Kapow!"). Using these as titles suggests that those features of Bollywood that could be considered unrealistic and hyperbolic have in many cases been incorporated into the cinephilic celebration of Bollywood within Bollywood films themselves.

Intertextuality

Beyond their titles, Bollywood films also make active reference to other Bollywood films, references which are usually extradiegetic and have little meaning within the films' plots, and thus serve as expressions of cinephilia that enhance viewing pleasure when they are noticed and recognized. These references range from small throwaway lines to substantial sections of plot. Sometimes the references are indirect, as in the references to *Purab Aur Paschim* (1970) and *An Evening in Paris* (1967) in the 2014 film *Queen*. More explicitly, *Main Hoon Na*'s (2004) whole college setting and the subplot featuring the tomboy Sanjana are clear references to *Kuch Kuch Hota Hai* (1998), one of the first Bollywood films set on a college campus and one of Shah Rukh Khan's most successful early films, and which also featured a tomboy character. In *Chalti Ka Naam Gaadi* (1958), when Renu, played by superstar Madhubala, shows up at Mannu's garage late at night, he jumps and says, "Hum samjha koi bhoot-woot hoga" ("Oh, I thought it was a ghost"), referring to Madhubala's earlier film, *Mahal* (1949), in which she played a ghost. Likewise, the end sequence of *Amar Akbar Anthony* (1977) with the three brothers all paired up with their lovers and driving in a car together seems directly inspired by almost exactly the same sequence at the end of *Chalti Ka Naam Gaadi*.

Perhaps the most commonly referenced film in Bollywood is the iconic *Sholay* (1975), one of the most successful Bollywood movies of all time. As we have seen, the title of *Gabbar Is Back* (2015) references Gabbar Singh, the notorious villain in *Sholay*, but the protagonist also ends the film by giving a rousing speech that includes the line, "Ab tera kya hoga Kaliya?" ("Now what will happen to you, Kaliya?"), which is one of Gabbar Singh's most famous lines in *Sholay*. In *Main Hoon Na* (2004), a fight scene takes place outside a cinema hall showing *Sholay*, and the rickshaw that Ram uses to chase the bad guys has "Dhanno" written on the back, referring to the name of Basanti's horse in *Sholay*. In addition, after capturing one of the bad guys, Ram says to him, "Jodidaar toh chale gaye. Ab tera kya hoga Kaliya?" ("Your mates have all disappeared. What's going to happen to you now, Kaliya?"), again referring to Gabbar Singh's famous line in *Sholay*. In *Andaz Apna Apna* (1994), Amar says to the villain, in false flattery, "Janta tha, main rota tha toh meri maa kya kehti thi? … Kehti thi ki so jaa, Amar bete, so jaa, varna Gogo aa jayega" ("You know what my mother used to say to me when I cried? She used to say, 'Go to sleep now, Amar, otherwise Gogo will come'"), a line that references Gabbar Singh's line in *Sholay* in which he menacingly brags, "Yahan se pachaas pachaas kos door, gaon mein jab baccha raat ko rota hai, toh maa kehti hai bete so ja, so ja nahin toh Gabbar Singh aa jayega" ("In villages as far as fifty miles from here, when a child cries at night, his mother tells him, 'Go to sleep, otherwise Gabbar Singh will come'"). And in *Baazigar* (1993), when Priya reprimands the servants, Babulal jokingly calls her "Gabbar behn" ("sister Gabbar").

Another commonly referenced film is *Dilwale Dulhania Le Jayenge* (1995). In *Dil Bole Hadippa!* (2009) Rohan tries to impress Veera by dressing up as *Dilwale Dulhania Le Jayenge*'s Raj and singing "Tujhe dekha toh yeh jaana sanam," one of the popular songs from that film. In the comedy *Dil Toh Baccha Hai Ji* (2011), a waiter tells Milind, who just got dumped, that he once saw in a movie that if a woman is walking away and looks back, it means she likes you, referring to a scene in *Dilwale Dulhania Le Jayenge*. Repeating "Palat, palat" ("Turn around, turn around") under his breath, just as Raj did in *Dilwale Dulhania Le Jayenge*, Milind waits for his beloved to turn around, but in this case, unlike in the original, she never turns; the waiter suggests that maybe she didn't see the same movie! In *I Hate Luv Storys* (2010), when Jay finds out Simran's name, he jokes, "Kaafi filmi naam hai, na? … Listen, tumhara koi boyfriend vagaira nahin hai, jiska naam Raj hai?" ("That's a pretty filmi name, isn't it? Listen, you don't have a boyfriend too, whose name is Raj?"), referencing the couple in *Dilwale Dulhania Le Jayenge*. When she admits her boyfriend's name *is* Raj, he replies, "But seriously, tumne socha hai tumhare bacchon ka kya haal hoga? School mein teacher poochegi, 'Bete, tumhare parents ke naam kya hain, Raj aur Simran? Bete, kya woh bhi kheton mein gaane gaate hain?'" ("But seriously, have you considered your children? In school the teacher will ask them, 'Your parents are named Raj and Simran? Do they also sing songs in fields?'"), referring to an iconic scene in *Dilwale Dulhania Le Jayenge* in which Raj and Simran meet after a long separation and sing a song in the mustard fields of the Punjab. In *Chennai Express* (2013), Meenamma tries to run onto a moving train as

Simran did at the end of *Dilwale Dulhania Le Jayenge*, and while she is running, the theme song from the earlier film plays in the background. Rahul, played by Shah Rukh Khan, who also played Raj in *Dilwale Dulhania Le Jayenge*, reaches out his arm to help Meenamma get on the train, and when she thanks him, he says, "It's ok. Maine pehle bhi kiya hua hai aise" ("That's ok. I have done this before"). The train scene from *Dilwale Dulhania Le Jayenge* is also referenced in *Shubh Mangal Zyada Saavdhan* (2020) with two male lovers, thus queering that iconic scene. *Dilwale Dulhania Le Jayenge*, moreover, has its own references to other films: in the engagement party scene, Baldev Singh sings a few lines to his wife from the song "Meri Zohra Jabeen" from the film *Waqt* (1965) – a song that is one of the rare Bollywood love songs meant for an older man to sing to his older partner – and imitates the dance moves of the original scene as well.

Intertextual references abound in Bollywood more generally; most of these are meant to be humorous or entertaining and have little meaning for the plot or theme of the later film. In *Andaz Apna Apna* (1994), Amar calls the villain, Crimemaster Gogo, "Mogambo ka bhatija" ("Mogambo's nephew"), referring to the evil villain in *Mr. India* (1987). In *Gunday* (2014), when Bala and Bikram first decide to start a life of crime, we see a movie theater in the background playing *Zanjeer* (1973), a film also set among gangsters. Later, when the friends go to the movies, *Mr. India* (1987) is playing, and Nandita dances in front of the screen, replicating the moves of the famous wet sari song sequence of that film (Figure 5.5).

Andaz Apna Apna (1994), in particular, is full of references to other Bollywood films. In the film, which stars Aamir Khan, we hear a refrain from "Papa Kehte Hain," a song in Aamir Khan's first film, *Qayamat Se Qayamat Tak* (1988). The twin brothers are named Ram and Shyam, after the twins in the

Figure 5.5 Nandita dancing to the wet sari song in *Mr. India* (1987) while the sequence, originally starring Sridevi, is screened in the background, in *Gunday* (2014).

well-known film *Ram Aur Shyam* (1967). Later in the film, Anand asks Prem, played by superstar Salman Khan, whether he has seen *Sholay* (1975), and Prem responds, "Ten times." In response, Amar tells Anand, "Uske baap ne likhi," which literally means, "His father wrote [the film]," but in colloquial language means he knows *Sholay* very well. The joke here is that *Sholay* was indeed written by Salim Khan, Salman Khan's father, so the dialogue works on multiple levels of cinephilia. Moreover, inspired by *Sholay*, Amar and Prem decide to flip a coin to decide who gets to make the first move toward a woman they both like. However, whereas in *Sholay* the coin toss represents inseparable friendship, here, they are merely trying to one up each other. Amar promises, before they flip the coin: "Jo jeeta wohi Sikandar," a saying that means whoever wins the toss gets to be boss, but is also a reference to another Aamir Khan film called *Jo Jeeta Wohi Sikandar* (1992). And when Amar finds out the woman he loves is actually someone else, we hear a few lines of the song "Kya Se Kya Ho Gaya" from the film *Guide* (1965), a song about betrayal, but whereas in *Guide* the sense of betrayal was central to the film, here it is a joke and made light of.

At other times, the references to earlier films are deeper and more meaningful. *Om Shanti Om* (2007) makes several references to *Karz* (1980), but is also an homage to that film. In *Karz*, Ravi is killed by his wife Kamini and gets reincarnated as Monty, a successful singer. As he begins to experiences flashbacks from his previous life, he realizes that he has been reborn in order to avenge Ravi's murder. In *Om Shanti Om* (2007), junior artiste Om Makhija is killed and then reborn as Om Kapoor, the son of a film family. Om similarly experiences flashbacks and takes it upon himself to avenge the earlier Om's death. *Om Shanti Om* purposely borrows several plot elements from *Karz*, such as the trap the characters set up to prove that Kamini killed Ravi, and the narrative song that tells the story of the murder as a means of disconcerting Kamini, both of which take place between Om and Mukesh in the later film as well. Even the tune for the latter film's song, "Daastan-e-Om Shanti Om," is influenced by the tune for the earlier reveal song, "Ek Haseena Thi." *Om Shanti Om* also has a scene in which Om is actually watching the shooting of *Karz*; so rather than an adaptation or a remake, we could see the later film as a multi-layered, cinephilic homage.

Likewise, *Dostana*'s (2008) reference to an earlier film is both cinephilic and meaningful. Sam's mother believes her son is gay and at first threatens to disown him. But after Neha convinces her that she should accept her son's sexuality, she officially welcomes his partner into the family by offering a prayer, with the title song from *Kabhi Khushi Kabhie Gham* (2001) playing in the background – a song which in the earlier film had served as the background to Nandini welcoming her son Rahul home after a long absence. When Sam walks in, however, and asks his mother what she is doing, we realize that her friend is playing the soundtrack from *Kabhi Khushi Kabhie Gham* on her iPod and she quickly turns it off. This is both a humorous and surprising reminder of the circulation of Bollywood songs through technology, but also offers a new idiom in which to incorporate queer relationships into the epic Bollywood family romance.

The director Karan Johar, whose films were discussed in Chapter 4, also makes generous use of intertextuality and references to other films, not only in his repetition of the Shah Rukh Khan–Kajol pairing but also through explicit references; in *Kabhi Khushi Kabhie Gham* (2001), for instance, Rahul and Anjali (named after the Rahul and Anjali of Johar's earlier film *Kuch Kuch Hota Hai*) say, "I don't like jokes" and "I don't like you" which is the same dialogue the characters had spoken in the earlier movie. In addition, in a break in the song "Suraj Hua Maddham" we hear the bridge from the title song in *Kuch Kuch Hota Hai*.

Bollywood characters also sing or dance to songs from other films. Sometimes these have no purpose in the plot at all. For instance, in *Dostana* (1980), a character sings the "Hum Tum Ek Kamre Mein Band" song from *Bobby* (1973). In *Lamhe* (1991) Viren is feeling particularly morose and Pooja and Prem try to cheer him up by acting out a medley of songs from old Hindi films. In *Mr. India* (1987), the children humorously adapt the lyrics of "Na Mange Sona Chandi" from *Bobby* (1973) as a way of apologizing to Seema for interrupting her work, and they have a back-and-forth, with Seema and the children cleverly repurposing lines from other classic film songs such as "Awaaz Main Na Doonga" from *Dosti* (1964) and "Sawan Ka Mahina" from *Milan* (1967) to argue about whether Seema should return the children's football. In *Raja Hindustani* (1996), Chachaji hums a song from the 1955 film *Shri 420* to himself. In *Darr* (1993) during the Holi song "Ang Se Ang Lagana" there is a break in which we hear a couple of lines from the famous Holi song "Rang Barse" from *Silsila* (1981), and in *Kal Ho Naa Ho* (2003) the grandmother's tone-deaf singing group performs a painful rendition of *Devdas*'s (2002) "Maar Daala." In *Fanaa* (2006), Zooni and Rehaan play the game Antakshari (discussed in Chapter 3) with old film songs and Zooni's mother recites the lyrics from the title song of the film *Kabhi Kabhie* (1976). In *Gunday* (2014), the song "Chalo Dildaar Karo" from *Pakeezah* (1972) is playing on the radio and in *Seeta Aur Geeta* (1972), a car drives by with "Dum Maaro Dum," from *Hare Krishna Hare Ram* (1971), blasting on the stereo. In *C.I.D.* (1956) the characters play musical chairs to a medley of film songs. In *Bunty Aur Babli* (2005), during the wedding scene, the song "Kabhi Kabhie" from the 1976 film of the same name is playing in the background and in another scene, we can hear the song "Dil Cheez Kya Hai" from the 1981 film *Umrao Jaan*. At other times, the use of film songs is supposed to be playful and even funny. In *Padosan* (1968), when Bindu rejects Masterji, he woefully sings a line from "Awaaz Main Na Doonga" from the film *Dosti* (1964), registering his sadness at being dumped. In *Kal Ho Naa Ho* (2003) the characters humorously sing the song "Chale Chalo" from *Lagaan* (2001) – whose lyrics are about national unity – while they work to remodel Jennifer's New York City restaurant to serve Indian food. And in *3 Idiots* (2009), Raju sings the song "Kuch Na Kaho" from *1942: A Love Story* (1994) while Rancho is professing his love to Piya. These multiple, playful references – indeed, their very proliferation – suggest a sustained commitment to intertextuality that is quite unique to the genre.

The affectionate parody

Recently we have seen more films that explicitly parody Bollywood conventions. I call these affectionate parodies, however, to emphasize that they poke fun at these conventions not as a means of moving beyond them or mocking them from a critical distance, but as a form of intimacy, love, and homage. In most cases, the films end up using the very conventions they parody. In *Andaz Apna Apna* (1994), Robert, one of the villains, asks his friend, "Yeh Hindi filmon mein gangster ko, villain ko, aisa buddhu, bewaqoof type kai ko batata hai?" ("Why do they make gangsters and villains in Hindi films so stupid?") when he is in fact an incredibly stupid villain. *Shamitabh* (2015) parodies the creation and titles of films such as "Thappad!" ("Slap!") whose hero's title move is slapping his enemy. In *Main Khiladi Tu Anari* (1994), Deepak is an actor hanging out with Karan, a policeman, in order to learn how to play a cop in films. In *Aiyyaa* (2012), as in *Main Hoon Na* (2004) discussed below, music starts playing and a breeze begins to blow through Meenakshi's hair every time Surya walks into the room, parodying conventions around the representation of Bollywood love.

Director Farah Khan is especially known for the fun she has with Bollywood parody. Her directorial debut, *Main Hoon Na* (2004), self-consciously parodies the practice of stars (especially male stars) playing characters much younger than them. (For instance, Aamir Khan played a recent college graduate in *Qayamat Se Qayamat Tak* [1988] when he was 23, another recent college graduate in *Dil Chahta Hai* [2001], 13 years later, and yet another in *3 Idiots* [2009], when he was 44!) In *Main Hoon Na*, Shah Rukh Khan plays Major Ram, an army officer who is supposed to go undercover on a college campus in order to protect a general's daughter whose life is under threat. At first he refuses, saying "Bahut ajeeb lagega" ("It will look really strange") and "Main student nahin lagta hoon!" ("I don't look like a student!"). However, when forced to impersonate a student nonetheless, Ram dresses in unfashionable clothes and tries and fails to fit in with the youth. The film pokes fun at the fact that even in 1998, when Khan played Rahul on a similar college campus in *Kuch Kuch Hota Hai*, he was far too old for the role. But here, that practice is exposed; all the other students in *Main Hoon Na* call him "Uncle," poking fun at his age, and referencing this practice of unrealistic Bollywood casting in an entertaining way.

Farah Khan's second directorial venture was *Om Shanti Om* (2007), an extended parody of Bollywood conventions that is simultaneously a celebration of Bollywood conventions. Set in a film studio and featuring a protagonist who is a devoted fan and lover of film, *Om Shanti Om* is cinephilia par excellence, from every aesthetic and visual choice to its story, which is a reincarnation plot that, as discussed above, is also an homage to the earlier reincarnation film *Karz* (1980). The film's protagonist, Om, feels such intense devotion to cinema that he cannot draw a line between his own life and the movies: thus, the first scene of the film shows him watching a shooting and imagining himself as the star performing in the song sequence. Many representations are parodic, for instance when Om, played by Shah Rukh Khan, gets nominated for the Filmfare Award for two different movies in which he plays a character named Rahul, and as the signature move of each film, he embraces his lover in front of a backdrop of the Swiss Alps – parodying how Shah Rukh Khan has played characters with the same name across films. *Om Shanti Om*, set mostly on film sets, also parodies industry practices like the star showing up late and telling the director how the story should proceed, extreme melodramatic storylines to the point of ridiculousness, and other Bollywood conventions like item songs and repeated gestures.

The technology of filmmaking

Another aspect of cinephilia is the representation of and the taking pleasure in the technology of filmmaking. Sometimes this is simply humorous, as in *Ram Aur Shyam* (1967), in which Shyam gets kicked off a film shoot because he actually punches his opponents in the filming of a fight scene rather than faking it. Many Bollywood films that are set, or partially set, on film sets partake in this form of cinephilic enjoyment, including *Guddi* (1971), *Main Khiladi Tu Anari* (1994), *Rangeela* (1995), *Main Madhuri Dixit Banna Chahti Hoon* (2003), *Khoya Khoya Chand* (2007), *Om Shanti Om* (2007), *Shamitabh* (2015) and others. In these films there is a pleasure in seeing the otherwise invisible mechanics of film production in front of the camera. We discussed earlier how in *Guddi* the audience watches with pleasure as Kusum gradually begins to understand the technologies of filmmaking, even if that film's ultimate goal is cinematic disenchantment. *Main Madhuri Dixit Banna Chahti Hoon* takes the opposite tack; the more time Chutki spends on film sets, the more she is enchanted by the world of the cinema. The same is true in *Om Shanti Om*. Throughout that film we see the technology of filmmaking, whether it is the pulleys that allow a superhero to fly, the fan that makes a female hero's hair blow or the constant shouts of "Action!" and "Cut!" that make up the soundscape of a film shoot. In the song sequence "Dhoom Tana," images of former superstars Sunil Dutt, Jeetendra, and Rajesh Khanna are digitally layered over the filmed sequence, so that Shanti appears to be dancing with those stars, thus both evoking the history of Bollywood cinema and crossing time through the use of technology. And in *Gunday* (2014), Bala starts a fight in a cinema projection room, and when he shoots the man, he falls backwards through the screen, allowing a glimpse of the technology of projection.

One of the most notable celebrations of film technology and materiality is director Farah Khan's end credits performances in all four of her films. In these credits sequences, she brings on screen not only the actors, but the entire team of people who worked on the film, including the lyricist and the music director, who might be well-known but are rarely shown on screen, and also crew, hair designers, accountants, art directors, camera operators, lighting technicians, spot boys, makeup artists, and producers. These collaborators are shown in an extended scene that is supported by music and dance and thus reads as part of the film (Figure 5.6).

Figure 5.6 Not just the stars, but camera operators, costume designers, makeup artists, lighting technicians, and many others get a shout-out in the credits sequences of Farah Khan's films. Here, a frame from the end credits of *Main Hoon Na* (2004).

This cinephilic gesture foregrounds all the different people and types of labor that go into making a film and serves as a democratizing gesture that refuses the hierarchies of labor upon which the star system operates.

There are also cinephilic elements that call attention to the sonic quality of Bollywood.[23] Sudhir Mahadevan reads *Kaminey* (2009), whose director Vishal Bhardwaj is also a composer and singer, as a cinephilic consideration of the sonic landscape of Bollywood. The title of the song "Dhan Te-Nan" refers to the classic tune that defines a 1970s action sequence. Later in *Kaminey* two gangsters have an aural gun battle, in which they pretend to shoot each other by voicing Bollywood gun noises like "dishkiyoon," "dichkaun, dichkaun," "phiskyu," and "jujujujujuju" while laughing hysterically. The song "Fatak," in which the title word is repeated several times, refers to the *sound* of a whip crack. These references to the technologies of filmmaking enhance the cinephilic quality of Bollywood, embracing the pleasures and joys of the medium in both serious and parodic ways.

As this chapter has shown, cinephilia is not simply a theme of some Bollywood movies but so prevalent across so many films that it might well be seen as a defining feature of the genre as a whole. Understanding this element of Bollywood offers a different interpretation of the repeated tropes, intertextual references, and parody that are sometimes seen as contributing to Bollywood's repetitive quality – not signs of a lack of originality but as generic conventions in their own right. Moreover, identifying cinephilia requires reading *across* a large number of texts rather than simply deeply into a few, a reading practice that emphasizes patterns rather than ruptures across films.

Part II

6 Nationalism

Nationalism is probably the most commonly discussed theme in teaching and scholarship on Bollywood. The question of the nation matters especially in India, because, as in many other countries that were formerly colonized (i.e. postcolonial), national affiliation is not a self-evident reality. India's massive diversity – of language, religion, and ethnicity – made it harder than in more homogeneous places for its residents to see themselves as Indian. Nationalism had to be invented in India, and then the population had to be convinced that nationalism mattered – that allegiance to the massive institution of the nation was as important than allegiance to one's family, village, community, or region. In many scholars' accounts, the popular cinema was an important tool in constructing and reinforcing this national unity, beginning in the early postcolonial decades and continuing until today.[1] In this line of argument, Bollywood serves an essentially normativizing role in securing the public's ideological support of the Indian nation. Cinema is a particularly important medium in doing so because of India's largely non-literate population and because of cinema's proximity to other popular modes like the Parsi theater and folk theatrical forms, epic oral storytelling, and mythical and theological tales.

This chapter takes a somewhat different view, arguing that Bollywood films are not simply expressions of a conservative, homogenizing, or militaristic Indian nationalism.[2] It is true that some films touch on national themes or feature patriotic characters, especially those released right around independence in 1947,[3] but the question of what it means to love your country is contested within most films themselves. As we shall see, many films are actually quite critical of the homogenizing impulse of Indian nationalism, as well as of the Indian state's failure to improve conditions for most people. Even where we see the expression of "Indianness," there is actually a striking variety, across films, regarding what Indianness actually means. Sometimes films offer quite radical ideas of what it means to be Indian – ideas that refuse a conservative nationalism, such as, for instance, the valuing of all of India's religions, not just the majority Hinduism, or that advance a desire for peace, rather than war, with neighboring Pakistan. Thus, by centering Indianness but offering new definitions of what Indianness means, some Bollywood films are both nationalist *and* offer new understandings of nationalism that can be actually quite open and liberal.

Moreover, the fact that in Bollywood love is the most important value, even more than national belonging, shows why Bollywood's generic features must mediate any understanding of a film's politics. As discussed in Chapter 2, love is Bollywood's central feature, and any reading of films that foregrounds its political meaning over its belief in love has the potential to misread these formulaic and melodramatic films – films that engage primarily at the level of heart and body rather than mind – as conservative or nationalist. Reading political themes through the lens of love, however, offers new understandings of Bollywood's politics.

The nation as mother

As we saw in Chapter 1, the mother is often the moral center of Bollywood films. This is in part because of the association of the mother with the Indian nation, which was popularized in the nineteenth century through the widely disseminated image of Mother India, a female goddess posed over the map of India. Slogans such as "Bharat Mata ki jai!" ("Long live Mother India!") were similarly popular during the anti-colonial movement. The centrality of the mother to nationalist discourse has led many scholars to read Hindi films as national allegories, swapping in India for the mother to argue that Indian nationalism is the true meaning of all films that feature a mother as the moral center. This interpretation is supported in films themselves by the fact that the mother is often presented as pure, virginal, uncorrupted, and allegorical, as in the film *Mother India* (1957), when one of the villagers says to Radha: "Tu toh hamari maa hai, saare gaon ki maa hai" ("You are our mother – the whole village's mother"), or in *Amar Akbar Anthony* (1977), where the mother is named Bharati, which means Indian (Bharat referring to one of the names for India). However, looking at these films more closely shows that the relationships among morality, motherhood, and nation are actually more complex than they might initially seem. Motherhood in Bollywood often becomes a way of complicating, rather than only confirming, a narrow nationalism.

Case study: Mother India *(1957)*

The fact that one of Bollywood's most well-known and iconic films is called *Mother India* seems to confirm the idea that Bollywood expresses nationalist sentiments. The film, released ten years after Indian independence, centers on Radha, who lives in a small village and tries to make a life for herself and her family. Besieged by one hardship after another, from the predatory interest rates of the moneylender to drought and then flooding, Radha suffers stoically even when her husband abandons the family and one of her sons grows up to be a troublemaker and a thief. The film is seen by many critics to valorize a model of ideal femininity based around motherhood and the mother's complete and utter devotion to her land, i.e. to India.[4]

However, a closer look at the film suggests that it does not simply valorize the allegorical role of motherhood. In fact, *Mother India* presents a quite troubled relationship of the protagonist to the nation. From the title and Radha's positive qualities, the moral universe is established with her at the center. However, the nature of the various disruptions in the moral universe suggests that she is not merely a surrogate for the nation. This is apparent early in the film; when asked to inaugurate a dam that, it is hoped, will better the lives of poor farmers, Radha at first refuses to participate, and when she does, the water rushing through the dam appears to her as blood. This is because her relationship to the land she loves is in fact undercut by hardship and pain; the dam, which represents modern progress for the nation, is revealed to have come at a huge cost for the nation's mother. The film then moves to flashback, where we see the early days of her relationship with her husband Shamu, filled with flirtation and romance, but cut short by all the hard work they both had to do to pay off the debt that Radha's mother-in-law incurred to pay for their wedding. Thus we are introduced early on to the two primary disruptions of the film's moral universe: (1) the mother-in-law's "betrayal" of the land by mortgaging it, thus cutting off the family from its birthright; and (2) the whole system of predatory lending, by which the moneylender charges an exorbitant interest, taking, for an originally ₹500 loan, 75 percent of the family's harvest every year for several decades into the future.

The nature of these two disruptions of the moral universe is significant. The first disruption is significant because it is also caused by a mother – Shamu's mother – but, in this case, one who is misguided, mortgaging her land and thereby not recognizing its value, thinking of it as a commodity defined by its exchange value, i.e. its convertibility into money. This is a mother who *misunderstands* the value of land, a flaw associated with capitalism. The second disruption in the moral universe is also associated with capitalism, in addition to greed, as the moneylender represents self-interest and monetary gain, lacking in any sense of community or collectivity. Later, the moneylender attempts to convince Radha to become his mistress in exchange for writing off her debt. Radha refuses, even though one of her children is literally dying of hunger. This shows the moneylender as not only greedy but also someone who thinks love can be bought and sold, another immoral trait in Bollywood, as discussed in Chapter 2.

Moneylenders such as Sukhilal are common to India's villages, and they have been insufficiently prosecuted by the Indian state. Thus, the film's critique of the moneylender might also be read as an early critique of the ineffectiveness of the Indian state in adequately protecting India's farmers. In addition, the fact that Radha's experience of motherhood is cut through with pain and sacrifice complicates any sense that the film is simply a valorization of motherhood in relation to the nation.

As we can already see, *Mother India* is hardly a straightforward celebration of Indian nationalism. Rather, by using familiar tropes and a Manichean moral universe, it is able to both valorize Radha's devotion *and* criticize the failures of the new nation by associating the latter with the disruption in the moral universe. Likewise, it is able to celebrate Radha and criticize the capitalist greed that the new nation was unsuccessful in abolishing.

This critique is furthered by the third disruption in the moral universe, which is Radha's husband Shamu's abandonment of her and their sons after he loses his arms in an accident and is taunted for his impotence by the other villagers. Shamu's abandonment of the family is represented as a disruption of the nuclear family, which might also be seen as allegorical for the loss of leadership or loss of vision by India's founders. Shamu's departure takes a toll on Radha, who must now raise her three children by herself *and* do all the work on the family's land. Although she tries to do all this stoically, the hardships she goes through, including the death of her youngest child, are hardly unthinking valorizations of her plight. The film also underlines Shamu's fundamental character flaw – his inability to follow through on his obligations to his family that is at least in part caused by a crisis of masculinity: by not having arms, he no longer feels that he has any value.

The father's abandonment precipitates yet another moral crisis. Lacking a father, the dynamic between the mother and the two brothers becomes disrupted, leaving a vacuum in the father's place – both in terms of patriarchal authority but also sexually – that it is up to one of the brothers to occupy. There is no actual incest plot, but the unsettling of the nuclear family throws up all sort of unresolved couplings, something we will see in other Bollywood films centering around mothers as well. In this case, Birju tries to take his father's place, becoming a bandit and stealing things in order to replace the bangles Radha had to pawn and then, in a scene that shows how intensely he wants to replace his father, putting the bangles onto Radha's wrist much as his father had done in one of the film's earlier scenes – a gesture that, in Bollywood, often stands in for sexual contact (as discussed in Chapter 2). At first, Radha is pleased with Birju's attention, but she soon realizes what Birju has sacrificed in order to take the place of his father. This new dynamic between Radha and her son, with Birju straddling the roles of (rightful) son and (transgressive) lover, further marks motherhood in this film as something *problematic* rather than as a straightforward allegory of the nation.

For the multiplicity of disruptions in the moral universe, and for the transgressive nature of especially the final one, *Mother India* is unique in that, unlike in most Bollywood films, here the moral universe is never quite restored. Rather, the disruptions are so severe that the film cannot end happily. Birju's morality becomes further compromised, and when the moneylender takes Radha's bangles to give to his own daughter and Birju forcibly and violently tries to take them back, Radha finds that her own son has not only broken the law but is violent toward women – transgressions that her sense of morality simply cannot permit. Thus in a remarkable ending, Radha stops Birju at gunpoint after he has kidnapped the moneylender's daughter and tells him to let the girl go, and when he refuses she fatally shoots him. This is, obviously, the worst thing a mother could ever have to do: kill her own son. But the fact that she does it suggests a moral universe so far disrupted that it cannot be restored – or rather, more precisely, that in order for the moral universe to be restored, Radha has to make the ultimate sacrifice: ironically of her own motherhood. Far from unthinkingly valorizing motherhood, the film ends by presenting it as a violently unstable category.

This analysis, founded in an understanding of Bollywood's moral universe rather than in simply reading the politics of a film from its title or its ostensible theme, shows that even so seemingly nationalistic a film as *Mother India* raises significant questions surrounding the relationship between motherhood and nationalism. Certainly Radha is an idealized hero for her stoicism, self-reliance, and devotion to her land, but her journey is ultimately a deeply painful one rather than a nationalist triumph. Returning to the opening scene then, we see why she is hesitant to inaugurate the dam, even though in the film's present time she is considered a village matriarch. The blood in the river represents her loss, and thus the title, "mother India," might be reconsidered as deeply ironic.

In *Deewaar* (1975), the position of the mother, Sumitra, is similarly unsettled by the abandonment of the father and by a system that is fundamentally immoral. Compelled to choose one son to love and nurture while abandoning the second one to criminality and fate, Sumitra, like Radha, is ultimately faced with an impossible decision, as one of her sons, Ravi, becomes a policeman and the other, Vijay, a criminal, and she is forced to choose sides. She ends up siding with the law, actually handing Ravi the gun he will use to kill his brother and blessing him so that his hand will not shake when shooting it. Yet immediately afterwards she goes to meet Vijay at the temple where, presumably, she knows he will take his final breaths. The line she speaks – "Aurat apna farz nibha chuki hai, ab Maa apne bete ka intezar karne jaa rahi hai" ("A woman has fulfilled her duty, now a mother is going to wait for her son") – reflects a profound split in the figure of the mother that radically undercuts the figure's idealization in Hindu cosmology, in Indian nationalist iconography, and in Bollywood morality.

In *Amar Akbar Anthony* (1977) as well, we see the mother's failure to live up to the ideal of nation-as-mother. Contrasted with *Mother India*'s Radha, who stoically puts up with whatever fate has in store for her, Bharati (whose name's proximity to Bharat, one of the names for India, indexes her potential allegorical value, which is, as we will see, then ironized) abandons her children early in the film with a hurried note that announces her planned suicide. Although Bharati's decision is not entirely her fault, the film suggests that even the incorruptible mother is not immune to external forces. Thus Bharati's weakness is that she cannot live up to the ideals of motherhood and of her allegorical name. Although she ultimately comes back into the fold and regains her place as matriarch, it requires the unfolding of a series of events of which she is neither the center nor the lead: the restoration of the secular order and the poetic justice that will impede capitalism and corruption. The mother is thus presented as subject to the overall larger political and social crisis rather than an uncorruptible moral paragon.

Corruption and capitalism

As *Mother India* (1957) and *Deewaar* (1975) demonstrate, where Bollywood cinema has engaged with political issues, it has long presented capitalism and corruption as profound disruptions to the moral universe. Corruption refers to both individual and government corruption, and capitalism is most often represented not as an economic system per se, but as an obsession with money and the belief that morality and love can be bought and sold. Especially in early Bollywood films, money was seen as inherently corrupting, and excessive wealth as compromising a character's morality. This is in part because, as Tejaswini Ganti writes, Hindi cinema in the 1950s was influenced by progressive trends in culture at large, specifically the Indian People's Theater Association (IPTA) and the All-India Progressive Writers' Association (AIPWA) which were formed in 1943 and 1936, respectively.[5]

We see a sustained critique of capitalism and corruption in the films of well-known director-producer Guru Dutt, which straddle the Bollywood/art films divide, using some Bollywood conventions but generally being more visually and narratively subtle and more explicitly politically oriented. *Pyaasa* (1957), for instance, is the story of Vijay, a struggling poet who battles against a corrupt and commercial society. His first love left him in order to marry a rich man, a loss that opens Vijay's eyes to the fact that society is full of hypocrisy and the selling of virtue. He also realizes that real art has no chance at success when the market dictates what gets published. A subplot of the film takes Vijay into a brothel, where he sees first-hand the exploitation that women face there. The lyrics of the song he sings in this scene, penned by progressive lyricist Sahir Ludhianvi, are explicitly critical of the failures of the Indian nation and in particular of those who claim to be patriotic but do not see the misery in front of them:[6]

> Yeh kuchhe, yeh neelaam, ghar dilkashi ke
> Yeh lutate hue kaarvan zindagi ke
> Kahan hain, kahan hain, muhafiz khudi ke
> Jinhein naaz hai Hind par, woh kahan hain?
> Kahan hain, kahan hain, kahan hain?

> [These lanes, these houses of auctioned pleasure
> These ravaged caravans of life
> Where are they, where are they, the guardians of dignity
> Those who claim to be proud of India?
> Where are they, where are they, where are they?]

While Dutt's film *Mr. and Mrs. 55* (1955) is less explicit in its politics, Dutt plays a similar role as in *Pyaasa*: a struggling artist unable to understand why money is so important to people. When his character Pritam goes to the doctor, he is diagnosed with "bhook aur bekari" ("hunger and unemployment") – two ills, the doctor says, "plaguing the twentieth century." Pritam's disinterest in money represents both a valorization of the true lover, as discussed in Chapter 2, as well as a critique of a society in which value and morality are judged via material wealth.

Raj Kapoor is another director–producer whose early films critiqued social hypocrisy and the commodification of human relationships. *Shri 420* (1955) is the story of a man who comes to Mumbai (then Bombay) with little in his pockets except a medal he had won in university for his honesty and his college degree. But what he finds in Bombay is a ruthless world where space is bought and sold and where people are always out to cheat one another. In Kapoor's *Awara* (1951) as well, the protagonist Raj has to resort to petty crime because of the cruel disregard of the rich. And in *Boot Polish* (1954), two poor children are abused by their aunt and struggle to make ends meet on the streets.

In other 1950s films that were less explicitly political, social issues are sometimes referred to obliquely. For instance, Prakash is an alcoholic and abusive husband in *Paying Guest* (1957), but the film's plot revolves around Chanchal's unhappy marriage and she actually uses Prakash to help her woo Ramesh; the love plot thus ends up side-lining the social issue of the mistreatment of women. There is another critique of moral corruption in *Chalti Ka Naam Gaadi* (1958), in which Renu's father arranges her marriage with a man who is impersonating a prince just to get her money. When Raja Hardayal, the scam's mastermind, is asked why he is scheming to get more money when he already has so much, he replies, "Jab tumhare paas daulat aa jayegi, tum samajh jaoge. Daulat-walon hi ko daulat zaroorat hai" ("When you get rich, you'll understand. It's the wealthy who lust for more wealth"). At the heart of this film is a cross-class marriage – the center of the moral universe – between Renu the heiress and Mannu the mechanic. Although Mannu's oldest brother Brijmohan seems to take a strong stance against love, resulting from a broken affair many years ago, it is soon revealed that his lover is not dead, but has been kidnapped by the same conmen who are now trying to trick Renu. Thus the true moral disruption in the film is greed and excessive wealth rather than Brijmohan's stubbornness or lack of faith in love.

In *Sahib Bibi Aur Ghulam* (1962) we see a similar critique of wealth and feudal despotism; the rich family whom Bhoothnath becomes imbricated with are represented as debauched and frivolous, with absurd expenses like spending ₹10,000 on a cat's wedding and being so focused on pigeon-flying that they don't pay attention to the world around them. They are also pictured as alcoholics and lust-driven. Choti Bahu, who didn't know what kind of family she was marrying into, stays up all night and sings sad songs while her husband debauches with courtesans. Finally, in a desperate attempt to regain her husband's affections, she asks Bhoothnath to buy her alcohol, which he refuses at first, but then finally does. It is downhill for Choti Bahu after that; she becomes a full-fledged alcoholic. Bhoothnath remains the innocent hero, and thus his shock at their depravity and the corruptibility of extreme wealth mirrors the viewer's stance.

Criticisms of capitalism and corruption – both explicit and subtle – continued in Bollywood films throughout the 1970s and 1980s. Echoing *Pyaasa* (1957), in *Deewaar* (1975) (discussed more fully below), a young Ravi hungrily stands outside a schoolyard where the children are singing the patriotic song

"Saare Jahan Se Accha" just as his mother is telling him she cannot afford to send him to school; here, the song that extols India as better than any other country in the world is put to ironic use as children are shown having to work instead of attending school. In *Mr. India* (1987), the hero fights government corruption and the greed, profit, and corruption of Indian businessmen on behalf of ordinary Indians who suffer because of food adulteration and lack of access to credit, which lead to hunger and starvation. Although this film's central villain is the evil Mogambo, India's business leaders are equally criticized for their greed and disregard for ordinary people. We see a similar critique of the corrupt partnership of government and big business in *Jaane Bhi Do Yaaro* (1983) and *Main Azaad Hoon* (1989).

It has been noted that in 1990s Bollywood, explicit critiques of capitalism became less common, and many have identified a move toward a celebration of consumption and capitalism as a reflection of the liberalization of the Indian economy in that decade. It does seem to be the case that if we see Bollywood as repurposing old plots with new moral valences, then at least the most commercially successful films of the 1990s seem to have moved away from explicit social critique. However, beginning around 2000 we have seen a shift back in the other direction. For instance, there have been several sports-themed Bollywood films that are deeply critical of the way national-level sports are mismanaged due to government corruption. In *Chak De India* (2007), India's national hockey association is represented as devaluing and underfunding women's sports, and in *Dangal* (2016), when Mahavir Singh Phogat asks the local government sports office for money to buy his daughter a mat to practice wrestling, he is laughed at. In response, he tells the officer: "India medals is liye na jeet pata hai, kyunki kursi pe aap jaise officer baithte hain" ("India doesn't win any medals because officers like you are in power"). Both films use the language of nationalism – of building India's sports pro-wess – to offer deep criticisms of the callousness of the state, empty nationalist rhetoric, and government officials using the state apparatus for personal profit. Additional examples of more recent political films are discussed below as well as in Chapter 8.

Police corruption and the vigilante

Police corruption is a particular kind of government corruption that features in many Bollywood movies. In Bollywood generally, the police are repre-sented as weak, corrupt, incompetent, immoral, easily bought, and unable to stand up to violence, villainy, and illegal activity. This is sometimes comedic, as in *Seeta Aur Geeta* (1972) or *Bunty Aur Babli* (2005), but other times it has serious consequences for justice, as in *Prem Kahani* (1975) or *Mardaani* (2014). At times, the police are simply criminals, as in *Kaminey* (2009). Across films, Bollywood portrays the Indian state as weak and inef-fective, maintaining the impulse to criticize the failures of postcolonial India that began in the 1950s.

In this context, some Bollywood films suggest, it is up to regular people to stand up to injustice, a sentiment that has given rise to many vigilante plots across the decades. The vigilante rose to prominence in the 1970s and seems to have resurged again in the 2000s. At one level, the vigilante represents the valorization of extra-legal violence. But vigilante justice also opens up the moral universe to question and even contest the state's claim to have a monopoly on morality and justice. By representing the police as a *disruption* in the moral universe which the vigilante must set right, Bollywood films refuse the state's inherent morality, further calling into question the claim that Bollywood cinema is straightforwardly nationalist.

Indeed, although the vigilante acts illegally, s/he acts on behalf of social justice, for instance against the rich and on behalf of the poor, or to avenge crimes that the state is too weak or corrupt to adjudicate. Even when s/he is merely avenging a personal injustice, the vigilante is represented as driven to act outside of the law only because of the law's blatant failure to enact justice. Sometimes, as in *Zanjeer* (1973), *Sholay* (1975), or *Mardaani* (2014), the vigilante is a member of the police force, but, frustrated at the constraints put on her/him by the law, acts illegally anyway. In *Mardaani*, when Shivani finally catches the sex trafficker she has been pursuing, she decides not to give him up to the police, assuming that justice will not be served. Instead, she gives him over to the women he has sold into the sex trade, who beat him to death. Yet despite endings such as these, vigilante action is usually represented as morally ambiguous: while it might be understandable that a character would act when the law fails to, a world of vigilante justice is never presented as entirely desirable, and oftentimes even when the vigilante has justice on her side, she has to die at the end of the film in order for the moral universe to right itself.

This moral ambiguity is evident in one of Bollywood's most famous vigilante films, *Sholay* (1975), in which the vigilantes are played by two of the 1970s' biggest stars: Amitabh Bachchan (as Jai) and Dharmendra (as Veeru). Jai and Veeru are criminals, but they are also compassionate and fiercely loyal to one another, and their intense friendship (discussed in Chapter 7) suggests an inherent morality. They are hired by a former police officer to seek vengeance against Gabbar Singh, a villain who had killed most of the officer's family and whom the state had been unable to keep imprisoned. The idea that our heroes would be thieves, remain thieves, and still be our heroes, and that their work involves extra-legal vigilante justice, offers a complication to conventional Bollywood morality. The moral universe has to be adjusted to account for this new social concern around the failure of the state to maintain morality.

Sholay is a characteristic plot of the 1970s, when disillusionment with the legal system was at its height.[7] As one scholar writes:

> Morally ambiguous characters … captured the Zeitgeist of the seventies, when the idealism of the freedom struggle and the optimism of newly independent India were things of the past; when politicians and bureaucrats had lost the respect of the people, and the young had come to believe that while it was desirable to be good, it was more important to be effective.[8]

The vigilante figure of the 1970s is often referred to as the "angry young man" – angry at the failures of the system, disillusioned by the inability of the state to adjudicate morality, and therefore willing to take the restoration of the moral universe into his own hands. But, as mentioned above, this results in an ambivalent rather than straightforward morality; Jai dies at the end of *Sholay*, suggesting that a fully happy ending is not quite possible under these conditions. The angry young man was often played by the superstar actor Amitabh Bachchan, whose outsider status (he was not born into a film family) and his unconventional good looks made him an ideal figure to play this rogue hero. As Ranjani Mazumdar writes:

> Bachchan's rise to stardom was epitomized by his complex and varied portrayals of the "angry man," a screen space occupied by the star for well over a decade. Bachchan's dialogue delivery, sense of timing, and superbly crafted restraint in acting ushered in a new kind of anger on the screen, an anger generated primarily by his physical gestures and movements. The brooding, inward-looking yet outwardly searching, vulnerable anger of Bachchan was symptomatic of its time.[9]

Case study: Gabbar Is Back (2015)[10]

The title of *Gabbar Is Back* is a reference to *Sholay*'s notorious villain, Gabbar Singh, but the two films have more in common than that. *Gabbar Is Back* is part of a resurgence of vigilante films in the 2000s that, like the angry young man films of the 1970s, give voice to a widely felt frustration at the incompetence of the police and the judicial system in stemming crime, and at government corruption overall. *Gabbar Is Back* is the story of Aditya, a college professor who moonlights as Gabbar, a vigilante, kidnapping and even assassinating government officials who have been found to be corrupt. He began this work in the wake of his pregnant wife's death; she had been killed in the collapse of an apartment complex built on unstable soil that was declared safe by corrupt government inspectors bribed by the builder. Aditya had collected evidence against the powerful builder but quickly realized that no one was going to hold him accountable. His frustration at the complete impunity of the builder and the government officials he had paid off compels him to move toward more extreme solutions to corruption. Like *Sholay, Gabbar Is Back* also raises questions of morality, such as, what counts as a moral action in a fundamentally immoral world? Is it better to sit by and watch an immoral system, or take action, even if that action involves violence? These questions are reinforced by Aditya's choice of pseudonym; by naming himself after a paradigmatic Bollywood villain but establishing himself as this film's hero, he raises the question of whether conventional standards of morality still apply when the very avenues to seek out justice have themselves been corrupted. As Aditya says, "I am neither sarkari, nor gher qanuni. Na neta hoon, na koi terrorist. Kaam se hero, naam se villain" ("I am neither a government employee, nor illegal. I am not a leader, nor a terrorist. My work makes me a hero, my name a villain"). Unlike in *Sholay* and other 2010s vigilante films like *A Wednesday* (2008), *Kahaani* (2012), *Mardaani* (2014), *Angry Indian Goddesses* (2015), and *Madaari* (2016), Aditya is punished at the end of *Gabbar Is Back* for his transgressions and condemned to be hanged. He gives a final rousing speech to a large crowd of supporters urging them to take on the cause of fighting government corruption and to all become "Gabbars."

This film too uses vigilante justice as a way to imagine alternatives to the status quo, challenging the government's ineptitude and corruption. This extreme case, where vigilante justice is enacted not despite the government but actually *on* government officials, offers a powerful anti-government stance that further refuses any sense of Bollywood being simply nationalist. While Gabbar's final speech does include lines about making India better, these lines are, like so much other ostensibly nationalist sentiment in Bollywood, about imagining what India could be, while deeply critical of what India is.

The secular nation

In India, the term secularism refers to the embrace of all religions rather than, as in the west, the separation of religion from the state. The ideal of secularism instituted at independence promised that despite the fact that India was a majority Hindu country, all religions were to be treated equally, and religion would not be the basis of citizenship. In reality, this has not always been practiced; throughout India's postcolonial history, majority religion has been an excuse for discrimination and violence, in the form of anti-Muslim and anti-Sikh riots, along with the persecution of Christians. The cultural and political marginalization of Muslims and Islamophobia specifically are long-standing problems in India.

The primary opponent to secularism is the force of Hindu nationalism, a movement that has been gaining mainstream popularity over the course of the twentieth and early twenty-first centuries. Hindu nationalist ideology claims that India has been and always should be a land for Hindus, and anyone who is not a Hindu is fundamentally an outsider. Mohandas K. Gandhi, India's most internationally recognized freedom fighter in the anti-colonial struggle and a strong believer in the equality of all religions, was assassinated by a Hindu nationalist, who believed Gandhi's secular views were anti-Hindu because they did not assert Hinduism as superior to other religions.

Despite the increasing role of Hindu nationalism in Indian politics, secularism has been and continues to be a heroic trait in Bollywood cinema, a quality which again calls into question the interpretation of Bollywood as straightforwardly nationalistic, patriotic, or chauvinistic. At the most basic level, Bollywood offers positive representations of Muslim and Christian characters as true nationalists and heroes, representations which undermine the idea that people of minority religions are somehow outsiders to India, less Indian, or less patriotic. In *Prem Kahani* (1975), Sher Khan is a Muslim minor character who works underground for the freedom movement. He sings a patriotic song and exhibits significant bravery to save the hero's life, saying: "Sirf tumhare yahan paida ho jaane se yeh mulk tumhara nahin ho jaata" ("The country doesn't become yours only if you are born here"), a line that refutes nativist under-standings of belonging. Later, when Sher Khan is captured by the police, he refuses to give up the hero's whereabouts even under torture. Inspector Salim in *Sarfarosh* (1999) is another Muslim character whose loyalty to India is unwavering, even as he faces discrimination and mistrust on all sides. In *Pyaasa* (1957), it is the Muslim Abdul Sattar who helps Vijay escape from the asylum where he has been unfairly imprisoned by his villainous brothers. And in *Bobby* (1973), it is the Christian Jack Braganza who convinces the Hindu Prem Nath that Bobby and Raj's love should be accepted despite their different religions. In films such as *Sarfarosh* (1999), *Chak De India* (2007), and *My Name is Khan* (2010), anti-Muslim prejudice is explicitly represented and criticized.

But beyond individual positive representations of non-Hindu characters, secularism itself is a marker of heroism and morality in Bollywood. As discussed in Chapter 1, Bollywood heroism is established through formulaic gestures or qualities, and many of these qualities are associated with secularism. Thus when Vijay (who is Hindu) kisses his badge with the number 786, a holy number in Islam, in *Deewaar* (1975), and when Veer finds himself prisoner number 786 in *Veer-Zaara* (2004) (which leads Saamiya to say, "Yeh khuda ka banda hai" ["This one is a man of god"]), and when Om wears a lucky necklace that contains an Om symbol, a crescent and star, and a cross (Figure 6.1) in *Om Shanti Om* (2007), all these immediately index these characters' virtue: you know a character is morally good when she embraces the values and symbolism of a religion that is not her own. In *Kabhi Khushi Kabhie Gham* (2001), we know Rahul and Anjali's love is destined because it is expressed through a song at a Muslim wedding even though both of them are Hindu; their love story is enhanced by this embrace of secularism. In *Raja Hindustani* (1996), Raja

Figure 6.1 Om wears a necklace featuring the symbols of India's three main religions in *Om Shanti Om* (2007).

explains his adopted last name, "Hindustani," which means "Indian," by saying that it stands for the common man of any religion or caste. Even in *Purab Aur Paschim* (1970), a more explicitly nationalist film than most, when Bharat takes Preity to India to show her all its spiritual features, one of the sites he takes her to is the Jama Masjid, the famous Delhi mosque, showcasing and taking pride in India's multi-religious heritage. In *Naseeb* (1981), Johnny's full name is "John Jani Janardhan," with each part of the name referring to a different religion, and in one song he sings, "Yeh teenon naam hain mere/ Allah, Jesus, Ram hain mere" ("These three names are all mine/ Allah, Jesus and Ram are all mine"). In *Amar Akbar Anthony* (1977), Anthony conveys his moral virtue, despite being a small-time gangster, by saying, "Apun sab dharam ko manta hai; mandir jaata hai, masjid jaata hai, church jaata hai, gurudwara jaata hai" ("I believe in all religions; I go to the temple, to the mosque, to the church, and to the gurdwara"). When Bharati gets her sight back in the same film, the miracle occurs in a Muslim dargah (shrine) where devotees are praying to Sai Baba, a Hindu saint who was known for his syncretic beliefs and his embrace of both Hinduism and Islam. In Akbar's song in praise of Sai Baba, he uses both the words "khuda" and "bhagwan" for God, with Muslim and Hindu associations, respectively, and describes celebrating both Eid and Diwali. And the significant number of courtesan films in Bollywood also celebrate secularism, as "cinematic courtesans embody Indian hybrid culture in a distinctive way … Women from different communities lived together in courtesan households, engaging in a mix of religious practices. They catered to men of different communities, and many courtesans were the offspring of inter-community liaisons and marriages,"[11] and were thus represented "as both Hindu and Muslim."[12]

Spaces of religious mixing and syncretism are magical spaces in Bollywood, enabling the restoration of the moral universe in almost miraculous ways. In *Kuch Kuch Hota Hai* (1998), the Hindu child Anjali prays to Allah to give them more time to find her father's true love, and it is suggested that the syncretic nature of the prayer is so powerful that it causes the Hindu astrologer in another part of the country to postpone the adult Anjali's wedding, which eventually allows the lovers to reunite. Cross-religious prayer is always coded as morally good. Thus in *Dilwale Dulhania Le Jayenge* (1995) when the goofy Raj sneaks in a prayer before leaving a church in Switzerland, it is one of the first times we see him as the film's rightful hero, and when Vanraj prays at a church for Nandini's recovery in *Hum Dil De Chuke Sanam* (1999), we realize it is he who is meant to be with her, not Sameer. Likewise, when Zaara comes to India to immerse her nanny's ashes in *Veer-Zaara* (2004), she wants to participate in the Sikh ritual despite the fact that she is Muslim. In fact, here it is Veer who assumes that the Sikh priests will deny her entry, but he is proven wrong, as Zaara is welcomed to perform the rituals alongside the priest. Veer's father Bauji too is even more effusive in his welcome of Zaara when he hears that she is from Pakistan: "Kamal ho gaya! Tusi saade extra special mehman ban gaye ho!" ("How wonderful! You have become our extra special guest!"). Across the board, Bollywood heroes are those who embrace secularism rather than cling to narrow, bounded, mutually exclusive, or singular religious identities.

This is most evident in films that have secularism as their overt theme. Probably the most famous of these is *Amar Akbar Anthony* (1977), the story of a family that is separated, and the three brothers found and adopted by men of India's three main religions: a Hindu policeman, a Muslim imam, and a Catholic priest. The boys are raised by their adoptive fathers to practice their respective religions, and through a series of coincidences they eventually reunite with their lost family. But the reunion of the family, which represents India's secular possibility, now includes a son and a daughter-in-law from different religions; thus the reunited family is not narrowly defined, but broadly inclusive. The film literalizes the idea of being "brothers" with people from other religions; as Amar says at the film's end, referring to his new-found family but also clearly referencing the nation at large: "Hindu, Muslim, Sikh, Isaai, sab hi toh hain bhai bhai" ("Whether Hindu, Muslim, Sikh or Christian, all and all are brothers").

This idea that brotherhood across religious difference will make India stronger is a theme in several Bollywood films. In *Lagaan* (2001), the Indian team organized by the villagers to defeat the British colonial team in a game of cricket is a mix of Hindus, Muslims, Sikhs, and high and low castes. The primary lesson here is that only by coming together as a team can they defeat the British at their own game; the lyrics of one of the songs is "Toot gayi jo ungli utthi/ Paanchon mili toh, ban gaye mutthi" ("When one finger alone would break/ Five fingers together make a fist"). As Bhuvan succeeds in teaching the other villagers, the fear of difference makes India weak, while unity across caste, religious, and linguistic lines makes India strong. We see a similar theme in *Chak De India* (2007), another sports movie in which the true nationalist sees India's internal diversity as an asset rather than a liability. These examples underline the importance of cross-religious solidarity as a way of making the nation stronger. Again, these are nationalist films insofar as they advocate for strengthening the nation, but in doing so they necessarily draw attention to the failures and divisiveness of the actual nation and its leaders.

PK (2014) is explicitly critical of religion, in this case of the popularity of so-called godmen – Hindu religious leaders who prey on superstitious followers to make lucrative careers for themselves. PK is an alien who comes to earth from another planet and cannot understand why humans have divided themselves up according to the arbitrary differences of religion and nationality. This story of a perspective from the outside is another way of advancing Bollywood's belief in secularism *as* a nationalist project.

Partition and the question of Pakistan

The foremost crisis of Indian secularism took place at the very moment of India's birth in the form of the Partition, the division of the Indian subcontinent into two independent countries, India and Pakistan, in 1947. Muslim-majority regions in India's eastern and western areas were designated Pakistan, a nation that was supposed to offer protection to Muslims who would suffer in a Hindu-majority India. The announcement of the Partition led to mass migrations, with Hindus and Sikhs crossing the new borders into India and Muslims traveling in the opposite direction to Pakistan. The Partition turned neighbors against neighbors, and because of the horrific violence and huge loss of life it spawned, continues to cast a shadow over both countries.[13] Several Muslims in the Bombay film industry left for Pakistan, and for those who remained, their loyalty felt continuously tested. Superstar Dilip Kumar, formerly Muhammad Yusuf Khan, changed his name to a recognizably Hindu one, reflecting the alienation many Muslims felt during this time. Despite the profound importance of this historical event on the region, Partition has not been a common theme in Bollywood. It was a kind of national trauma that was repressed and silenced rather than spoken about; there is, however, slightly more representation of Partition in Indian parallel cinema.[14]

It was only really at the turn of the millennium that Pakistan started being named as an enemy state in Bollywood cinema; before that, national enemies were more vaguely defined, and issues around secularism within India became a way of talking about religion without actually talking about Pakistan. In *Sangam* (1964), Sundar goes to war, which is likely with Pakistan, but the enemy remains unnamed, as does the location, which is described only as the "valley." *Hindustan Ki Kasam* (1999) and *Sarfarosh* (1999) seem to have been the first films to name Pakistan; *Sarfarosh* is about a Pakistani terrorist who sells weapons to adivasis and others in order to foment dissent in and thus weaken India. This straightforward grafting of a Pakistani Muslim character as a national enemy seems to negate the secularism of Bollywood at large. However, the villain is portrayed as a Muslim who had felt betrayed by Partition on one hand, which destroyed India's secularism, and Pakistan's discrimination against so-called mohajirs, or Muslim migrants from India, on the other. Thus his violence is political rather than inherent to his religion. In addition, as Kavita Daiya argues, *Sarfarosh* represents the discrimination faced by Indian Muslims through the character of Salim,[15] a patriotic Indian police officer whose motives, as a Muslim, are constantly doubted. *Gadar* (2001) is another action film in which Pakistanis are depicted as generally bloodthirsty and violent. There is a cross-border love story, but it falls narrowly along nationalist lines, involving an Indian man saving a Pakistani woman from the bloodlust of other Pakistanis. The film also mostly shows violence from Muslims on Hindu and Sikh victims, when in reality there was inordinate violence committed by all sides.[16]

However, such jingoistic and one-sided films are the exception rather than the rule. The overwhelming ethos of Bollywood continues to be secular, and most of the few films that represent Pakistan are oriented toward peace rather than war. *Veer-Zaara* (2004), *Main Hoon Na* (2004), and *Bajrangi Bhaijaan* (2015), the first two of which are discussed below, present a moral universe in which India recognizes and values Pakistan's legitimacy, and in which the disruption to the moral order comes from those who hate peace. Even high-adrenalin action films like *Ek Tha Tiger* (2012) and its sequel, *Tiger Zinda Hai* (2017), promote Indo-Pakistan peace rather than enmity. *Gold* (2018) is a recent sports film that focuses on the pre-Partition time when Hindus and Muslims played sports together, and details the way Partition weakened the subcontinent by dissolving this unity.

Since 2010, there have been a few Pakistani actors who have starred in Bollywood films such as Fawad Khan, Mahira Khan, and Ali Zafar. These actors, who have become quite popular, have helped break down the stereotypes and prejudices held by some Indian audiences, although there has been some backlash from the right-wing government, including a recent ban on Pakistani actors working in India.[17]

Case study: **Veer-Zaara *(2004)*

In this cross-border love story, made in a period of increasing political tension between India and Pakistan, Indian Veer falls in love with Pakistani Zaara. Because it is a love story, we know that their love is the center of the moral universe, and because Bollywood values love so centrally, we know that their union is more important than the fact that they are from different religions and live on opposite sides of the border. The film presents their love as epic and transcendent − not a thing of this world − and so we are asked to believe that no border can divide them. On the other hand, we know that the enmity between India and Pakistan is also deep-seated. Thus the film becomes an extended battle between two powerful forces: national enmity versus love. For the moral universe to be restored, so that their love can prevail, the film must necessarily contest India–Pakistan enmity. Thus the use of Bollywood formulas promises a progressive resolution to the political divide.

Veer-Zaara offers an alternative to India–Pakistan enmity through the aestheticization of the Punjab, the region most directly affected by the Partition. Punjab has a culture and long history of Hindus, Muslims, and Sikhs living together as neighbors, speaking the same language, and participating together in folk traditions like the festivals of Basant and Lohri. This syncretic culture was violently and traumatically destroyed by Partition, not only by the literal splitting of the region into two warring nations, but also in the mistrust and suspicion it planted that, unfortunately, continue until this day. Even the Punjabi language was partitioned, with Punjabi in Pakistan being written in the Nastaliq script instead of the Gurmukhi script it was historically written in, so today, Punjabis from one side cannot read literature or newspapers from the other. While the historical partitioning of Punjab along religious lines destroyed the sense of shared culture and history, in *Veer-Zaara*, the two Punjabs are figuratively reunited, the Punjabi language is given voice, Punjabi festivals and folk dances are featured, and the fertile landscapes of the region are visualized as sites of productivity and futurity, despite the border that divides them.

For instance, in "Des Mera" ("My Land"), a song sequence that takes place when Zaara visits India, she and Veer sing together about the Punjab. Veer begins by describing the beauty of his land, "des mera," which has the double meaning of my country, i.e. India, *and* my land, meaning my region, i.e. the

Punjab. This dual meaning is exploited in the song to suggest that he is singing potentially about *both* India and Pakistan:

> Dharti sunehri ambar neela, har mausam rangeela
> Aisa des hai mera, ho … aisa des hai mera …
> Mere des mein mehmaanon ko bhagwan kaha jaata hai
> Woh yahin ka ho jaata hai, jo kahin se bhi aata hai.

> [The golden land and the blue sky, each season is colorful
> That's what my land is like …
> In my land we treat guests like gods
> Wherever they come from, they belong here.]

And the lyrics continue in that vein, celebrating the beauty and hospitality of the land. At the end of the song, Zaara joins in:

> Tere des ko maine dekha, tere des ko maine jaana
> Jaane kyun yeh lagta hai mujhko jaana pehchaana
> Yahan bhi wahi shaam hai wahi savera
> Wahi shaam hai wahi savera
> Aisa hi des hai mera jaisa des hai tera
> Waisa des hai tera haan jaisa des hai tera.

> [I have seen your land, I have understood your land
> I don't know why it feels so familiar to me
> It's the same evening here, and the same morning
> So my land is just like your land.]

Zaara's lyrics reflect a recognition that all the positive and welcoming traits of Veer's "des," whether that means India or Indian Punjab, are also visible in her "des," which is Pakistan and/or Pakistani Punjab. This use of a beautiful and poetic song and the double meaning of the term "des" assert love for one's country, but allow a much more expansive idea of what that might mean, first suggesting that one's land might in fact cross national borders, and, second, suggesting that other people have equivalent love for their country, something which is nationalist but refuses the exceptionalism that comes with most nationalisms, and is particularly significant in the context of the Partition.

Moreover, in a twist on the arranged marriage plot, here Veer's father Bauji actually advises Veer to marry Zaara, transforming the idea of arranged marriage as occurring only within one's own religion, caste, and community into marriage based on a shared sense of *place* – in this case the Punjab – even if that place crosses religion and country. Bauji's marriage to Maati, who is South Indian while he is Punjabi, *and* the fact that they are adoptive, rather than biological, parents to Veer, further affirms forged bonds of love and kinship as equally, if not more, important as seemingly natural ones.

Case study: **Main Hoon Na** *(2004)*

The importance of moving on from the past rather than bearing Partition as a never-ending grudge is the core message of *Main Hoon Na*, also from 2004, and which, together with *Veer-Zaara*, were the two highest grossing films of the year. In *Main Hoon Na*, which innovates on a number of Bollywood formulas, the current enmity between India and Pakistan is allegorized via a broken family.

Major Ram is an officer in the Indian Army working on Project Milaap, a plan to return Pakistani prisoners languishing in Indian jails to their homes in Pakistan. The prisoners had all been farmers or shepherds arrested for accidentally crossing India via an unmanned border, but treated like criminals, spies, or terrorists. The general in charge of Project Milaap hopes that by releasing the prisoners, Pakistan will reciprocate and do the same for those Indians wrongfully held in Pakistani jails. However, he is impeded in this peace gesture by Raghavan, an ex-officer who hates Pakistan so much he wants continual war with them. Raghavan tries to kill Ram in an effort to stop the prisoner exchange. This action plot is layered with Ram's quest to reunite his father's broken family. On his deathbed, his father tells Ram that Ram was the product of an extramarital affair. When his wife found out about it, she had kicked him out of the house, leaving him and Ram to live apart from his wife and other, legitimate son. Now, after his death, he wants the two half-brothers to immerse his ashes together. Yet when Ram approaches his father's other family, he finds that they maintain utter contempt of him and his father, even so many years later. Unable to forgive her husband for his betrayal, the mother tells Ram there is no place in her family for him.

The mother's grudge – her sense of lasting betrayal – is allegorical for India's unwillingness to forgive Pakistanis for Partition. Even though Ram is the product of the betrayal rather than its cause, much like today's Pakistanis are the product of Partition rather than its cause, the mother's inability to think of him as part of her family, and as a brother to her biological son, is presented as a moral failing. In contrast, Ram is the moral center, both for his commitment to India–Pakistan peace and for his belief in the sanctity of the adoptive family. Ultimately, Ram's moral centrality compels the mother to realize that she has been wrong and to accept him into her home, just as, the film suggests, India should do for Pakistan. This family reunion coincides with the success of Project Milaap, furthering the sense that a better future of peace between the two countries is possible. The fact that *Main Hoon Na*, along with *Veer-Zaara*, both performed very well at the box office even in a period of heightened enmity between the two countries suggests that, at times, Bollywood cinema might allow for the articulation of progressive sensibilities or feelings that are as yet inadmissible in the public sphere.

Kashmir and the margins of the nation

The state of Kashmir is central to the Bollywood imaginary because of the long-standing tradition of filming Bollywood songs in Kashmir. This is due to the state's natural beauty and sublime landscapes, which are markedly different from those of most of the rest of India and thus enhance Bollywood's visual aesthetics. While most films set in Kashmir do not explicitly name the place, there have been a few films that are explicitly set in or about Kashmir. One is *Kashmir Ki Kali* (1964), in which Kashmir represents a space distant from bourgeois domesticity and aestheticized through its folk traditions. The film begins with Rajeev gaining control over his father's textile mill, but since he is uninterested in work or money, he immediately gives huge bonuses to all the workers, angering his mother, and decides to go on a trip to Kashmir instead. For Rajeev, Kashmir represents a place outside the boundaries of restrictive society, where a person can be free of work, family, and social ties. There, Rajeev meets and immediately falls in love with Champa, a local flower seller, and the film follows their travails as they try to escape a villain who wants to marry Champa himself and learn secrets about both their pasts.

More recent films specifically address the political conflict in Kashmir. Since independence, Kashmir has been essentially an occupied territory of India rather than a state with equal rights. Kashmiris were promised and then denied autonomy over their own politics and economy, and the calls for self-determination, and in some cases independence, have only increased in recent decades. These have been met with a violent response from the Indian Army and, at times, full-on military occupation, including the shutting down of the internet in Kashmir for seven months in 2019–20. The Indian government has deemed calls for autonomy "terrorism," stereotyping Kashmir – which is India's only majority-Muslim state – using a globally circulating language of Islamophobia. While song sequences like "Jiya Re" in *Jab Tak Hai Jaan* (2012) can be seen as making light of this conflict using regular Kashmiri men, women, and children as props, other contemporary representations of Kashmir in Bollywood engage to some degree with the contested political reality on the ground there.

Fanaa (2006), for example, is the story of lovers Rehaan and Zooni. Zooni does not know that Rehaan is working for a terrorist group committed to Kashmiri independence. In a departure from earlier representations, this film does not depict Kashmir only as a space of natural beauty; thus although Zooni's family's house is in a lush valley, most images of Kashmir in the film include Indian Army trucks or soldiers at the margins of the frame, and news stories about Kashmir's independence struggles are playing on television in the background of several scenes. The Indian government's betrayal of Kashmir is mentioned by a top government officer, even though the leader of the terrorist group is portrayed negatively and Rehaan's morality is called into question because of his belief in violence as a path to Kashmiri self-determination. The hero of this film is therefore not Rehaan, but Zooni, a woman who ostensibly has to choose between her love and her country. However, any analysis of this film must account for the love story that is, arguably, more central than the political story. This feature of *Fanaa* will be discussed in the next section.

Another film centering on the experience of military occupation in Kashmir is *Haider* (2014). Although made by a Bollywood director, it lacks many of the generic features of Bollywood cinema, and is instead a chilling representation of forced disappearances and the everyday violence that Kashmiris face. This film is unflinchingly critical of the Indian occupation and the treatment of Kashmiris by Indian forces and thus offers a possible new direction for the representation of Kashmir in Bollywood cinema.

Love and the nation

Patriotism is an important moral value in Bollywood, but as we have seen, what it means to love one's country can shift to accommodate surprisingly inclusive or radical nationalisms. In many of the examples above, nationalism must accommodate itself to encompass Bollywood's true heart, romantic love. Seeing love as central, rather than peripheral, to these stories offers alternative readings of these films and of nationalism in Bollywood as a whole.

Sometimes the relationship between love and the nation is presented humorously, as in *Padosan* (1968), when Bindu asks her lover Bhola to sing her a song, and because he doesn't know any songs, he sings the first few lines of a patriotic song from the film *Kismet* (1943), whose lyrics go "Door hato, door hato, ai dunyawalon, Hindustan hamara hai" ("Step away, people of the world, India is ours"). But upon hearing this, Bindu quickly cuts Bhola off, pouting, "Lo, yeh bhi koi geet hai? Yeh toh koi marching song hai … Mujhe koi pyar-bhara geet sunaoge?" ("What kind of song is that? That's some marching song … Can you sing me a love song instead?")

Other times, the conflict between romantic love and nationalism is central to a film's story. In *Prem Kahani* (1975), which is set during the anti-colonial nationalist movement, Rajesh is presented as an ideal lover, while his brother is a patriot who writes nationalist poetry that bores the other youths. His brother lectures Rajesh: "Is 1942 mein, ishq ki shairi karna ghaddari ki barabar hai" ("In 1942, writing poetry about love is akin to treason!") to which Rajesh responds that love is more important than politics. However, this view changes when his brother is fatally shot by a British officer at a protest, inciting Rajesh to join the nationalist movement and end his relationship with his beloved Kamini, along with his poetry career. Taking revenge on the British man who had killed his brother, Rajesh is now a wanted man and has to live in hiding. He returns to Kamini's house to hide, but she has moved on and married his best friend Dheeraj; his return to her space suggests that he is unable to completely turn his back on love, even as a patriot. As Dheeraj wonders, "Vatan se wafadari ki yeh shart kab nikal aaya ki aadmi apne pyar se ghaddari kare?" ("Since when does serving the nation mean a man should betray his love?"). Indeed, the film presents Rajesh as at least partially at fault for thinking that nationalism is more important than love; Kamini reprimands him: "Aap ko us ladki se sach bolna chahiye tha. Mumkin hai kisi ki biwi bankar jeene ke bajay aapki bewa bankar jeena woh zyada pasand karti" ("You should have been honest with your lady [referring to herself]. It's possible that she would have preferred to be your widow than someone else's wife!"). Thus although her-oically fighting for his country, Rajesh is also presented as a lover who loses faith in love, a moral failing that mitigates the former success.

In *Sangam* (1964), Sundar joins the Air Force, but he does it only to prove himself a worthy lover for Radha. In *Ek Tha Tiger* (2012), Tiger is a special agent in the Indian government. He works hard and thinks of nothing else besides his work and has no social life. He finally meets a woman, Zoya, and falls in love with her, but he then discovers that she is a special agent for Pakistan. He is told in no uncertain terms that he has to end the relationship as it is compromising national security. But in the end, he quits his job instead, choosing love over the nation. In *Fanaa* (2006), Rehaan is trained to be a sol-dier committed entirely to the cause of a free Kashmir, but when he meets and falls in love with Zooni, he is distracted from this single-minded idealism; love is presented as Rehaan's "kamzori" ("weakness"). His grandfather, a militant leader, berates him for getting distracted, leading Rehaan to abandon Zooni and promise to stay the course, until he accidentally runs into her again and falls back in love. The film shows Rehaan's struggle between devotion to his cause, which has no place for love, and devotion to his beloved. The last part of the film shows the intensity of this internal debate, and we watch as Rehaan comes increasingly close to renouncing his politics for the sake of love. By centering Rehaan's role as a lover, his death becomes not, as some scholars see it, merely a victory for a nation that now has one less terrorist, but rather the inevitable outcome of an impossible situation: love *or* politics.

Case study: Dil Se (1997)

Dil Se, which was released in 1997, the fiftieth anniversary of India's inde-pendence, similarly presents nationalism as a metaphor for love, rather than – as most scholars see it – the other way around. Amar first meets Meghna at a far-flung train station, presumably in India's Northeast, and immediately falls in love with her. He falls hard, becoming a classic *aashiq* (lover) from Urdu poetry: he cannot stop thinking about her and when he runs into her a little while later, he pursues her, even when she makes it clear that she is not interested. Amar's love, as we saw in Chapter 2, borders on obsession; he cannot think of anything besides Meghna, he cannot focus on his family or on his work, and he is drawn to her almost instinctively, as a moth to a flame. He starts behaving irrationally; for instance, after being badly beat up by a group of men, he is jubilant – even while hospitalized – when he discovers that they are her brothers and not her husband.

Amar works for All-India Radio, India's national radio network, and he is in the Northeast – one of India's politically and culturally marginalized regions – to interview residents on whether they think India has made any progress in the 50 years since independence. He interviews, among others, a militia leader who is involved in separatist activity because he feels that India only cares about its centers and big cities like New Delhi, not its far-flung and less populated regions. Many others he meets are similarly skeptical about whether India's progress has really helped people's lives. Amar is surprised by what he finds in his travels. His father having been in the army, and Amar himself now working for the government, the views he encounters conflict with the mainstream understanding of Indian nationalism that he had been taught, in which the nation is necessarily and unproblematically good.

It also turns out, unbeknownst to Amar until the very end, that Meghna is actually involved with a separatist militia from India's Northeast, which she joined because her village was raided by the army when she was a child, her father was killed, and she and her sister were raped by soldiers. Now, in recognition of 50 years of this internal colonialism, she and her group are planning a suicide attack at the annual Republic Day parade in New Delhi.

Dil Se thus does two things at once: it tells a love story of obsession and passion, and it narrates a battle between India's center and its margins. It is tempting to make the first a metaphor for the second, in that Amar's irrational pursuit of Meghna is symbolic for India's irrational pursuit of its margins. However, that reading assumes that the love story is the scaffolding for the political plot, which is the "real" point of the film.[18] But understanding Bollywood through its generic conventions – which includes recognizing love as the central moral fixture of the narrative – suggests the opposite, that the political story is in fact the scaffolding for the love plot. From this perspective, the story of the terrorist action and the state's attempt to defuse it serves as a means of enhancing the obsessive and all-consuming nature of Meghna and Amar's love. Likewise, the dramatic ending reflects the unrequitable nature of pure love rather than Amar somehow saving the Republic Day parade. It is politics that intrudes on love, rather than the other way around. Thus when the militant leader, suspecting Meghna might be reciprocating Amar's feelings for her, tells her to stop thinking about love and focus on politics, he is becoming an enemy of love like so many other Bollywood villains. "Pyar mein nasha hota hai. Hamare liye nahin bana hai" ("Love is intoxicating. It is not made for us"), he tells her, referring to those who have sacrificed their lives for a political cause. But Meghna, like Rehaan in *Fanaa*, is not sure. Indeed, interpreting *Dil Se* primarily as a political film would replicate the same mistake as the militant leader: thinking that politics is more important or more fundamental than love, even when the evidence says otherwise.

The nation and the diaspora

Representations of NRIs (referring to Non-Resident Indians, NRI is the commonly used abbreviation for Indian citizens living abroad) have been seen by critics as a major site of Bollywood's nationalism. Although Bollywood films set outside of India are not very common, representations of Indians living abroad, when they occur, are often criticized for relying on stereotypes of western decadence and immorality that ultimately shore up simplistic notions of Indian authenticity and culture.

Perhaps the starkest contrast between western and Indian cultures is evident in *Purab Aur Paschim* (1970), whose title translates as "East and West." This film begins in the period of the nationalist movement, with snatches of well-known patriotic songs such as "Sarfaroshi Ki Tamanna" and "Vande Mataram" playing in the background. Om is a freedom fighter assassinated by a British solider, his whereabouts having been revealed by his duplicitous brother, Harnam, who takes the money he earns as a reward and moves abroad with it, vowing that "main apne bacchon ko waise palunga, jaise Angrez palte hain" ("I will raise my children as the English do"). By contrast, Om's son Bharat – named after one of the names of India – grows up as a patriot. The film is filled with patriotic songs and images of the army and fighter planes, which contribute to a particular kind of nationalist imaginary that, in its specificity and focus on the state and the military, is actually quite foreign to Bollywood visuality. Even more strikingly, the diaspora is represented as hyperbolically immoral; for instance, the NRI Sharma's son Shankar nicknames himself "Orphan" as a joke (going against Bollywood's valuing of kinship), talks back to his father, and conveys a complete alienation from anything Indian. Sharma's daughter, Preity, dyes her hair blond, smokes cigarettes in front of her parents, and knows nothing about India. Bharat has to explain Indian culture piece by piece to these two alienated youngsters. Likewise, all the Indians living in London are presented as completely lacking any moral compass. Mohan has a wife back in India but is having an affair with a white woman, and when his father-in-law comes to find him, he beats the old man up. London itself is represented as completely morally debased, made up only of rock music, cabarets, sexually depraved parties on boats, race tracks, and extramarital sex. In the film, these "immoral" attributes can only be reformed by the patriotic Indian, Bharat, who takes on Preity and Shankar as his project, encouraging Preity to give up smoking, teaching Shankar Gandhi's favorite religious song, and ultimately bringing about Harnam's return to India and Preity's last-minute decision to stay in India, which are presented as the restoration of the moral universe. The morality of this film is thus *explicitly* nationalist in a way that is actually quite exceptional to Bollywood morality as has been discussed in this chapter.

Moreover Bharat, the hero, is presented as such a true patriot that his love for his country is even more important than his love for Preity. Rather than the conventional Bollywood hero who puts aside everything for his love (see Chapter 2), Bharat refuses to get waylaid from his desire to return to India, even though Preity actively tries to convince him to stay in England with her instead. When she refuses to return to India with him, saying she cannot live there, he easily talks of leaving her: "Tumhare liye apna desh bhi toh nahin chod sakta." ("Even for you I wouldn't abandon my country"). By contrast, Preity speaks the more typical Bollywood line: "Main bhi aise aadmi ke saath shaadi nahin kar sakti, jis se mujh se zyada apne desh se pyar ho" ("I wouldn't marry a man who loves his country more than me"). Even when he relents to living in England with Preity, under the condition that she visit India with him first, it is less because he has realized the importance of love than because he believes in India so much that he is sure that once Preity visits, she will want to live there (a prediction which turns out to be correct).

However, even in this seemingly straightforward nationalism, there are some more subtle politics that complicate the idea that nationalism is always chauvinist. For instance, when the old teacher laments that young people go to the west for *gyaan* (wisdom) when they used to be able to find it in India, Bharat corrects him to say, "Gyaan nahin, Guruji, vidya, science. Aaj zaroorat hai, na?" ("Not for wisdom, Guruji, for science. We need that, don't we?") thus showing how science and modernity have something to offer India along with its own cultural heritage. Conversely, the NRI characters are portrayed as sitting around in London talking about India as a faraway and dystopic place, characterized by nothing but poverty, charity, starvation, and backwardness. As Harnam asks Bharat rhetorically, "Hai koi aisi baat tumhare desh ki jis par sar unche kar sako? Nahin. My dear boy, tumhare desh ne kuch nahin diya. India's contribution is zero, zero and zero" ("Is there anything in your country about which you can feel proud? No. My dear boy, your country has contributed nothing"). The constant negativity around India coming from NRIs is meant to be critical of an elite class who abandons the country and criticizes it from afar, rather than participating in its contemporary life. When Bharat announces his intention to return to India after completing his studies, Preity's mother is shocked, saying "Tumhein wapas jaane ka khayal kaise aaya? India se students yahan aate hain. Pad kar yahin reh jaate hain, yahin kaam karte hain" ("What do you mean go back? Students come here to study, then they stay forever!") The film's criticism of NRI culture as unable to see any futurity in India cannot quite be reduced to a chauvinistic nationalism. Thus when Preity comes to love India, the nature of her revelation is significant: "Yeh bhi suna tha ki yahan khane ke liye roti nahin hai, pehne ko kapda nahin, rehne ko ghar nahin. Sabhi kuch toh hai. Aur phir har mulk mein kisi na kisi cheez ki kami toh hoti hi hai" ("I had heard there's no food, no clothes, no houses here. But everything is here. Also, every country has deficiencies"). This can be interpreted as an important revaluation of global hierarchies that refutes colonial and postcolonial perceptions of the global South as irreducibly backward and abject.

Indeed, Anglophilia – and, since the 1990s, Americophilia – is often satirized in Bollywood films, in part because it captures a certain sensibility held by Indian elites who are enamored with the west and almost instinctively critical of everything in their own country. In *Raja Hindustani* (1996) when Aarti's stepmother laughs at her decision to go to the Indian hill station Palankhet for a vacation, telling her Switzerland would be a better option, we are confirmed in our sense that the stepmother is morally corrupt, not because there's anything wrong with Switzerland, but because her prejudice reeks of snobbery and elitism, manifesting in an instinctive dislike of anything Indian. The stepmother also has a fake, Anglicized accent when she speaks Hindi, another trait shared by a number of villains such as the jailer in *Sholay* (1975) and Robert in *Amar Akbar Anthony* (1977), all of whom are presented as aspiring to be something they are not. In *3 Idiots* (2009), Chatur is not a complete villain, but he is an unthinking lover of all things American, which leads him to act snobbish to everyone around him. Later Rancho, the film's hero, criticizes the fact that so many students enroll in Indian engineering colleges only because they want to find a job in America. This helps us understand lines like Raju's in *Nagina* (1986), who says, regarding his return to India after 15 years abroad, "Jis ped ki jade yahan ho, woh itni door hara-bhara kaisa reh sakta hai?" ("How can a tree whose roots are in one place flourish so far away?"). While it is tempting to dismiss such lines as nationalist sentiment, they in fact run against the grain of a fetishization of living abroad or an unthinking Anglophilia, tendencies which appear throughout India's modern history.

At the same time, the prevalence of representations of NRIs should not be exaggerated. Bollywood films are far more critical of homegrown villains – who exist in almost every film – than they are of villains with foreign values. Likewise, all references to places outside of India should not be read as symbolic or allegorical. Western locales sometimes represent westernization or the loss of Indian culture, but more often, they are simply locations. *An Evening in Paris* (1967) is set almost entirely in Paris, but the city is presented neither as exotic nor as morally corrupting but just as a place Deepa travels to, convinced that "Hindustan mein ab koi saccha chahnewala nahin raha" ("there are no real lovers in India anymore"), and that "jisne Paris mein mohabbat nahin kiya, woh duniya mein kahin nahin kar sakta" ("if you don't fall in love in Paris, you won't ever"). *Love in Tokyo* (1966) is set in Tokyo, where Ashok's brother had married a Japanese woman and had a mixed-race son, Chikoo. Far from questioning Chikoo's morality because he is not "fully" Indian, when Ashok tries to retrieve his nephew after his brother's death and take him back to India, telling Chikoo, "Main Hindustani hoon, mera vatan Hindustan hai" ("I'm Indian, my country is India"), Chikoo responds, "Main Japan mein paida hua, mera vatan Japan hai" ("I was born in Japan, so my country is Japan"), legitimating diasporic identity rather than seeing it as secondary to true Indianness. In *Lamhe* (1991), Viren is living in London and returns to India periodically. While he is represented, for much of the film, as somewhat weak and morose, this is not attributed to his life abroad but to his inability to marry the woman he loves. In all these cases we might say that living abroad has no value, either positive or negative, but is just an opportunity to diversify background and setting, no more meaningful than the fact that Viren comes from a Rajput background.

In the 1990s there were more films set among Indians living outside of India, most often in Europe or the United States. In some of these films, questions of Indianness featured centrally, in that one or several characters struggled to come to terms with their Indian identity even while living abroad. In these films, such as *Pardes* (1997) and *Aa Ab Laut Chalen* (1999), we see a return to some of the themes of *Purab Aur Paschim* (1970), but also we see critiques of capitalism, of the commodification of love, and of unthinking Anglophilia. While these qualities may be more common in the west, the films show Indian characters who are easily seduced by them. These critiques are apparent, though in a more subtle way, in *Swades* (2004), the story of Mohan, a NASA scientist who returns to India to bring his former nanny to the US to live with him. She is living happily in a village but Mohan feels the need to rescue her nonetheless, convinced that life in the US is inherently better than life in India. At first, Mohan finds the living conditions in the village unbearable, renting a mobile home instead of sleeping in the village, drinking bottled water, and generally thinking himself more sophisticated than the villagers. However, we gradually learn that his life is quite lonely in the United States, and in the village, he learns what community is – and, ultimately, falls in love. Moreover, his work as a scientist allows him to make real changes, for instance bringing electricity to the village. While his move to India might be summed up as a nationalist message, in fact the question of nationalism is grafted onto the larger questions of the value of science, social alienation vs. community, and what it means to live a good life.

But *Pardes, Aa Ab Laut Chalen*, and *Swades* are largely exceptions; even in the 1990s diaspora films, we see a significant range in how the west is treated. In *Hum Dil De Chuke Sanam* (1999), Europe is presented as mildly dangerous (Nandini and Vanraj get robbed), but otherwise, it is used as a location distant from family and society, where a different kind of love story can legitimately take place, which has nothing to do with western ideas or influence. In *Dil Bole Hadippa!* (2009), Rohan is from London and is forced to learn so-called Indian ways in order to impress his love interest, but this is more of a joke than a genuine worry about Indian values: what he learns is to seduce Veera in "nautanki-style" ("drama queen-style"), in this case dressing up like Raj in *Dilwale Dulhania Le Jayenge* (1995) and serenading her with the theme song from that film and then playfully aiming a slingshot at her backside in reference to the same flirtatious action in *Hum Aapke Hain Koun* (1994). In other words, Indianness here is more akin to filminess than any authentic cultural value. In *Queen* (2014), Rani travels to Paris and meets Vijayalakshmi, an Indian Parisian who smokes and is openly sexual, thus seeming to be the stereotypical NRI in the model of *Purab Aur Paschim*. However, this film goes in a different direction altogether, and Vijayalakshmi turns out to be a true friend to Rani. *Kal Ho Naa Ho* (2003) is set entirely in New York City but no mention is made of Indianness, except in the one scene in which Aman revives Jennifer's failing diner by convincing her to sell Indian food instead of generic diner fare. In fact, New York is largely rewritten as an Indian city, thus precluding the question of diasporic (un)belonging. In *Dil Chahta Hai* (2001), characters move back and forth between India and Australia, but the question of Indianness never features. Many action and underworld films are also set abroad with little allegorical significance, such as *Company* (2002) in Kenya, *Dhoom 2* (2006) in Rio de Janeiro, *Dishoom* (2016) in Dubai, and so on.

Case study: **Dilwale Dulhania Le Jayenge** *(1995)*

In probably the most well-known and beloved Bollywood film of the 1990s, Simran lives with her family in London. She falls in love with Raj on a trip with her friends around Europe, and when her father, Baldev Singh, finds out about their affair he sends her back to India to marry the son of his old friend, horrified by the thought of his daughter's marriage to someone living in London, despite the fact that Raj is himself an NRI.

Baldev's desire to control his daughter's marriage reflects patriarchal and nationalistic values that conflate identity with place in a simplistic way. These values are captured in the song "Ghar Aaja Pardesi," whose lyrics include the lines, "Ghar aaja pardesi, tera desh bulaye re" ("Come home, stranger, your country is calling you") and thus construct the NRI as a stranger and India as his only possible home. However, these values are actively questioned as part of the plot of this film. Indeed, Raj and Simran are our heroes as they represent true Bollywood love. So immediately the viewer understands that anyone who gets in the way of love will be disrupting the moral universe, even if it is in the name of love for one's country. In this case, it is Baldev, the patriarchal and nationalistic father, who plays the role of love's enemy. Thus, for the moral universe to be restored, Raj and Simran's love must win over Baldev's prohibitions. So immediately the idea of nationalism, or at least a simple nationalism that equates living in a place with having the values of that place, is called into question.

Rather than elope, Raj proves his heroism by trying to convince Baldev that he is worthy of Simran by altering the patriarch's understanding of what it means to be a patriot, which is a *limited* notion, as opposed to Raj's broader understanding of nationalism, which says that an Indian can live anywhere and remain a true Indian. In other words, in contrast to the lyrics of the song, the stranger does not need to "come home" – and, even more suggestively, the migrant is no stranger but can actually be one of our own. This offers a different version of nationalism, one that is delinked from physical location, replacing a narrow nationalism with a more inclusive one. In this context, the moral universe can only be restored when the villain – the patriarch, and the enemy of love – realizes that one does not need to live inside the nation to espouse nationalist values.

All these examples suggest that like other political or socially relevant aspects of Bollywood films, nationalism must be understood *through* Bollywood conventions, not simply inferred from a film's title, its explicit theme, an individual dialogue, or the behavior of one of its characters. Seeing nationalism as mediated through song, love, and visuality decenters this theme from the central place it has long been given in Bollywood film criticism while also showing how alternative formations of the nation might be born in Bollywood's love-centered morality.

7   Gender and sexuality

It is commonly said that all Bollywood films end with a lavish wedding, but that does not mean that the genre as a whole is simply a celebration of heteronormative and reproductive sexuality. Many Bollywood films feature weddings but simultaneously offer representations of alternative, non-normative, homosocial, and even queer sexualities that cannot be reduced to the marriage plot. We have already seen how the kind of love discussed in Chapter 2 is at times so unrealistic, so transcendent, and so distanced from the world that it cannot be requited in marriage. Thus, we might say, there is already something queer about Bollywood love in its most ideal form, as it transcends the modern and national projects of reproductive heteronormativity.[1] Likewise, as we saw in Chapter 2, the way love overpowers individuals, especially men, driving them to despair and even death, complicates the assumption that Bollywood love is simply patriarchal. We also saw in Chapter 3 that weddings can be the sites for alternative romances due to the use of proxies in wedding songs. Moreover, generic qualities like song-and-dance sequences allow female characters to express sexual desire and films to develop an erotic imaginary that exceeds the limits of bourgeois domesticity.

This chapter looks at the various counter-trends of gender and sexuality in Bollywood. Identifying these formulations will require new modes of reading than we conventionally bring to texts – modes of reading that are perhaps better suited for popular genres than for more realist or modernist literature or art cinema. For instance, it is sometimes tempting to read the gender politics of a text as determined by its ending: It showed a strong female character, *but in the end*, she got married. The idea that a representation is not meaningful unless it is carried through all the way until the end will lead many viewers to conclude that most Bollywood films are not politically progressive. As we saw in Chapter 1, Bollywood films tend to abide by a formulaic structure in which a relatively straightforward moral universe is established, then disrupted, then restored. There is not much room in this formulation for surprise endings, unconventional heroes, or plot twists. Therefore, in understanding the politics of a Bollywood film, we have to be attentive to what happens in particular moments, especially moments of interruptions,[2] transgressions, or diegetic rupture (like song-and-dance sequences), even if they never appear to get folded back into the main narrative. This will become clear in the queer readings of Bollywood described below.

The kinds of intimacies described in this chapter are only in rare cases named; most often, they are portrayed but not identified as gay, lesbian, queer, homosocial, or transgressive. Bollywood shows relationships that it cannot name, and in doing so offers a world of erotic possibility that stops short of cohering into stable identities.

Gender roles

On the surface, characters in Bollywood might seem to conform to fairly rigid gender roles, especially within the family context. However, these roles are not always as straightforward as they seem, especially when it comes to the ideal lover, and in particular the male lover, who is susceptible to love and highly emotional rather than patriarchal or rational. The questioning of conventional gender roles has increased especially in the last 20 years (recent female-centered films and new masculinities are discussed in more detail in Chapter 8).

However, even early Bollywood called into question simplistic ideas of male heroism. The heroes of the 1950s tended to be down-and-out lovers, educated but underemployed, dreamers rather than ambitious, and in this way offer a much more sentimental and poetic form of masculinity than might be expected. In *Andaz* (1949), Dilip is supposed to be a businessman, but he spends most of the film sulking around when he realizes Neena does not love him. Guru Dutt's films in particular present male heroes who try to opt out of a modern world they find corrupted by money and greed. In doing so, his characters largely reject the trappings of conventional patriarchal masculinity.[3] In *Pyaasa* (1957), Vijay wants to write poetry but finds that there is no market for his art. In *Mr. and Mrs. 55* (1955), Pritam has no ability to handle money and ends up indebted to his close friend. We can see similar characterizations in other 1950s and 1960s films as well. In *Paying Guest* (1957), Ramesh is incompetent and underemployed and thus cannot pay his rent; Shanti has to go to work to support them. Raju in *Guide* (1965) also lives off Rosie's income. And in *Sahib Bibi Aur Ghulam* (1962), Bhootnath is a sort of befuddled, weak hero, who is in love with Choti Bahu but unable to express it and who is powerless against her various demands on him.

Female characters have also questioned traditional gender roles from the beginning. In *Mr. and Mrs. 55* (1955), Anita is a rich heiress worried about men using her for her money and her aunt is a staunch feminist who mistrusts men. In *Chalti Ka Naam Gaadi* (1958), both Renu and Sheila refuse traditional gender roles; Renu drives herself and her father around, and Sheila knows how to repair cars. Neither of these practices is ever questioned or criticized. Sheila expressly states that she wants a dim-witted ("thoda sa buddhu") husband so that she can control him: "Mujhe toh aisa chahiye: Jo main kahoon, 'Utho' toh uth jaye, main kahoon 'Baitho' toh baith jaye" ("I want it so that when I say get up, he gets up, and when I say sit down, he sits down"). In *Sahib Bibi Aur*

Ghulam (1962), even though Choti Bahu lives in a depraved and repressive household, she is presented as having a sexuality that has no outlet because her husband is more interested in courtesans than her. Although her ending is tragic, this film features the fascinating character of a dynamic, pleasure-seeking woman hemmed in by the restrictions of the zenana and by traditional patriarchy. Rosie in *Guide* (1965) is a strong woman who leaves her adulterous and neglectful husband, embraces her role as a dancer, and moves in with a man who is not her husband. The song she sings right after leaving her husband, "Aaj Phir Jeene Ki Tamanna Hai," reflects on the joys and the fears of female freedom, with the eponymous refrain translated as, "Today I finally have the desire to live." Unlike many other female protagonists of the time, Rosie also embraces her sexuality, despite living in a world that tries to shame her for doing so. Thus when she confronts her husband for his neglect and adultery, she does so by dressing up as one of the courtesans he has been seeing and thus in a sense uses her own sexuality as a way to criticize his hypocrisy. In this scene, the very anklets which had been a source of shame when Rosie wore them become arousing to Marco – that is, as long as he thinks a courtesan is wearing them, but when he finds out they are being worn by his own wife, he is disgusted. The film is critical of marriage as constraining women's freedom. In *Waqt* (1965), it is Renu who teaches Vijay to drive rather than, as we may expect in the 1960s, the other way around. In *Ram Aur Shyam* (1967), Anjana is presented as a woman who knows what she wants; she stands up for herself and insists on having control over her own marriage even as various men try to force her to marry a man she has never met. In *An Evening in Paris* (1967), Deepa is a young heiress who chooses to move to Paris to find true love there. There are few restrictions based on her gender, and when her lover Sam tells her that "acchi Hindustani ladki kabhi sharab nahin peeti" ("good Indian girls don't drink alcohol"), she responds, in English, "Will you please tell him to mind his own business?" and takes a sip just to spite him. In *Seeta Aur Geeta* (1972), Geeta is the character with the most agency; she saves her sister, and she has several fight scenes where she shows her physical prowess as well, including one in which she repeatedly smacks the sexual predator Ranjit across the face with a ping-pong paddle. Throughout the 1980s and 1990s, actor Sridevi was also known for her strong gender roles, such as "working women who were irreverent and left men flummoxed and often emasculated."[4] In *Fanaa* (2006), the head of the anti-terrorist squad is female, and the film shows how much sexism she faces from the men she supervises.

But even when films do conform to seemingly strict gender roles, these gender roles should be seen as part of the formula apparatus of Bollywood films – in other words, they exist in part so they can be innovated on to produce new plots even over formulaic structures. For instance, in *Damini* (1993), the eponymous protagonist witnesses her brother-in-law rape a housemaid and tries to tell the police. But her husband's family threatens her, saying it will damage the family's reputation. The film's conflict arises precisely between the family's idea of appropriate gender roles – i.e. the daughter-in-law should obey the patriarch – and Damini's sense of moral outrage at having to silence the truth. Since the moral universe is centered on Damini, the rigid gender roles she is forced to conform to constitute its disruption.

Sometimes, rigid gender roles ironically allow female characters to assert their own agency. *Dilwale Dulhania Le Jayenge* (1995) has a scene set during the Hindu holiday of Karva Chauth, when wives traditionally fast all day for their husbands' well-being and, once the moon is sighted, are served their first sip of water by their husbands. But Simran uses this patriarchal holiday to assert her own choice of lover against her father, who has arranged her marriage to a man of his choosing. Thus when it is time for Simran to have her first sip of water, her fiancé tries to give it to her and she pretends to faint, so that Raj, her actual lover, can jump in to feed her the water instead and thus claim his place as her rightful husband. In this case, Simran is able to use the one-sided tradition to assert her own romantic agency.

In *Kabhi Khushi Kabhie Gham* (2001), it is the seemingly weak mother who changes the patriarch's mind and she does so specifically by using the language of patriarchy against him. Yash's disowning of his son because of his choice of wife seems stubborn and intractable. Nandini tells him, "Maa hamesha kehti hai, pati parmeshwar hai. Woh jo kahe, woh jo soche, sab sahi … Par ab hamara parivar bikhar gaya … Phir pati parmeshwar kaise hua? … Mera pati pati hai, sirf pati, parmeshwar nahin" ("My mother used to say, a husband is like god. Whatever he said, whatever he thought was right … But now our family has been scattered … So how is a husband like god? … My husband is a husband, just a husband, not a god"). Here, Nandini uses the patriarchal idea of a husband's intrinsic morality to point out Yash's failures. Moreover, she uses this antiquated idea to defend her son's freedom of whom to love and marry, thus refuting the limited, weak, patriarchal concepts like tradition and family loyalty that Yash had earlier wielded to defend disowning his son. Indeed, this speech of Nandini's is the only thing that successfully changes the stubborn patriarch's mind.

Extramarital pregnancy stories also offer alternative roles for female characters. In *Aradhana* (1969), Vandana is pregnant when her fiancé dies in a plane crash; she has no option but to put the child up for adoption because of fears of social sanction. Even though the film stars Rajesh Khanna – one of the most popular stars of the time – as both Vandana's lover and then as her adult son, the film remains centrally about Vandana, who remains the center of the moral universe despite her transgressive actions. A few decades later, *Kya Kehna* (2000) tells another story of a woman who gets pregnant before she is married. In this case, she is rejected by the child's father and faces social ridicule but goes through with the pregnancy nonetheless. Once she has the baby, the father agrees to marry her, but this time she rejects him and marries her true love instead.

Courtesan films offer another alternative to traditional female roles.[5] While these films' female protagonists are courtesans, tawaifs, and/or prostitutes, the period films in particular show a context in which these women had a surprising amount of power in society. As Veena Oldenburg writes, although being a sex worker involved exploitation, pre-1857 tawaifs were free of some of the limitations put on women at the time.[6] Indeed, courtesan films are often the most clearly female-centered, and they offer some of the most interesting spaces for representing transgressive sexuality outside of domestic hetero-normativity. That does not mean that things end happily for them; in *Umrao Jaan* (1981), the eponymous protagonist loses her lover when he gets married, and even when she is older and established, her family continues to reject her. However, despite these circumstances and the importance Bollywood films put on family, it is the courtesan Umrao Jaan who remains at the moral center of the film.

Homosociality and male friendship

Homosociality, especially male friendship, is a space where non-normative or queer erotics can be represented without necessarily being named as queer. Close friendship, known as *yaarana, dosti,* or *dostana,* is a heroic quality in Bol-lywood films; if a character has a close friend, it is likely he is a hero, and conversely, it is rare that a villain or even semi-villainous character will have a close friend.[7] The language of friendship is often intimate; in *Prem Kahani* (1975), Rajesh and Dheeraj call each other "yaar," a Hindi-Urdu word that originally referred to a lover, although it is now used colloquially to mean "buddy."[8] Exploiting the double meaning of this word, close friendship in Bollywood can often involve significant intimacy. This intimacy is not intended to be sexual, but the persistent representation of two men touching, putting their arms around each other, embracing, and holding hands suggests something more than what is conventionally understood by the term "friendship," even if it is not named as queer.

At times male friendships can be expressed in song sequences. As we saw earlier, song sequences are often spaces for the development of romance, so for two male leads to share a song suggests, if not literal romance, at least an intensified, even eroticized, friendship that exceeds what we usually understand by that term. In *Chalti Ka Naam Gaadi* (1958), the three prota-gonists are brothers, but the aesthetic is more of a buddy film, especially because they have no parents, and throughout the film, they look out for one another without the heavy baggage that sometimes comes from being biologically related. They sing the first song of the film together, which includes lyrics such as, "Hilmil ke chalna yun hi saathi/ Arré band mutthi lakh ki/ Aur khule toh pyare khak ki" ("We'll always stay together like this/ United we stand, divided we fall"), showing the enormous importance of male friendship here and in Bollywood more generally. In "Tu Mujhe Suna" in *Chandni* (1989), Rohit and Lalit tell their love stories to each other, neither of them knowing that they are in fact love with the same woman. The physical intimacy founded in this mutual confession contains queer resonances (Figure 7.1). And in *Main Khiladi Tu Anari* (1994), Deepak and Karan are close friends who share a song about their friendship.

Figure 7.1 Rohit and Lalit enjoy an afternoon sharing their love stories with one another, in *Chandni* (1989).

At times the queerness of friendship is mentioned, even if disavowed. In *Lamhe* (1991), Prem and Viren are close friends. When Viren tells Prem he is thinking of getting married, Prem, who is known for his sense of humor, jokes, "Mujhe aisi baatein mat kiya karo, main waisa aadmi nahin hoon" ("Don't talk to me like that, I'm not that kind of guy") and when Viren asks him to be serious, Prem responds, "Tumhein kya lagta hai, Daijaan hamari shaadi ke liye raazi ho jayengi?" ("What do you think, will Daijaan [Viren's ayah] approve of our marriage?"). While this can be dismissed as humor, and perhaps even homophobic humor, it is also interesting to note what the comment *does* suggest, which is that underlying any male friendship might be repressed erotics. We see this in more recent films in which characters seem to make fun of queer relationships by pretending or faking them. In *Kal Ho Naa Ho* (2003), close friends Aman and Rohit are humorously caught by Kantabehn, Rohit's maid, who finds them snuggling next to each other in bed in the morning, Amit with his shirt unbuttoned. Here, homosexuality is implied through Kantabehn's homophobia. While mostly for the purpose of humor, it is notable that neither character defends himself to Kantabehn; Aman even arguably plays up the misunderstanding when he later melodramatically – and parodically – announces to Kantabehn that "Main mar jaunga lekin Rohit ko nahin chodunga!" ("I will die but never let Rohit go!"). This scenario is developed further in *Dostana* (2008), in which homosexuality is named, and the possibility of two men being married is articulated, even though again the scenario is one of humor, as the two friends are faking being gay in order to appease a landlady wary of single men. I will return to the topic of naming queerness in Bollywood later in this chapter.

Male friends do not just joke and play around with each other; they exhibit intimacy and even love. Friends make sacrifices for one another, as in *Dostana* (1980), when Vijay discovers that he and his close friend Ravi are in love with the same woman, and he tells her to marry Ravi instead of him. They might also use the language of love; in *Main Khiladi Tu Anari* (1994), Deepak is completely in awe of Karan, saying things like "What style!" and "You're terrific!" and calling himself Karan's "deewana" – which can be translated as fan, but also refers to a besotted lover. We are rarely given the *source* of a friendship or any psychological depth as to why the friends love each other or what binds them. Rather, Bollywood presents us with a category – friendship, or *dosti* – which has a morality in and of itself.

Friendship is one of the few values that might in certain cases be even more important than love. In *Dostana* (1980), Sheetal complicates the friendship between Ravi and Vijay by inciting their jealousy, but the film's moral universe is centered on the friendship, not the love. In *Gunday* (2014), Bikram and Bala have a close, intimate friendship forged in a difficult youth. They become gangsters and unthinkingly defend each other when needed. There is a queer frisson to their relationship, and unlike films of the earlier generations, the two men do not try to make their friendship seem heterosexual and thus socially acceptable: they are seen drinking from the same glass (which happens to be heart-shaped [Figure 7.2]), sleeping in the same bed (wearing matching pyjamas) and sitting next to each other in wet clothes while they discuss love. At first it seems that heterosexual love will put a strain on their friendship, especially since they end up being in love with the same woman, Nandita. They reassure themselves that "Whoever she chooses, it shouldn't affect our friendship," and proudly tell her that "Hum pyar karte hain aap se" ("We love you"); when she asks, "Donon?" ("Both of you?") they both reply, "Haan" ("Yes"). However, when Nandita ultimately chooses Bikram, it causes a rift. It is certainly suggested, in the epic tantrum Bala has in the wake of Nandita's choice, that he is not only possessive over Nandita but also facing the potential loss of Bikram in his life. Their conflict comes to a head in a shirtless duel in which Bala and Bikram fight it out with their muscled, oiled chests gleaming. But ultimately they discover that Nandita is a cop who was purposely trying to weaken their gang by destroying their friendship; thus, here as well, in the end,

Figure 7.2 Best friends Bala and Bikram share a drink as they watch a dance performance, in *Gunday* (2014).

heterosexual romance is represented as a potentially dangerous distraction from true homosocial *dosti*. It is only when Bikram and Bala realize the strength of their friendship that the moral order can be restored.

Bollywood friendship might be traced to the intimate friendship between Arjun and Krishna in the Hindu epic the *Mahabharata*. As Ruth Vanita writes, "Krishna clearly states that Arjuna is more important to him than wives, children, or kinsmen – there can be many spouses and sons but there is only one Arjuna, without whom he cannot live."[9] Krishna is Arjun's chariot driver; the *Mahabharata*'s chariot becomes a space of closeness and physical intimacy.[10] While all Bollywood friendships do not refer directly back to this friendship, some do, and it is possible to read the motorcycle that Jai and Veeru share in *Sholay* (1975), where they sing a song about the unbreakable bond of their friendship, as an interpretation of Arjun and Krishna's queer chariot (Figure 7.3).

Similar to when a character loses faith in love, as discussed in Chapter 2, it is also possible for a character to lose faith in friendship, constituting the disruption in a film's moral universe. In *Dostana* (1980), Ravi and Vijay are intimate friends, but through a misunderstanding Ravi believes that Vijay stole his girlfriend, and so turns against him, saying the worst thing one friend can say to another: "Toot gaya woh dostana. Aaj hum dost nahin, dushman hain" ("Our friendship has ended. We are no longer friends, but enemies"). This fickleness regarding friendship is presented as a weakness, and the moral universe can only be restored when Ravi realizes how wrong he was. The fact that male friendship is presented as intensely and with as much of a sense of fatedness as romantic love suggests a queering of friendship in the genre as a whole.

Case study: **Sholay** *(1975)*

One of Bollywood's most famous homosocial friendships is Jai and Veeru's friendship in *Sholay*. They even sing an entire song about their friendship:

Figure 7.3 "Khana-peena saath hai, marna-jeena saath hai" ("We'll eat and drink together, live and die together"); close male friendship in *Sholay* (1975).

Yeh dosti, hum nahin todenge
Todenge dum magar tera saath na chhodenge
Aye meri jeet teri jeet, teri haar, meri haar
Sun aye mere yaar
Tera gham mera gham, teri jaan meri jaan
Aisa apna pyar
Khana-peena saath hai, marna-jeena saath hai
Saari zindagi.

[Nothing will break this friendship
We might lose our lives but we won't leave each other
My victory is your victory, your loss is my loss
Listen, my friend
Your sorrow is my sorrow, your life is my life
That's how our love is
We'll eat and drink together, live and die together
Throughout our whole lives.]

The potential queerness of this friendship is confirmed in a later scene when Veeru is flirting with Basanti, while Jai is playing a sad rendition of this same song, "Yeh Dosti," on his harmonica, suggesting an unarticulated melancholy around Veeru's heteronormativity. At the end of the film, Jai dies in Veeru's arms, and the camera centers on Veeru's grief more than it does on Radha's (Jai's female lover).

Likewise, the morality of the film centers around their relationship. Jai and Veeru are first introduced as criminals, but once we hear this song, witness their physical intimacy, and understand the extent of their friendship – how they protect each other but also how they joke with each other – the inherent morality of friendship trumps the immorality of a life of petty crime. Their closeness and physical intimacy, their fierce loyalty, their faith in each other's love, and of course, Jai's final sacrifice of his own life at the end of the film all make them the moral center of the film, even in a film that reflects a larger world of uncertain morality.

More recent buddy films revolve around a group of male friends, usually three, who have fun and enjoy life together. The newer buddy films might seem to lack the kind of intense intimacy and homosociality that we see in the longer tradition of Bollywood friendship, epitomized by Jai and Veeru. Many friend groups are supported by a heterosexual unit, meaning the three male friends end up paired off with three women by the end. Nevertheless there is a psychosexual element to buddy films that suggests that friendship has particular qualities that are not merely the foil for eventual heterosexual coupledom. Thus in many buddy films, we see a strong friendship that gets disrupted by some external or internal force, and then is restored when the friends realize how important their friendship is. In *Dil Chahta Hai* (2001), the disruption is an argument between Akash and Sid after Sid announces that he is in love with a woman who happens to be older and a divorcée. Akash dismisses this as lust and laughs at Sid, a dismissal that Sid is not able to forgive. The fact that the break in their friendship comes from a misreading of Sid's sexuality suggests a libidinal dynamic to even the more recognizably heterosexual buddy film.[11]

Female friendship

Films centered around the dynamics of female friendships are more rare in Bollywood, even as female friendships themselves are quite common. In *Andaz* (1949), Neena and Sheela are *saheliyaan*, or best friends, who confide in each other and are often physically intimate, draping their arms around one another or looking into one another's eyes. In a scene in which Neena is singing, ostensibly to Dilip, she is facing Sheela and it is as if she is singing to her instead (Figure 7.4). Radha and Sakina are close friends in *Sangam* (1964), and Deepa and Honey form a fast friendship in *An Evening in Paris* (1967); Honey introduces Deepa to the romance that is everywhere in Paris and counsels her on her love life. The two plan a women-only picnic together – because, as Deepa says, "I hate boys!" – that is then crashed by the group's boyfriends. In *Padosan* (1968), Bindu is often surrounded by her group of girlfriends and the song "Main Chali," where the group ride bicycles to the local park, celebrates the

Figure 7.4 Close friends Neena and Sheela share an intimate moment during a song in *Andaz* (1949) while Dilip accompanies them on the piano.

perils and pleasures of love from the perspective of close female friends. In *Kati Patang* (1971), Madhu and Poonam meet after Madhu has run away from home, and Madhu pretends to be Poonam's sister so that "hum donon milke sukh-dukh baant lenge, aur is Munne ka sahara ban kar, zindagi guzaar denge" ("we can pass the days, in happiness and in pain, and raise Munna [my son] together"). Although *Andaz Apna Apna* (1994) is centrally about two men, Raveena and Karishma are also close friends. In *Queen* (2014), Rani and Vijayalaxmi develop a close friendship that has potentially queer undertones, with the latter's name similar to that of Vijay, Rani's former fiancé, and in the way they visit romantic sites together as they travel around Paris.

Veere Di Wedding (2018) is a rare film that explicitly centers on female friendship. "Veer" is a Punjabi word used for "brother" and the four friends refer to each other as "veer" throughout the film, suggesting a deliberate transferal of the buddy genre to a woman's plot (a translation of the film's title would thus be something like, "My Buddy's Wedding"). The potential queerness of this self-designation is supported by the fact that the protagonist Kalindi's uncle is in a gay relationship. Conversely, her heterosexual parents have a broken relationship, souring Kalindi on marriage overall. The film tracks the friends' conflicts and their ultimate resolution; the moral is the importance of friendship – in particular female friendship – and supporting each other through various romantic and professional travails. This is the theme of *Angry Young Goddesses* (2015) as well, a film that shows how friends, despite small tensions between them, ultimately have each other's backs when faced with sexual violence and a larger patriarchal and misogynistic state.

Love triangles

Love triangles are quite common in Bollywood, introducing a complication into love stories that also potentially queers them. There exist in Bollywood both kinds of love triangles: two men in love with one woman, and two women in love with one man (as in *Kuch Kuch Hota Hai* [1998]), although the first is more common. On one level, the love triangle is simply enjoyable to watch, when lovers talk at cross-purposes, for example, or through a spokes-person (who might also be part of the love triangle), creating entertaining misunderstandings. This is the case in *Purab Aur Paschim* (1970), in which Shyam loves Gopi but Gopi loves Bharat, and since Bharat and Shyam are best friends, Bharat tries to seduce Gopi on Shyam's behalf and Gopi misunder-stands. But love triangles can also complicate ideas of heteronormative love because in involving three figures in the romantic universe, including two of the same gender, they can allow for the representation of queer erotics even when a plot seems strictly heteronormative. Such films often set up a triad of erotic relationships, which at times is focused narrowly on the female lead but also allows for erotically charged encounters between the two men or, in rarer cases such as *Andaz* (1949), between the two women. At times, it is even possible that the love triangle might be a way to render a queer relationship legitimate. In these cases, the apparently central figure – the character whom the two others are fighting over – might serve as a sort of third wheel, a front to make legitimate what is actually an unspeakable queer love.

For instance, in *Prem Kahani* (1971), Rajesh and Kamini were lovers until he left her to join the nationalist movement. Coincidentally, she ends up married to Rajesh's best friend, Dheeraj. When Rajesh comes to stay with the couple, all sorts of sexual tensions are unleashed, between former lovers Rajesh and Kamini, and, because Dheeraj remains in the picture, among the three as well. Although Dheeraj does not know about the couple's history together, he seems to sub-consciously want them to be together; at one point, he sends them on a long drive together, and because Rajesh is in hiding from the police, he has Rajesh dress up in his clothes, as if gesturing to the two men's intimacy and interchangeability.

In *Silsila* (1981), Amit and Shekhar are orphan brothers and best friends;[12] Shekhar dies in a fighter jet crash and Amit feels pressured to marry his pregnant fiancée. This is not quite a love triangle, since Amit and Shobha never feel strongly for each other, and Amit remains in love with Chandni, but the arrangement does nevertheless expose a latent queerness in Amit and Shekhar's relationship.[13] In an early scene, Amit tells Shobha about his relationship with his brother (Shobha's fiancé) as one that exceeds friendship and certainly brotherhood:

AMIT: Bhai mujhse ded saal bada hai, aur hum donon taqriban dost hain. Hum donon ne cigarette peena ek saath shuru kiya, phir sharab bhi hum donon ne ek hi saath ek hi glass mein pi, aur usse pehle, hum donon ne ishq bhi taqriban ek saath hi shuru kiya …

SHOBHA: Balki ek hi ladki se …

AMIT: Aap janti hain? Good. Aur usse pehle hum donon ek saath nange nahaya karte the.

SHOBHA: Sun chuki hoon.

AMIT: Dekha nahin hoga … [both laugh]

[AMIT: My brother is one-and-a-half years older than me, but we're friends. We started smoking together, and we started drinking alcohol together, at the same time, from the very same glass. But even before that we fell in love at about the same time …

SHOBHA: With the same girl …

AMIT: You know that already? Good. And before that we used to shower together naked.

SHOBHA: I heard that.

AMIT: You must not have seen it … [both laugh]]

The word "bhai," which Amit and Shekhar use to refer to each other, has loose connotations: it can be used for a brother or a close friend. And indeed, in this dialogue, Shobha becomes the conduit for Amit to describe his intimate relation-ship with Shekhar, and the suggestive line, "You must not have seen it …" implicates Shobha in their sexual intimacy. Indeed, later in the film there is actually a scene of Amit and Shekhar showering together which suggests that this was not only a childhood game but a continuing form of intimacy (Figure 7.5), and in another scene, they joke that Amit should find a bride and they should all take their honeymoons together. This last comment is even too much for Shobha, and she laughingly indicates that this is taking the men's friendship too far.

Kal Ho Naa Ho (2003) is a slightly different kind of love triangle; Aman and Rohit are both in love with Naina, but Aman knows that he has only a few more weeks to live, so he pretends not to love Naina so that she will reciprocate Rohit's love instead. But here as well, when Aman is on his deathbed, he falls asleep holding Rohit's hand rather than Naina's, suggesting a queer undercurrent to this love triangle as well.

Case study: Sangam *(1964)*

Sangam explicitly centers on the transgressive dynamics that can characterize the Bollywood love triangle. Sundar, Gopal, and Radha are best friends since childhood, but even in childhood their threesome was marked by unequal dynamics. In an early scene, the young Sundar builds a toy house and announces to Radha that "maine ek ghar bana diya hai. Gopal ke liye bhi kamra hai. Ab toh rahogi na mere ghar mein?" ("I've made a house. There's

Figure 7.5 While showering together, Shekhar drops a bar of soap and jokingly asks his brother Amit to pick it up, in *Silsila* (1981).

even a room for Gopal. Now will you stay in my house?"), to which she responds, "Nahin rahungi … meri marzi hai. Mujhe nahin accha lagta tumhara ghar" ("I won't stay there, it's my decision. I don't like your house"). Sundar seeks both of their affections; while he imagines himself as Radha's husband, all his domestic arrangements include Gopal as well. Later as an adult, Sundar becomes a persistent lover, following Radha everywhere and trying to steal her clothes when she is swimming (recalling Lord Krishna's stealing of the gopis' clothes in Hindu mythology), but these actions irritate Radha, who is in love with Gopal. When Gopal realizes both he and Sundar are in love with Radha, he backs off for the sake of their "dosti" ("friendship"), which he values more than his love for Radha. The two men speak to each other in the language of love; Gopal says, "I could even give up my life for you" and Sundar tells Gopal, "Tumhari hansi bahut khoobsurat hai" ("Your smile is very beautiful"). This film presents the homosocial relationship as more important, long-standing, and intimate than either of the men's relationship with Radha. In a break from Bollywood conventions on love, the wrong couple gets married (Radha and Sundar), but this is in fact a success for Sundar, who gets to have *both* love and friendship at the same time. He invites Gopal to join them on their honeymoon, telling him in a letter, "Europe aur phir Radha saath mein, lagta main … kisi swarg mein hoon. Lekin … ek kami hai, wahi tumhari mere yaar, tumhari" ("Being with Radha in Europe, I feel like I'm … in heaven. But … there is still something missing, and that's you, my friend, you"). When Gopal joins them, the situation is understandably awkward for him and for Radha, but Sundar is thrilled. Back at home, Sundar places a photograph of Gopal right between the two portraits of him and Radha on his mantle. For Sundar, this threesome is the ideal – like the domestic scene he had imagined as a child. However, he soon learns that Radha had another lover and is overcome with jealousy. He discovers that the other lover was Gopal, which drives him even further into insanity, but it is not clear whether he is more possessive over Radha or over Gopal. This precarious libidinal economy cannot survive, so in the end, Gopal has no choice but to kill himself, taming the transgression his very body poses to the heterosexual romance.

Relationships with no name

As mentioned above, queer or transgressive relationships are rarely named in Bollywood, and, ironically, this allows them to offer characters a kind of liberation from the kinship and romantic designations (most prominently, husband–wife) that dictate conventional Bollywood morality. It was Tara in *Dil Chahta Hai* (2001) who defined her erotic but never requited relationship with Sid as, "Kuch rishte hote hain, jinka koi naam nahin hota" ("There are some relationships which have no name").[14] But long before this film, Bollywood has given moral centrality to relationships that cannot be named, even potentially transgressive ones such as queer or other forms of love – cross-class, inter-age – that exceed established kinship terms or social sanction.

In *Guide* (1965), for instance, Rosie and Raju cannot name their intimate relationship because Rosie is already married. Thus their love resides outside the boundaries of respectability; it is an impossible love – radical and unstable, but nonetheless, the heart of the film. In fact, it is never called love and therefore lies at the limits of – and from there puts pressure on – the existing romantic imagination.

The same could be said of Amit's and Shekhar's relationship in *Silsila* (1981), discussed above. Although they are brothers, that term is not able to contain the true nature of their relationship. The film encourages this reading by representing no parents or other siblings and no images of their past or their childhood together, thereby allowing viewers to think beyond the kinship structure in which their brotherhood is legible as such.

Mothers and sons

Some unnameable relationships are impossible or transgressive. The sexual tension between mothers and sons, for instance, a sublimated expression of impossible desire, exists across films as diverse as *Mother India* (1957), *Deewaar* (1975), and *Kapoor & Sons* (2016). There is never actual sex between family members; rather, the mother–son dynamic underlies the sexual unconscious of Bollywood cinema as a whole and offers a queering of otherwise seemingly family-friendly plots.[15]

Mother India was discussed in Chapter 6; in that film, the disruption of the moral universe is caused by the mother-in-law's misunderstanding of the value of land and a fundamentally unjust social structure. But the family also undergoes another upheaval resulting from the abandonment of Shamu, the father, a trope which is repeated across several Bollywood films. The departure of the father effectively unsettles the harmony of the domestic unit made up of the mother, the father, and the children. When the father leaves, he leaves a vacuum that is often filled by one of the sons, who sees himself as now having to occupy the role of the patriarch. But obviously this is a transgressive role, as in taking the place of the father, he has to readjust his relationship with his mother. The mother, too, ends up loving this transgressive son more than her other son, who remains a child, further disrupting the libidinal economy of the nuclear family.[16]

This plays out in a number of films in interesting ways. In *Mother India*, even years after Shamu's departure, Radha continues to fantasize about his return. In one fantasy, she sees Shamu walking into her compound with two oxen but then, as he gets closer, she realizes it is her son Ramu walking toward her, not her husband. Her temporary conflation of son and husband suggests transgressive libidinal dynamics existing just under the surface of Radha's consciousness; this transgressive confusion is registered in quick cuts between her face and images of her son and then her husband. For his part, her other son Birju finds himself obsessed with filling the role of patriarch as he witnesses the hardships and sacrifices his mother has to undergo. He steals cotton and trades it for a pair of bangles to replace the bangles his mother had to sell. When he brings the bangles to her, he puts them on her in a gesture that replicates the gesture earlier in the movie when Shamu had put bangles on Radha right after their marriage. Again, the son's attempt to play the father's role – and here the explicitly sexual role of bangle-endower – reveals potentially transgressive sexual dynamics.

Indeed, even after Radha discovers that the bangles were stolen, she devotes her full attention to Birju, although his downfall is already underway. He becomes the privileged son, and she consistently takes his side over Ramu even when it is clear that he is in the wrong. At one point Ramu tells her point blank: "Tera beta chor hai" ("Your son is a thief"), an idea that she cannot bear. This theme of loving one son more than the other is repeated in several Bollywood movies, and awakens darker dynamics that lie beneath the surface of the supposed familial ideal. From this perspective, Radha's final act of murdering her own son might be seen as a violent response to the danger of their transgressive love.[17] This somewhat provocative reading is nonetheless supported by the fact that during the shooting of *Mother India*, Nargis, who played Radha, became romantically involved with Sunil Dutt, who played her son Birju, and eventually they were married.

In *Aradhana* (1969), the mother–son relationship is also extradiegetically eroticized due to the fact that while Vandana's husband Arun dies early in the film and she is separated from her son, the film skips forward two decades, when she is reunited with her son who is played by the same actor, Rajesh Khanna, who had played her husband. This results in an interesting dynamic. During their courtship, Vandana and Arun's relationship is highly erotically charged, as shown in the "Roop Tera Mastana" song they overhear in a room next to theirs, which arouses them and leads them to make love for the first time. Twenty years later, Suraj, her son, is engaged to Rupa, but the eroticism we had earlier seen between the two actors, Sharmila Tagore and Rajesh Khanna, remains as a trace that disrupts Suraj's relationship with Rupa, even though now Sharmila Tagore is playing Suraj's mother. This afterglow of the earlier relationship seems to affect the characters as well; Suraj says to Rupa regarding Vandana (who he does not yet know is his mother), "Na jaane kya baat hai unmein, par jab bhi meri taraf dekhti hai, mujhe kuch ho jaata hai" ("I don't know what it is about her, but whenever she looks in my direction something happens to me"). This comment makes Rupa jealous, so she quickly responds, "Aur jab main dekhti hoon?" ("How do you feel when I look at you?"), suggesting that the earlier relationship continues to haunt this one in the spectral body of Rajesh Khanna/Arun/Suraj. To underscore this, and unlike the Arun–Vandana relationship earlier in the film, Rupa and Suraj are represented as having little chemistry, and the two actually seem quite mismatched.

Other films gesture to this transgressive dynamic as well. In *Deewaar* (1975), after the father's abandonment of the family, the mother only has enough money to send one child to school. Vijay makes the sacrifice and says he will work so that his younger brother, Ravi, can go to school. Vijay thus steps in to take over the role of the patriarch, an action which, once again, unsettles the libidinal economy of the film.[18] Here, the mother openly admits to loving Vijay more than Ravi, a transgression that also results in a violent action, where she essentially gives Ravi the gun to kill his brother while saying the line, "Bhagwan kare, goli chalaate waqt tere haath na kampe" ("God willing, may your hands not tremble when you pull the trigger") – a line that Priya Joshi reads as a way for the mother to absolve herself of her transgressive love.[19] In *Bobby* (1973), this erotic dynamic between mother and son is framed in a more psychoanalytic manner: early on in the film it is mentioned that Raj's mother did not nurse him when he was a baby, a relinquishing of motherly duty that disrupts the moral universe and sets the stage for an unresolvable impasse between the son and his parents.

In *Kapoor & Sons* (2016), a film that moves away from typical Bollywood aesthetics, we nevertheless see a recrafting of this same mother/sons dynamic, suggesting more of a Bollywood influence than might initially be perceived. Both Rahul and Arjun are writers; their mother loves Rahul more than Arjun, so much so that she is willing to steal a story that Arjun had written to give to Rahul, ensuring the latter's professional success. This family too is effectively abandoned by an adulterous patriarch, an abandonment which opens the door to this kind of intra-family betrayal and the uneven apportioning of love among the various men. While in *Kabhi Khushi Kabhie Gham* (2001), this transgressive unconscious is poked fun at, with Rahul joking to his brother Rohan that "Maa mujhe tujhse zyada pyar karti hai" ("Mom loves me more than you"), in these other examples we see how this transgressive dynamic seriously troubles the libidinal economy of the heterosexual romance.

Queer Bollywood

There are very few Bollywood films that contain uncloseted queer characters. Over Bollywood's history, the closest we have seen is the sporadic representation of hijras, members of India's third sex, who could also be understood as transgender or intersex. *Tamanna* (1997) and *Shabnam Mousi* (2005) are two films that feature a hijra as the protagonist. *Tamanna* is the story of Tiku, a hijra who finds an abandoned baby and raises her as her own daughter. When Tamanna grows up and wants to find her birth parents, she discovers that her biological father had left her outside to die because he had wanted a boy. She confronts her father and ultimately exposes him; when her apologetic birth mother invites her back into the family, however, Tamanna refuses, saying that her real home is with her hijra mother and her mother's lover, Salim Khan. Although *Tamanna* is not explicit about Tiku's relationship with Salim Khan, it is clear that they are romantic partners. So the moral universe is centered around the queer, adoptive family and in the end they remain united.

More commonly, hijras play minor characters who represent a kind of sexual excess that is usually coded as good on Bollywood's moral spectrum. In *Amar Akbar Anthony* (1977), a group of hijras participate in Akbar's public protest against his father-in-law, Tayyab Ali, who has forbidden his daughter from marrying Akbar, and thus is labelled, by Akbar and the hijras, as a "pyar ka dushman" ("enemy of love"). In *Mom* (2017), Devki enlists the help of two hijras to enact revenge on one of her step-daughter's rapists by kidnapping, drugging, and then castrating him. In both films, the hijras are on the side of love and justice and take a stand against patriarchal violence.

In *Nagina* (1986), Raju falls in love with a woman, Rajni, who casts a spell on him that takes him out of the domestic world of his mother, his family's prestige, and normativity. He becomes obsessed with Rajni, and his obsession takes him further and further from the rational world. We learn that Rajni is in fact a rein-carnation of a snake, who returned to earth initially to get revenge on Raju for the death of her snake-husband, but who ends up falling in love with Raju instead. Raju's mother finds out Rajni's secret and is horrified; but when Raju finds out, he begs his mother to accept Rajni into their family nonetheless. In a sense, he wants his mother to accept the queer, multi-species family they will become as an alternative to the heteronormative future she had imagined for him. When the mother cannot accept this – secretly calling the snake charmer to try and control and capture Rajni – it is she who ends up dying, allowing her son and Rajni to live "happily ever after," as the final title announces. This is a rare case when the mother has to die in order for the romance to prosper, and it is likely related to the fact that, as a queer romance, it exceeds even Bollywood's own idea of what can be contained within the extended family unit.

In the absence of explicitly queer characters or plots, queer possibilities more commonly emerge in the excessive moments of Bollywood cinema, in its incessant invocation of desire. Queer fans of superstar Sridevi found new possi-bilities for self-imagining in her excess. As queer activist Dhrubo Jyoti writes, "[Sridevi's] songs gave us fleeting glimpses of how the world would be if we could dance like we wanted to, and wear the clothes our hearts desired. In her often garish, kitschy performances, we saw the promise of a future where we wouldn't lie about who we were and what we liked."[20] This feeling is only intensified in song-and-dance sequences in which there is cross-dressing and men dance with men or women with women, which allows gender transgressions which might not be possible within the narrative. These show a latent queerness in the form itself.[21] While cross-dressing is often the source of comic mis-understandings, it can also allow for the representation of queer desire in Bolly-wood films. In *Love in Tokyo* (1966), Asha and Mohan exchange flirtatious banter while Asha is dressed up as a man, and in fact their love affair develops in this form. Asha seems to confirm the queerness of the scene when she says, "[Main] maa-baap da ek lauta. Mainu hi munda samjho, mainu hi kudi" ("I am the only son of my parents so they treat me as both a boy and a girl"). When Asha gets up to leave, Ashok, clearly attracted to her even in men's clothing, invites her to stay: "Arré yaar, itna bada palang pada hua hai, hum donon yahin so jayenge" ("Listen, friend, there's such a big bed sitting here, let's both sleep right here"). Later in the same film, Mahesh cross-dresses as a geisha and seduces Sheela's father in that role. While both misunderstandings get resolved, the enjoyment of both scenes lies at least in part in the queer excess they generate.

In the "Didi Tera Dewar" song in *Hum Aapke Hain Koun* (1994), the convention of wedding proxies discussed in Chapter 3 is queered to offer the representation of lesbian erotics.[22] The wedding song precedes Pooja's wedding, and in it her sister Nisha plays the bride while a female friend plays the groom; the two of them perform a madcap song anticipating the ups and downs of married life. The woman who plays the groom keeps grabbing female audience members around the waist and trying to kiss them, dances closely and suggestively with Nisha, and the couple dances together in a song that is flirtatious and fun (Figure 7.6). Although the fact that the woman is a proxy for the groom ties the song sequence to a heterosexual core, the queer erotics that emerge in this song sequence are entirely uncontained by that core.

In *Dil Bole Hadippa!* (2009) Veera dresses up as a man to join an all-male cricket team and falls in love with her coach, Rohan. Although it is the female Veera who interests Rohan, the scenes when she is dressed as Veer also contain a queer frisson. In *Bajrangi Bhaijaan* (2015), Pawan, Chand Nawab, and Munni pretend to be a family after illegally crossing the border to Pakistan; Pawan dresses up in a burqa, offering a glimpse of a queer family dynamic. All these cross-dressing characters animate a queer potential that underlies Bollywood cinema. Conversely, characters who regulate others' sexuality by criticizing cross-dressing are on the wrong side of the films' moral universe, as with Raja's father in *Main Madhuri Dixit Banna Chahti Hoon* (2003), who gets angry when his son dresses up as a woman to dance on stage. In all these cases, individual queer scenes offer viewing pleasures that are not reducible to the film's plot.

We also see drag sequences whose intention might not be queer but can certainly be enjoyed as such. In *Duplicate* (1998), Mannu dresses up as an escort in order to assassinate Dhingra, a man who had earlier betrayed him. The idea of drag as a ruse or disguise seems to contradict a more critical interpretation of drag as "effectively mock[ing] both the expressive model of gender and the notion of a true gender identity";[23] thus, reading the performance in relation to

Figure 7.6 The pre-wedding celebrations in *Hum Aapke Hain Koun* (1994) include a queer dance.

the plot does not give us much in terms of a queer reading. However, once again, the ultimate meaning or end result should not solely determine the impact of this scene. The fact is that the scene itself is intensely queer. We see Mannu enter the room from the back, and we think he is a woman. S/he enters and begins seducing Dhingra, who is immediately aroused. What follows is an extended scene of queer seduction and sexual arousal, with Mannu dancing and gyrating to entice Dhingra and Dhingra using a whip to engage Mannu. Dhingra kisses Mannu's knee and finally gets on top of him/her to fervently kiss his/her neck and chest (Figure 7.7). It is only when Mannu has Dhingra close, in a state of arousal and half-undress, that s/he pulls out a gun, takes off his/her wig, and shows Dhingra that s/he is Mannu. But even then, the image of Mannu we get is not the familiar Shah Rukh Khan but his queer and gender non-conforming avatar.

This extended sequence of queer sexuality exceeds the use of disguise in the plot. In fact, this scene is *more* graphic than most seduction scenes in Bollywood. It is almost as if it passes the censors precisely because it takes place between two men, and thus – to unimaginative censors – was not thought to threaten morality. This is ironic, of course, because it allows for a more graphic scene of a male–male sexual encounter than would likely be allowed of its male–female equivalent.

Dostana (2008) was discussed earlier as an example of a film that names homosexuality even if it ends up being a ruse. However, despite this ending, *Dostana* does offer new possibilities for queer representation within Bollywood. Sam and Kunal are pretending to be gay, and eventually Sam's mother finds out. At first, she is upset. However, she is convinced by Neha that she should accept their relationship and in the next scene, she greets Kunal with a prayer and by asking him to knock over a pot of rice, a custom for newlyweds. Then she gives him a pair of bangles, saying, "Yeh kangan maine apni bahu ke liye banvaye the … Ab sach pooch, toh main nahin jaanti ki tu meri bahu hai ya

Figure 7.7 Mannu seduces Dhingra while in drag, in *Duplicate* (1998).

damad, par jo bhi hai, meri taraf se shagun samajh ke rakh le" ("I had these bracelets made for my daughter-in-law … Now to be honest, I don't know whether you are my daughter-in-law or son-in-law, but whoever you are, take these as an engagement gift from me") (Figure 7.8) and asks him to keep the Karva Chauth fast the following year, a religious fast conventionally taken by wives for the health of their husbands. Thus, although Sam and Kunal are only pretending to be gay, the mother's acceptance of them is real, and thus despite the ending, the film actually offers a powerful possibility for parental acceptance of a gay relationship.

Bollywood films also sometimes include queer minor characters, whom Parmesh Shahani calls "gay sidekick[s]"[24] and whose representations are usually not considered queer, especially when they seem to exist primarily for comic relief. But some of these do seem to be ways to incorporate non-normative sexualities into the regulated space of Bollywood cinema and, more importantly, to associate them with the film's moral universe rather than as transgressive or threatening. Thus the two gender-bending servant characters in *Raja Hindustani* (1996), Gulabo and Kammo, are in part funny in their antics, and at first prank Raja, but ultimately come to stand with the protagonist Aarti in her resistance to her stepmother's snobbery and, at the end of the film, against the villain who is trying to steal Aarti and Raja's baby. Gulabo and Kammo are never named as queer, but they are clearly gender nonconforming, so when Raja angrily threatens to hit Kammo, and Gulabo shames him for hitting a woman, Raja says, "Aurat? Yeh aurat hai?" ("Woman? She's a woman?") and then asks Gulabo, "Aur tu kaun hai, uski behn?" ("And who are you, her sister?"), to which Gulabo answers, "How sick! Hum purush hain" ("I am a man"). The marriage of Kammo and the cisgender Balwant Singh also reads as potentially queer given that they flirt by having a wrestling match, as if two men, and when Balwant wins, he asks Kamal if she will begin to dress in women's clothes.

Figure 7.8 Sam's mother gifts Kunal the bangles that she was saving for her daughter-in-law, in *Dostana* (2008).

Recently there have been more explicit attempts at telling queer stories. *Shubh Mangal Zyada Saavdhan* (2020) is one of the first Bollywood films to centrally feature a gay love story and name it as such. Kartik and Aman are in love; while Aman has run away from his conservative family, Kartik craves acceptance from his. When Kartik's father discovers their relationship during his sister's wedding, he tries to keep the two men apart but ultimately realizes that love prevails over prejudice. This film also celebrates camp as an aesthetic that melds the queer with the filmi. *My Brother Nikhil* (2005) and *Kapoor & Sons* (2016) are less reliant on Bollywood conventions such as song sequences, and are more visually realistic, but both introduce gay protagonists. While *My Brother Nikhil* tells the story of a gay man who is diagnosed with HIV, *Kapoor & Sons* centers on a man who finally comes out to his family after hiding his identity from them for so long.

Case study: Ek Ladki Ko Dekha Toh Aisa Laga *(2019)*

Like *Shubh Mangal Zyada Saavdhan*, which came out a year later, *Ek Ladki Ko Dekha* is a more filmi celebration of queer love than what can be found in parallel cinema or in offbeat films like *Kapoor & Sons*. The title of this film is taken from a well-known song in the film *1942: A Love Story* (1994), and its meaning is "When I saw the girl I felt this way." In the original song, the lyrics go on to describe how the singer feels: "When I saw the girl I felt like a blooming rose, a poet's dream, a ray of light, like a deer in a forest, like a moonlit night, like the words of a song, like a burning flame in a temple." The assumption of the 1994 song is that the speaker who is seeing the girl is male. However, the film *Ek Ladki Ko Dekha* plays with this assumption by introducing a lesbian romance plot, in which the speaker, who feels all these emotions upon seeing her female beloved, is a woman.

Thus, *Ek Ladki Ko Dekha* actively uses Bollywood conventions to tell a lesbian love story. We are introduced from the very beginning to our protagonist, Sweetie, as a paradigmatic lover; she is always daydreaming about falling in love, even as a young child. She sketches pictures of brides and imagines her own wedding while watching the Bollywood romance *Hum Aapke Hain Koun* (1994) on television. The film actively cultivates the audience's heteronormative assumptions, only to debunk them later. For instance, in a scene when Sweetie is remembering her first crush as a child, the film flashes back to Sweetie in school where she is approaching her crush, Gurwinder, with a love letter, but then seeing Gurwinder holding hands with someone else, she runs away, disappointed. Viewers are led to expect that it was the boy of the couple whom Sweetie had been in love with, but later we learn it was the girl; the fact that Gurwinder is a unisex name adds to this actively elicited misunderstanding.

When Sweetie's brother and father discover she is gay, they are shocked and oppose her love. However, because the film abides by Bollywood conventions for representing love as the moral center, once Sweetie is established as the paradigmatic Bollywood lover, the viewer is necessarily on her side to requite her love. This is what it means to abide by a strict moral universe. Like more conventional romances such as *Dilwale Dulhania Le Jayenge* (1995) where the patriarch opposes the marriage, viewers of *Ek Ladki Ko Dekha* know that ultimately the patriarch *has to change his mind* in order for the moral universe to be righted. By maintaining the inherent morality of love and the inherent heroism of the lover, *Ek Ladki Ko Dekha* is able to incorporate an openly lesbian romance into the Bollywood formula.

Understanding Bollywood through its tropes and conventions allows for a more nuanced reading of its representation of gender and sexuality than a focus solely on the themes of marriage and family might allow. For a seemingly family-oriented genre, moments of queer potential are surprisingly common, and having the tools to interpret these moments becomes key to a full understanding of the genre.

Part III

8 The future of Bollywood

This chapter will assess post-2000 trends in Bollywood to begin to hypothesize on the future of Bollywood. A recent change in Indian movie-going practices has been the rise of the multiplex cinema, in which multiple films are shown at a time, as opposed to the single-screen theater which was common until the 2000s and continues to be dominant in rural areas and small towns. While the multiplex indexes increasing wealth inequalities in urban areas, it has also made possible new kinds of experiments with cinema, some of which put pressure on Bollywood conventions while also experimenting with new aesthetic and political possibilities. Building on the various generic features and themes discussed in Parts I and II, this chapter will show how the future of Bollywood is quite heterogeneous, involving not only more realistic and shorter films, but also more hyperbole and filminess: more melodrama, more fantasy, and more cinephilia. I argue that these new trends need to be seen as part of a larger contemporary landscape in India, which is a heterogeneous landscape in which reside multiple possible futures. Reading recent films both for their superficial differences from earlier Bollywood formulas *and* their continuities with earlier films offers a more nuanced reading of the contemporary landscape than is usually on offer in most deterministic accounts.[1]

The multiplex

Perhaps the most significant shift in India's cinematic economy in the last several decades has been the rise of multiplex cinemas in India's large and medium-size cities.[2] This is the result of significant changes in economic policy that took place in the early 1990s, most notably the liberalization of the Indian economy. Economic liberalization reversed the closed, import-substitution economy that India instituted at independence and ended restrictions on small businesses, opening India's markets to foreign investors and changing the focus of the economy to encourage consumption. While most of India's cinema halls continue to be single-screen theaters showing the big-budget film of the week in several showings throughout the day, the multiplex, because it has multiple screens, allows for several films to be shown at once, which incentivizes cinema halls to show smaller budget or art films that would likely not recover costs on a single screen.[3] Ticket prices are generally higher, but there is also a range of types of multiplexes, from upscale, expensive ones in and near posh neighborhoods where tickets can reach ₹500 to mid-range ones where the tickets are significantly cheaper and there is a still a significant amount of class diversity.[4]

The result of this change has been that filmmakers are more willing to take risks with the kinds of films they make, releasing smaller-budget films that need to sell fewer tickets to make money, and more financially risky films that break one or several Bollywood conventions. Such experimentation has become even more common with streaming platforms like Netflix and Amazon, who now produce their own original content that potentially has a wide international audience. Initially, these platforms' films did not even have to go through the bureaucratic process of getting a censor certificate, meaning they could essentially write their own rules, although that might well change in the near future.[5]

Bollywood no more?

Viewers of Bollywood will notice that some recent films seem to have definitively moved away from earlier Bollywood conventions,[6] evident in shorter running times, fewer song-and-dance sequences, less lip-synching, more realistic stories and settings, more character interiority, increased use of English, characters who are skeptical of love, more parody, more explicit sex, more transgressive sexualities, and more moral ambiguity. These films also often begin *in medias res* and are more subtle in their advancement of plot, allowing a greater ambiguity of meaning than conventional Bollywood, which presents its morality in visually deterministic ways. Indeed, many post-2000s films exhibit one or more of these features.

It can be tempting to read these shifts as symptoms of the Hollywoodization or westernization of Bollywood; however, that is not really the case. First of all, a close analysis of Bollywood conventions, as in the previous chapters, shows that they are not rigid rules but actually quite flexible and innovative of new plots and possibilities. It is not only in the 2000s that rules have been broken. Second, although it is tempting to think that these more realistic films are trying to appeal to international audiences, in fact Bollywood films, even these newer ones, still have a very small international audience. Most marketing outside of India, including on Netflix, appeals primarily to Indians who watch films on Netflix (Netflix became available in India in 2016), and secondarily to an Indian viewership overseas, rather than to non-Indian audiences. When Bollywood films do well abroad, as in South America and China, they tend to be classic Bollywood melodramas rather than those that move away from Bollywood conventions.

And lastly, and perhaps most importantly, the apparent move toward more realistic cinema is not the only path that Bollywood is taking. This chapter will show how there are likely multiple futures for Bollywood. One is a move away from Bollywood conventions to appeal to younger viewers, or to viewers with a more international sensibility; another is going even bigger, even more filmi than before. These changes reflect filmmakers' understanding that audiences and aesthetics change over time, and that films must change as well. However, filmmakers are simultaneously aware that Indian viewers want to keep the specificity of the Indian cinema rather than melding it into a generic Hollywood aesthetic. More to the point: Indian viewers, like viewers everywhere, want a choice. Even as more films are being made with a realist aesthetic, Bollywood blockbusters continue to make money, and innovation is taking place in *both* domains.

Hatke cinema

Film critic Rachel Dwyer defines "hatke" cinema (hatke is a slang Hindi word that can be translated as off-center or offbeat) as Indian films that are a little different from the mainstream. The term refers to films that are off-center from Bollywood conventions, displaying many of the new formal criteria listed above. Most hatke films do not have mass appeal, and when they make money it is because they were made on a small budget and can do well in a few small urban centers rather than across India.

Formally and narratively speaking, it might appear that hatke films do not count as Bollywood films but are more similar to art or parallel cinema; however, I am including them here because, at times, they do in fact make use of Bollywood conventions. For example, as discussed in Chapter 7, the hatke film *Kapoor & Sons* (2016) used the libidinal conflict between a mother and her two sons that is found in many Bollywood movies, in addition to the family as the moral center, as the basis for its much more realistic plot, presented via a more restrained visual style. Likewise, a hatke vigilante film like *Angry Indian Goddesses* (2015) mobilizes the morality of close friendship and the 1970s critique of an impotent state to advance a very contemporary critique of victim-blaming in the context of sexual assault. *Kaminey* (2009), although more gritty and dark than most Bollywood films, nevertheless builds on the convention of twins and double roles to tell a story about human corruptibility. As we saw in the previous chapter, a film like *Ek Ladki Ko Dekha Toh Aisa Laga* (2019) uses the convention of love as the moral center to tell a lesbian love story. Even contemporary films that poke fun at Bollywood conventions for representing love, such as *I Hate Luv Storys* (2010), are made more meaningful when seen in relation to those conventions: we then understand what they are parodying but also how much they end up relying on those very same conventions. Any of these contemporary, hatke films can be read on their own, but reading them as part of a longer history of Bollywood conventions enhances their meaning. Thus seeing hatke as a radical break from Bollywood conventions is less useful than seeing it as a further reconfiguration of those conventions for a new era.

At the same time, hatke films often allow for the emergence of new politics and sensibilities that sometimes could not be accommodated within Bollywood's traditional moral universe.[7] In *Queen* (2014), the protagonist travels to Europe on her own after her fiancé cancels their wedding, and, when she returns, makes the decision to stay single even when he wants her back. *Kapoor & Sons* and *Aligarh* (2015) feature protagonists who are gay, and *Aligarh* in particular deals with homophobic violence, persecution, and mental illness. *Margarita With a Straw* (2014) tells the queer love story of a woman with cerebral palsy. *Chandni Bar* (2001) focuses on the life of a bar dancer and *Chameli* (2004) sensitively tells the story of a sex worker. *Dum Laga Ke Haisha* (2015) is the love story of a woman who is overweight. *Newton* (2017) offers a searing critique of the marginalization of adivasis (indigenous people) during a national election. *Love Sex Aur Dhokha* (2010) is shot like a student documentary with a hand-held camera and amateur actors. *Taare Zameen Par* (2007) talks about learning disabilities in children. *Hindi Medium* (2017) is about the struggles families have in entering the middle class when they don't speak fluent English. *My Name is Khan* (2010) features a character who has Asperger's Syndrome and also addresses the issue of Islamophobia in the United States after September 11. *Gully Boy* (2019) is the story of a young rapper in Mumbai's burgeoning hip-hop scene. Hatke films also often represent sex more frankly and without coyness or euphemism. This marks a move away from the suggestive erotics of much Bollywood cinema into something more straightforward; it also destigmatizes sex and presents it as part of everyday life rather than something transcendent or spiritual. Women who have sex or desire sex are not seen as morally reprehensible in hatke cinema, and older people are allowed to have a sexuality, as in *Kapoor & Sons*, in which the elderly grandfather asks his grandson to download pornography for him on his iPad. In all these cases, we see new representations of people and topics that had largely been absent in conventional Bollywood cinema. For many young viewers in India, these films provide a refreshing change, even if they also enjoy more conventional Bollywood movies.

Blockbusters

Yet as this book has shown, new ideas can also be presented using Bollywood conventions. We have seen, for instance, how *Ek Ladki Ko Dekha Toh Aisa Laga* (2019) uses the Bollywood ideal of the lover to tell a lesbian love story. Blockbuster films like *Veer-Zaara* (2004), *Main Hoon Na* (2004), and *Bajrangi Bhaijaan* (2015) offer messages of India–Pakistan peace even as they make use of a hyperbolic visual style and a formulaic moral universe. These examples suggest that while hatke films are offering something new, they are not the only place where we can glimpse Bollywood's future.

A look at the largest money-makers of 2000–19[8] shows a surprising diversity of plots even for high-budget, mainstream films. *Lagaan* (2001) was massively popular but also offered a new kind of aesthetic to the Bollywood blockbuster. It mobilized nationalist sentiment, but did so by imagining an inclusive nation (rather than a chauvinistic one) and by bringing together the excitement of cricket, India's national sport, with an anti-colonial political message, all packaged via a stunning soundtrack, a love story, and dramatic visuals. *Krrish* (2006) was India's first homegrown superhero movie that utilized international-level special effects. *Ghajini* (2008) was a violent revenge story of a man with short-term amnesia. *3 Idiots* (2009), another blockbuster, was simultaneously a comedy and a poignant critique of India's intense and competitive education system. *Dabangg* (2010) offered an affectionate parody of the Bollywood vigilante film, while also being a vigilante police film. *Chak De India* (2007) and *Dangal* (2016) were both sports films featuring female athletes. These brief examples show the wide range of box-office success in Bollywood, and also shows a significant variety in storylines that belies any neat hatke/blockbuster divide.

Karan Johar and Farah Khan, discussed in detail in Chapters 4 and 5, are two directors who offer a futurity to Bollywood not by taming it into something more realist but by wholeheartedly embracing its excessive aesthetic and narrative qualities. Farah Khan especially, in structuring the moral universe of her film *Om Shanti Om* (2007) specifically over the love of Bollywood – so that the hero is a superfan and the villain believes the future is only in Hollywood – merges the love of the cinema with the characteristically Bollywood moral universe, allegorizing the futurity of Bollywood even while making an enjoyable film. *Om Shanti Om* is discussed in more detail below.

Case study: Aamir Khan[9]

Current Bollywood superstar Aamir Khan is a useful case from which to understand the multiple possible futures of Bollywood. On one hand Khan is appreciated as "the thinking man's hero"[10] for his choice of films and his progressive politics, which many think distinguish him from the mainstream of Bollywood stars. In addition, he has starred in, directed, and produced several small-budget and hatke films, which have led some critics to see him as a star who desires to move away from the formulaic plots of conventional Bollywood toward more realistic films, films without songs, films with themes not usually addressed by popular cinema, feminist films, and so on. This, combined with his commitment to method acting and authenticity – for instance, gaining more than 60 pounds for his role as a retired wrestler in *Dangal* (2016) and then losing it all at once – his stated dislike for awards shows, and his decision to commit to shooting only one film at a time,[11] has associated his name with a certain integrity and restraint, as opposed to the populism and overstatement that is seen to mark the rest of the industry.

Yet at the same time, Aamir Khan has starred in three of the nine highest domestic grossing Bollywood films of all time, *Dhoom 3* (2013), *PK* (2014), and *Dangal* (2016), and his *3 Idiots* (2009) is high on the list as well. Thus understanding his body of work as a teleology or a progressive move away from melodrama toward more "serious" art forms misses out on the hybridity that characterizes his work – a hybridity that suggests a more complex future for Bollywood as a whole. Indeed, Khan has always been interested in *both* mainstream and hatke films throughout his career. 1999 saw the release of *Earth* and *Sarfarosh*: the former a sensitive portrayal of religious conflict leading up to the Partition and the latter a thriller in which the villain is a Pakistani spy trying to wreak havoc in India. In

2001, *Lagaan* was a dramatic epic on the coming together of rural Indians to beat the British at a game of cricket, and the same year Khan starred in *Dil Chahta Hai*, an offbeat story of three friends living swanky lifestyles in Mumbai and Sydney. In 2006, *Rang De Basanti* criticized the political apathy of India's youth, and *Fanaa* had Khan playing a Kashmiri terrorist. In 2008 and 2009 he starred in *Ghajini* and *3 Idiots* respectively, both of which were commercially successful,[12] and the following year his production company released *Peepli Live*, a quirky, low-budget comedy that attended to the phenomenon of farmer suicides in rural India. Blockbuster *Dhoom 3* was a high-adrenalin action film and *PK* criticized godmen and religiosity in India. These are not, it seems, contradictions for Khan but part of an overall experimental mode. His works do not advance a narrative progress for Bollywood's improvement or for its homogenization into international norms but an experimentation with the possibilities of popular cinema itself. Aamir Khan's case suggests that hatke and blockbuster films need to be understood not as divergent paths but as part of Bollywood's inherent flexibility.

Social reform films

Another accusation made toward contemporary Bollywood cinema is that it unthinkingly celebrates India's turn toward capitalism by featuring only wealthy, urban characters rather than, as in the films of the earlier decades, characters from society's underclass, such as union leaders, dock workers, fishermen, and poets. The convention discussed in Chapter 1 in which excessive wealth is inherently corrupting is generally no longer operative, with Bollywood films of the twenty-first century much more comfortable showing their heroes living in grandeur.

However, in this domain as well we see multiple trends. There has been a recent spate of explicitly political films, many of which are set in India's small towns and rural areas and deal with social issues such as unequal access to electricity (*Swades* [2004]), government corruption (*Madaari* [2016]), sexual violence (*Pink* [2016]), women's lack of access to toilets (*Toilet: Ek Prem Katha* [2017]), the prohibitive expense of sanitary pads (*Pad Man* [2018]), caste discrimination (*Article 15* [2019]), and so on. These films address serious topics, but they still operate within a Bollywood structure, in which the hero is the character who overcomes the obstacles of social conservatism and a recalcitrant state to make the world better. These films mostly move away from urban settings and the use of English that we see in many hatke films, but have somewhat shorter running times (although still well over two hours), are less reliant on song-and-dance sequences, and are more realistic in their execution.

Questioning good and evil

While in the classic Bollywood film, there is a fairly clear distinction between good and evil, in recent years we have seen more of an attempt by some filmmakers to blur those lines. We saw intimations of this in the 1970s, as discussed in Chapter 6, when the hero pursued justice outside the law. In that decade, however, the hero of dubious morality often had to die by the end; he was not allowed a happy ending. By contrast, today we have more films in which conventional moral standards are called into question, and in which characters who embrace those dubious standards still get the possibility of a happy ending. Some of these are new vigilante films, which update the "angry young man" films of the 1970s to address new social crises that, these films suggest, cannot be resolved within the justice system, but require extrajudicial justice. Unlike the 1970s films, these often feature reluctant vigilantes, men and women who do not want to act outside the law but are, the films suggest, compelled to by an utterly inept police and judiciary. In *Viruddh* (2005), Vidyadhar is a jovial elderly man who waits for justice in his son's murder but gets increasingly disillusioned by the corruption of the police and courts. Finally, utterly helpless, he goes and shoots his son's murderer himself. In this case, he is acquitted of the murder when he explains the reasons behind his actions to the judge. We see a similar story in *Mom* (2017), in which the protagonist's daughter is brutally gang-raped and left for dead, and the accused men get away with it because of bribery and corruption. When Mom decides to take revenge herself, the private investigator who helps her admits, "Mujhe nahin pata jo main kar raha hoon, woh thik hai ya galat hai," ("I don't know if what I'm doing is wrong or right"), to which she replies, "Galat hai, lekin us se bhi zyada galat hai, kuch nahin karna. Galat aur bahut galat mein se chunna ho, toh aap kya chunenge?" ("It is wrong, but not doing anything is more wrong; between wrong and more wrong, which would you choose?") We see a similar sensibility in *Gabbar Is Back* (2015), in which Aditya, a college professor, moonlights as a vigilante who murders corrupt government officials. The question of whether his actions are justified is debated in the film, which shows people gathered in crowds or in trains or on social media debating what morality means in a fundamentally unjust system.

In *Gunday* (2014), the protagonists are criminals but also good guys. Even the police describe them as "aam logon ke liye massiahs" ("messiahs for the common people") for the way they provide for the poor. Conversely, the policemen act like villains; at one point Bikram says to the cop, "Ho aap vardiwale, par aap ke tevar hain gundon wale" ("You are a man of the law but you act like a criminal"). The ending of this film is a celebration of being "gunday" or gangsters, and even though the protagonists are shot by the police as they try to escape, we don't discover whether they are killed or not, thus allowing the possibility that despite their crimes, they can run free.

Kaminey (2009) – whose title can be translated as "Bastards" – shows a world in which everybody is out for themselves, and even the moral character Guddu – whose name is a play on the English "good" – has to work with gangsters and drug-dealing cops in order to advance his life plan. Here, crime is not separated from morality, but seen as part of the fabric of a corrupted moral universe. Thus although Guddu's twin brother Charlie fixes horse races and is involved in drugs and theft, in the end, his dream is allowed to come true with little consequence. In addition, there is no justice from the law; the policemen are completely in league with the international drug traffickers.[13]

Female-centered films

One of the most important trends in the multiplex era has been an increasing number of female-centered films. As we saw in Chapter 7, there is a longer tradition of strong female roles in Bollywood, but, as a whole, Bollywood becomes more outspoken about its feminism in the twenty-first century. Many female-centered films continue to revolve around love, even as they offer different interpretations of what love might mean to the contemporary woman. In *Queen* (2014), Rani's fiancé Vijay cancels their wedding at the last minute; although dejected, Rani decides to go on their honeymoon to Europe by herself, and the film traces her adventures there. This film specifically references and then upturns ideas of female passivity; when Vijay first leaves her, she desperately pleads with him to change his mind: "Vijay, aise khatam mat karo. Main, jaise aap kahenge, waise hi karungi … Main haath jodti hoon, aap mujhse shaadi karo, mujhse kaun shaadi karega?" ("Vijay, don't end it like this. I'll do whatever you want … I'm begging you, please marry me. Who will marry me now?"). However, when venturing out on her own, she gradually finds her own independence and ends up rejecting her fiancé when he comes back to her. The film ends with her realizing that being single is better than settling for a fickle and disrespectful man. *English Vinglish* (2012) is the story of Shashi, a housewife mocked for her poor English by her husband and daughter. When she travels on her own to New York for a wedding she secretly starts taking English conversation classes there. In the class she meets new friends and even a possible love interest. These two films end differently: in *Queen*, Rani decides to enjoy being single, whereas in *English Vinglish* Shashi returns to her husband after her adventures abroad, suggesting that there is no one path for feminist futures. In another female-centered film, *Aiyyaa* (2012), Meenakshi is the protagonist and lover, and it is she who pursues Surya, secretly trying to steal glimpses of his body while he is changing his clothes and fantasizing about them together through highly eroticized song-and-dance sequences. Even while Meenakshi is going through the motions of preparing for her arranged marriage, she fantasizes about being with Surya instead, and in the end makes sure she marries Surya rather than her fiancé. And in *Mom* (2017), Devki is the one who takes on avenging her step-daughter's brutal gang-rape by assassinating the acquitted rapists one by one. Again, this film plays off of sexist assumptions about women's agency, so that when the police notice that the rapists are being killed off, they immediately assume that it is Devki's husband who is having them killed, rather than her; they tail him, and ironically their sexism means she remains free to continue with her deadly plan.

Even in more traditional romances or love stories, more space is given to women's choice and agency. *Badrinath ki Dulhania* (2017) starts out as a conventional love story, with Badri, the son of a large feudal household, pursuing

Vaidehi after meeting her at a wedding. However, Vaidehi is determined to begin a career as a flight attendant before getting married and thus refuses Badri's proposal. Her family's financial hardships eventually compel her to say yes, but she does not show up on their wedding day. Angry at the abandonment, Badri goes so far as to kidnap Vaidehi to try to force her to marry him. But Vaidehi is insistent that her dreams matter to her more than marriage. As they spend time together in Singapore where she is in flight school, they grow closer and his ego and narcissism begin to be tamed. Finally she agrees to marry him only under the condition that she finish school first. In this case, the moral universe resolves only when Badri realizes that Vaidehi's career and aspirations are equally important to his pursuit. What begins as a vision of feudal masculinity ends with the reconciliation of love with female aspiration.

Veere di Wedding (2018) and *Angry Young Goddesses* (2015) are buddy films that explicitly center on the aggressions, both small and large, that women have to face. In the former, Avni's boyfriend rejects her when she kisses him on the dance floor, finding her too sexually aggressive. Sakshi's husband finds her masturbating and tries to blackmail her, threatening to tell her parents, until she finally just tells them herself. Kalindi, for her part, asks her fiancé, Reshab, "Who are we doing this wedding for? Us or your family?", thus suggesting the insufficiency of the traditional wedding for some twenty-first-century women. By foregrounding female characters and allowing women to speak for themselves, these films offer a new path for Bollywood in the twenty-first century.

Case study: Rani Mukerji

Rani Mukerji is a top Bollywood actor whose career trajectory spans the epic romances of the 1990s and the more hatke, female-centered films of the 2000s and 2010s. She made her name in romantic films such as *Ghulam* (1998), *Kuch Kuch Hota Hai* (1998), and *Har Dil Jo Pyar Karega* (2000). In 2002 and 2003 Mukerji played the lead roles in *Saathiya* and *Chalte Chalte*, both of which model a new kind of love story by featuring couples who struggle with post-marriage romance. These films highlight female subjectivity more than the traditional Bollywood romance. *Hum Tum* (2004) was another contemporary romance, in which the characters fall in love and then out of love. These new types of love stories changed the way love is represented in many films and challenged assumptions about female passivity and male aggressiveness in relation to love.

In this period, Mukerji also began to accept different kinds of roles for women that had not really been seen in Bollywood earlier. In *Veer-Zaara* (2004) she plays a Pakistani feminist lawyer who saves Veer from prison, in *Black* (2005) she plays a woman who is visually- as well as hearing-impaired, in *Bunty Aur Babli* (2005) she plays a thief and con artist, in *Kabhi Alvida Naa Kehna* (2006) she plays a woman in an unhappy marriage who begins an extramarital affair, in *Laaga Chunari Mein Daag* (2007) she plays a call girl, and in *Dil Bole Hadippa!* (2009) she plays a woman who loves cricket and dresses up as a man to join a team. In *No One Killed Jessica* (2011), she plays a tough and ruthless reporter intent on finding out the truth about a mishandled murder case, in *Aiyyaa* (2012) she plays a college librarian who gets obsessed with a painter she meets in the library, in *Mardaani* (2014) she plays a cop who becomes a vigilante to bust a child sex trafficking ring, and in *Hichki* (2016) she plays a teacher who has Tourette's Syndrome. Not content to play simply older women or mothers, the significant range of Mukerji's roles allows us to reimagine the range of roles given to women in their thirties and forties. Likewise, as shown by *Kabhi Alvida Naa Kehna*, *Dil Bole Hadippa!*, and especially *Aiyyaa*, middle age has not required Mukerji to give up on love or don an asexual persona. *Aiyyaa* is all about the sheer power of physical and sensory attraction and Mukerji plays the role of Meenakshi with humor as well as sensuality, offering a new model for middle-aged femininity for the twenty-first century.

The impact of #MeToo

The "casting couch" has long been a euphemistic way of talking about aspiring actors and models having to perform sexual acts in order to get ahead in the Bombay film industry. Recently, however, with the rise of the global #MeToo movement, such discussions are becoming much more open, and 2018–19 witnessed a large number of public accusations of sexual harassment against big-name Bollywood figures.

Intensified global conversations about sexual violence have also affected Bollywood plots. There is more awareness around issues of stalking and obsessive behavior, even though films about love continue to walk the line between representing love as an irresistible force that overwhelms the lover and acknowledging that a happy ending or requited love requires consent. On a 2014 episode of his television series *Satyamev Jayate* that focused on toxic masculinity, actor Aamir Khan presented a short video criticizing how Hindi cinema minimizes the importance of consent and hosted a discussion between three female actors on the issue. Khan admitted:

> Shayid maine bhi bahut sari gustakiyaan ki apni filmon mein, aur mujhe bada sharam hai, is baat ka … Sachmuch mein, us waqt hum samajhte nahin ki hum jo dikha rahe hain, ya jo hum scene kar rahe hai, us ka kya asar hoga, aur is baat ka ehsaas mujhe aaj hai.

> [Perhaps I too made lots of presumptions in my films, and I'm really embarrassed about it … Honestly, at that time we didn't understand that what we were showing, what scenes we were making, what effect those will have on people, but now I realize that.][14]

There have also been a number of films that take a much more contemporary perspective on sexual violence and rape, including *Mardaani* (2014), *Angry Indian Goddesses* (2015), *Pink* (2016), *Maatr* (2017), *Mom* (2017), *Bhoomi* (2017), and *Anarkali of Arrah* (2017). Most of these are quite realistic and some are starkly graphic in their representations of rape. They talk not only about sexual violence but how difficult it is for survivors to get justice in sexual violence cases. In *Mom*, high school student Arya is at a party and rebuffs a classmate who has been sending her sexually explicit texts. He complains to his older friends who then get back at Arya by kidnapping her, raping her, and leaving her for dead in a city sewer. The family tries to go to the police but they botch the case and the four accused men get acquitted, driving Arya into depression. Unable to watch Arya's misery, her stepmother Devki hires a private detective who tracks the acquitted rapists down so that she can take vengeance against them herself. She has one of the men castrated, kills the second, and frames the third man for the murder. Like the other vigilante films discussed in Chapter 6, vigilante action is presented here as the only possible form of justice in a thoroughly corrupt system. By foregrounding sexual violence and the lack of resource for its survivors, all these films respond to increased awareness of this issue while still using Bollywood conventions.

New masculinities

Along with new kinds of roles for women and a foregrounding of issues surrounding sexual violence and justice, we see in recent films experiments with new models of masculinity. Today's Bollywood characters struggle to figure out what masculinity looks like in the twenty-first century, freed as young people partially feel from static inherited conceptions of what it means to be a man. As discussed throughout the book, the figure of the lover is often male, and since love can be so debilitating, this often mitigates the hyper-masculine image of male heroism that circulates in Hollywood. However, the question of what it means to be a man in relation to changing gender roles becomes even more central to twenty-first-century Bollywood. In *Dil Chahta Hai* (2001) the three friends represent different understandings of what it means to be a man. Akash, for instance, is a goofball who finds chivalry outdated. In a scene in Sydney where Shalini gets scared when approached by a homeless man in an isolated subway station, Akash runs back as if to save her but then hugs the homeless man where it was expected that he might punch him or otherwise defend her honor, asking him, "You ok Mike? Did she scare you?" This humorous twist, underscored by the dramatic music when Akash turns toward the homeless man, deliberately plays with expectations for masculinity in Bollywood.

We see similar questionings of traditional masculinity across new films. In *Hum Dil De Chuke Sanam* (1999), when Vanraj announces his plan to go to Europe to find his wife Nandini's former lover, whom she is still in love with, his father yells at him, "Tum Rajput khandan se ho. Mard ho. Ek aurat ko kaboo mein nahin rakh sakte? Kahan gayi tumhari mardaanagi?" ("You're from a Rajput family. You are a man and you can't control a woman? What happened to your manhood?"), to which Vanraj rhetorically responds, "Kya mardaanagi aurat ko kamzor maan kar uski khushion par zabardasti kaboo karne mein hai?" ("Does masculinity mean assuming a woman is weak and forcefully restraining her happiness?"). In *Aiyyaa* (2012), alongside the main romance between Meenakshi and Surya, there is a second romance between Meenakshi's brother Nana and her colleague Maina, both of whom are somewhat eccentric. Nana shows no qualities of conventional masculinity; he flunks out of school, daydreams of opening a refuge for stray dogs, and is overall a ridiculous character, complaining, melodramatically, that "Is desh mein na kutton ke liye jagah hai, na kutton se jee lagane wale insaanon ke liye!" ("This country has room for neither dogs nor dog lovers!"). He falls in love with Maina at first sight and is happy to be led into her house full of strange sounds and images of Bollywood star John Abraham plastered everywhere. This non-normative romance puts pressure on conventional ideals of both masculinity and femininity. Likewise, in *3 Idiots* (2009), the protagonist Rancho cares little about material success. This film, which is a critique of an education system that focuses on churning out engineers rather than the real value of learning, offers, in Rancho, a model of masculinity that is generous rather than career-oriented. He is made fun of by a classmate for wanting to be a "mere" teacher rather than a businessman or engineer. Although, as discussed in Chapter 7, this is not entirely new as 1950s Bollywood heroes tended to not be very ambitious or driven, it does go against dominant ideas of masculinity that emphasize providing for the family; and it is this Rancho who gets the film's only love story, emphasizing his moral centrality. We see a similar reconfiguration of conventional masculinity in *Badhaai Ho* (2018), whose 25-year-old protagonist, Nakul, is shocked when his middle-aged mother announces that she is pregnant. As a young man, he feels that he should be the one in his sexual prime, but he cannot concentrate on his own romance because of the sudden realization of his parents' – and specifically his mother's – sexuality. The moral universe is disrupted here by the narcissism of the protagonist and it is only restored when he realizes that his devoted mother has a sexuality too. And of course, a film like *Shubh Mangal Zyada Saavdhan* (2020), discussed in Chapter 7, offers a model of masculinity that is openly gay.

Visually, too, men's bodies are represented differently in twenty-first-century Bollywood. Feminist film criticism has talked about how the cinematic camera is implicitly positioned to offer a male gaze, which means that the female body is necessarily treated in an objectifying way.[15] Even when films have a range of plots, this in-built feature of the gaze makes the cinema inherently misogynistic. While male stars in the early decades of Bollywood rarely danced and there was much less attention focused on their bodies, there has been an increasing attention to the male body, and an increasing trend for male stars to beef up their bodies. While this could be attributed in part to increasing pressures on body image, it also opens up the space for new, queer viewing positions rather than assuming an implicit heterosexual male viewer as the ideal spectator for Bollywood films. Along with this has been increased attention to male dancing, and an expectation that their bodies should look aesthetically pleasing when they dance, something earlier expected only of female actors. Moreover, men are also presented as scantily clad, at times even more so than their female counterparts; for instance, Aamir Khan is half-clothed in the "Guzarish" song of *Ghajini* (2008) and the camera focuses on his body more than his co-star Asin's (Figure 8.1).[16]

Choreographer and director Farah Khan plays with the reversal of the gaze in "Dard-e-Disco," a song sequence in *Om Shanti Om* (2007). In this song, it is Shah Rukh Khan's scantily-clad body that is the object of the filmic gaze, reversing the characteristic setup of the item number (Figure 8.2). In an interview, Farah Khan says she "kept telling [Shah Rukh], 'You're the item girl in the song,'" explaining further, "Maine Shah Rukh ko bilkul jaise koi male director heroine ke upar gaana picturize karega, aur woh heroine ko paani se nikaalega, ya heroine ko bighoega, maine Shah Rukh ko waise hi treat kiya hai" ("Just like a male director might picturize a song for a female item girl, asking her to emerge from water, or drenching her, I've treated Shah Rukh

Figure 8.1 The half-dressed male body offers the possibility of alternative viewing positions to the heterosexual male gaze, here in *Ghajini* (2008).

Figure 8.2 Shah Rukh Khan is the "item girl" in "Dard-e-Disco" in *Om Shanti Om* (2007).

Khan the same way").[17] By recalling conventions of representing the female body and by naming Shah Rukh the "item girl," Farah Khan deliberately queers the conventional Bollywood gaze.

The future of Bollywood

It is, of course, impossible to predict the future of Bollywood. This chapter has argued that although Bollywood films have tended to operate via a fairly rigid moral universe, new experiments and innovations, including the intensification of Bollywood aesthetics, might allow Bollywood to withstand cultural homogenization while also offering options to its viewers that cover a wider range of political and social issues that were not necessarily part of Bollywood's earlier repertoire.

Bollywood's futurity is best allegorized in Farah Khan's *Om Shanti Om* (2007), a film that simultaneously parodies and abides by Bollywood's formulaic moral structure and makes cinephilia the center of the moral universe. Om, the film's hero, is the ultimate fan; he loves everything about Bollywood, including its hyperbole and aesthetics of overstatement. Conversely, the villain is Mukesh, a film director who does many terrible things, including abandoning his pregnant girlfriend and marrying another woman because her father is going to invest in his studio. Then, in order to silence Shanti's complaints, he kills her. But in addition to greed, lust, betrayal, and murder, Mukesh is also guilty of another crime: he has no faith in Bollywood. When Shanti says she wants to marry him, he mocks her, criticizing her for being too easily influenced by movies. Then later, when he returns to India after a 25-year stint in the United States, he has completely lost faith in Bollywood. He changes his name to "Mike" and tells people, "Call me Mike, everyone in Hollywood does." This reference to Mukesh having acceded to Hollywood's hegemony is Farah Khan's way of criticizing those who predict Bollywood's death in a globalized world. Moreover, when Om suggests that they make a film on reincarnation, Mukesh/Mike scoffs at him, saying, "Reincarnation, poorna janam, aaj ke zamane mein, who's going to believe that?" ("Reincarnation, rebirth, these days who's going to believe that?"). Mukesh is the villain precisely because he doesn't believe in filmi lines or filmi emotions, in impossible plots or transcendent love.

By aligning the moral universe with cinephilia on one side and a mistrust of Bollywood on the other, *Om Shanti Om* makes a spectacular metacommentary on the overall critical sense, among educated audiences and critics, that Bollywood is outdated and irrelevant to the contemporary world. Mukesh scoffs at reincarnation, but even we the audience are surprised, in the film's ending, that the ghost of Shantipriya is in fact real, suggesting that we too might not have fully believed. The film suggests that viewing Bollywood with a skeptical eye is not a sign of sophistication, but an easy critique that reflects distance and disdain. By contrast, Bollywood cinema asks for an engagement founded in love and intimacy. It asks us to be full of faith – faith in magical transformation, in spectacle, in love, in Bollywood itself.

Notes

Introduction

1 The phrase "grammar of Hindi cinema" was used by Rosie Thomas ("Melodrama," 158) and Ashis Nandy (89). Although their two articles were written quite early in Hindi cinema studies, and need updating in terms of the films and issues they cover, both are influential to my approach in this book.

2 Scholars who have discussed the Bollywood production process include Rachel Dwyer and Divia Patel, Tejaswini Ganti (*Bollywood*, esp. 56–84, and *Producing*), Sangita Gopal (*Conjugations*); M. Madhava Prasad, Rosie Thomas ("Melodrama," 179–180), Ashish Rajadhyaksha, Ravi Vasudevan ("Meanings"), and Clare Wilkinson-Weber.

3 As Ashish Rajadhyaksha confirms, "The Indian cinema, of course, has celebrated its centenary, but the industry, in the current sense of the term, might be most usefully traced to the post-Second World War boom in production" (28); and later he elaborates that the post-World War II era is "when the Indian cinema first defined itself as a mass-culture industry" (31). See also Bhaumik, 2.

4 Ganti, *Producing*.

5 Rajadhyaksha, 30. Yet, as Sangita Gopal notes, "many of the features that we now associate with New Bollywood were already present in the *masala* film of the 1970s" (*Conjugations*, 11). Thus, I resist the call to define Bollywood only as a decade-long marketing phenomenon that, while founded in the cinema, goes beyond the cinema to refer to a global product (Rajadhyaksha, 28), or as "a transnational Hinglish media ecology" (Basu, "Dharmendra," 86). I also risk the "anachronistic usage of the term" that Vasudevan warns against, by referring to pre-1990s films as Bollywood, in my deliberate attempt to highlight commonalities within the genre across multiple decades ("Meanings").

6 "Don't Call." See also Vasudevan, "Meanings."

7 Anand, A21.

8 Elison, Novetzke, and Rotman, 16.

9 Gopal, *Conjugations*, 11.

10 Gopal, *Conjugations*, 14.

11 The name of the city was formally changed from Bombay to Mumbai in 1995. Thus although the "B" in Bollywood indexes Bombay, I will refer to the city as Mumbai.

12 Elison, Novetzke, and Rotman also define Bollywood generically rather than as a function of the political economy (16–17).

13 Ganti, *Bollywood*, 140.

14 Nandy, 90.

15 Rajagopalan, 2 and 15.

16 Dean; A. Iyer.
17 Rajadhyaksha, 29.
18 Mengying.
19 Hassan.
20 Anustup Basu argues that the 1950s was actually marked by many attempts at global collaboration – not literally remaking Bollywood films in English, but seeking out international partnerships. Most of these attempts were short-lived or unsuccessful ("Filmfare").
21 Ganti, *Bollywood*, 205.
22 Bhaumik, 1.
23 N. Majumdar, 161.
24 Bali.
25 Sarkar, 77–78.
26 N. Majumdar, 162.
27 Thomas, "Indian Cinema," 120.
28 C. King.
29 The next three largest, Hollywood, Tamil, and Telugu cinemas, each hold around 15 percent of the box office share (Laghate).
30 L. Iyer, 12–13.
31 As Iyer documents, Sridevi "made eighty-three films in Telugu, seventy-two in Hindi, seventy-one in Tamil, twenty-three in Malayalam, and six in Kannada" (L. Iyer, 45).
32 For more on parallel cinema, see Krishen, Dass ("Cloud"), Hood, and R. Majumdar. Rosie Thomas discusses how western critics view parallel/arthouse Indian cinema more favorably than they do Bollywood ("Indian Cinema," 118).
33 Ganti, *Bollywood*, 21.
34 Dwyer, "Zara Hatke," 199.
35 Vanita, *Dancing*, 147.
36 Nandy, 90; Prasad, 49.
37 Dissanayake, 1.
38 Thomas, "Indian Cinema," 130.
39 Ganti, *Bollywood*, 141.
40 Vasudevan, "Melodramatic," 30.
41 Gopalan, 11.
42 Thomas, "Indian Cinema," 120.
43 Quoted in Gehlawat, 6–7.

1. Structure

1 Thomas, "Melodrama," 159.
2 Braudy, 614.
3 Braudy, 619.
4 See also Thomas, "Indian Cinema," 117–119.
5 Thomas, "Indian Cinema," 120.
6 Braudy, 616.
7 Thomas, "Melodrama," 159; Nandy, 90–91.
8 Thomas, "Melodrama," 159 and 163.
9 Thomas, "Melodrama," 164.
10 Ganti, *Bollywood*, 106.
11 Thomas, "Melodrama," 165.
12 Thomas, "Melodrama," 160.
13 Thomas, "Melodrama," 168.
14 Wilkinson-Weber.
15 Thomas, "Melodrama," 172.

16 Malhotra and Alagh, 30.
17 Thomas, "Melodrama," 172.
18 Nandy, 91.
19 Creekmur, 181; see also Mishra, 29–30.
20 Vijay Mishra's extensive analysis of repeated tropes in *Amar Akbar Anthony* shows how certain microstructures of the film are repeated at various points to produce a form built on repetition (171–178).
21 Elison, Novetzke, and Rotman, 4.
22 Nandy, 92.
23 Nandy, 95.
24 Pinto, 53–54.
25 Thomas, "Melodrama," 165.
26 Thomas, "Melodrama," 166.
27 By "fictive" here I mean not false but, as in the dictionary definition, "created by the imagination."
28 Vanita, *Dancing*, 32.
29 Ganti, *Bollywood*, 149.

2. Love

1 Martin, 244.
2 Chintamani.
3 Chintamani, 74.
4 Orsini, 19.
5 Martin, 241.
6 Sinha, 66.
7 Johnson.
8 Martin, 244.
9 Creekmur, 176.
10 Prince Saleem in *Mughal-e-Azam* (1960), when reprimanded by his advisor for being distracted from issues of the state by his love for Anarkali, accuses him of harboring a "mohabbat ki dushmani" ("enmity toward love").
11 Gopal, *Conjugations*, 2.
12 Dwyer, "*Yeh Shaadi*," 72.
13 Dwyer, "*Yeh Shaadi*," 74.

3. Song and dance

1 Vohra, "Bodily."
2 "Chingari."
3 Cohan, 1.
4 N. Majumdar, 164.
5 N. Majumdar, 168.
6 "Round."
7 N. Majumdar, 169.
8 N. Majumdar, 170–171.
9 Mendonca.
10 N. Majumdar, 174–175.
11 N. Majumdar, 171.
12 N. Majumdar, 163.
13 N. Majumdar, 172.
14 N. Majumdar, 162.
15 Ganti, *Bollywood*, 90.
16 http://agentsofishq.com/tag/sexy–saturday–songs/, accessed June 9, 2020.

17 Dudrah, 296–297.
18 Vanita, *Dancing*, 67–68.
19 Dudrah, 298.
20 Dissanayake, 1.
21 Dass, "Cinetopia," 109.
22 Coppola, 900–901.
23 Dass, "Cinetopia," 114.
24 "Chammak Chalo."
25 "Zoya Akhtar."
26 Sharpe, 67.
27 A. Kabir, 154.
28 Dwyer, "Erotics," 159.
29 Mulvey.
30 As argued by Nijhawan, 106–107.

4. Visual style

1 Ganti, *Bollywood*, 84–87.
2 Nandy, 90.
3 Kapur, 211; Dwyer and Patel, 14; Mishra, 9.
4 Kapur, 211.
5 Dwyer and Patel, 102–180.
6 Raheja and Kothari, 74.
7 Dwyer and Patel, 57.
8 https://mrandmrs55.com/2012/09/18/what-is-eastman-color/, accessed May 20, 2020.
9 https://mrandmrs55.com/2012/09/18/what-is-eastman-color/, accessed June 1, 2020. As the authors write, Bollywood films used the less expensive Eastmancolor instead of the Technicolor that was being used in Hollywood at the time, which led to a significant amount of fading over the years.
10 Dwyer and Patel, 59.
11 Wilkinson-Weber.
12 Vanita, *Dancing*, 215.
13 Wilkinson-Weber.
14 Siddiqui.
15 Siddiqui.
16 Wilkinson-Weber; Dwyer and Patel, 97.
17 Dwyer, *100 Bollywood Films*, 71.
18 Wilkinson-Weber.
19 Dwyer and Patel, 59.
20 Dwyer, "Hindi," 196.
21 Mazumdar, 138.
22 Ahuja.
23 Ahuja.
24 Mandal.
25 Mazumdar, 144.
26 Sahota.
27 Ahuja.
28 "Devdas, the Making."
29 Creekmur, 186.
30 Khubchandani, 73–74.
31 Kapur, 221.
32 Kapur, 222.
33 "I Can Never."

34 Anjaria, *Reading*, 146.
35 Vanita, *Dancing*, 204.
36 Khubchandani, 73.
37 Muyiwa.
38 Khubchandani, 73–74.
39 L. Iyer, 74.
40 L. Iyer, 98.
41 L. Iyer, 65–66.
42 Khubchandani, 75.
43 Gopal, "Sentimental," 33. See also Dwyer and Patel, 45–46.
44 Prasad, 20–21.
45 Dwyer, "Hindi," 196.
46 Ganti, *Bollywood*, 122.
47 Joshi, 8.
48 Sangita Gopal considers this kind of frontal address as potentially democratic (*Conjugations*, 129).
49 Kapur, 220–221.
50 Kapur, 222.
51 Ghosh, 98; Ganti, *Bollywood*, 94–95.
52 Subramaniam.
53 Ghosh, 100.
54 Ghosh, 100.
55 Ghosh, 100.
56 Ghosh, 100.
57 Ghosh, 106.
58 Ghosh, 106–107.
59 Ghosh, 102.
60 Tuli.
61 Subramaniam.
62 Tuli.
63 U. Iyer, 180–181.
64 U. Iyer, 182–183.
65 N. Kabir.
66 Tuli. Also see U. Iyer, 183–185.
67 Vohra, "Bodily."
68 Gopal, "Sentimental," 17.

5. Cinephilia

 1 Fee.
 2 www.urbandictionary.com/define.php?term=filmi, accessed March 11, 2020. "Hinglish" is a colloquial term for a mixed, Hindi and English, vernacular.
 3 https://scroll.in/video/958131/watch-indian-police-foundation-video-about-cor onavirus-crisis-refers-to-dabangg-and-zanjeer, accessed April 22, 2020.
 4 B. King, 170.
 5 Thomas, "Melodrama," 167.
 6 Arora.
 7 Sharpe, 78.
 8 Chopra, 172.
 9 "DDLJ."
10 "He-Man."
11 "Hum Aapke."
12 Wilkinson-Weber.
13 "Variety."

14 "Amitabh Better."
15 Dickey, 148–172.
16 Unny.
17 As Prasad writes, "As we watch Guddi maturing into responsible middle-class womanhood, we too go through a process of maturation at the end of which we, and Guddi with us, become rational, intelligent film-goers" (171).
18 Khubchandani, 76.
19 Phukan; Kalra.
20 "I Feel Nice."
21 Shahani, 60.
22 Vanita, *Dancing*, 12.
23 Mahadevan.

6. Nationalism

1 See Chakravarty; Daiya; Malhotra and Alagh; Mishra; Prasad; Rajadhyaksha, 33; Sarkar; Srivastava; Thomas, "Melodrama," 160 and 162; and Virdi.
2 Virdi, 33. Virdi reads nationalism as hegemonic, whereas Prasad sees it, in Ranajit Guha's terms, as dominant without being hegemonic (Prasad, 12). Chakravarty sees Bollywood nationalism as inherently unstable, constituted by "notions of change-ability and metamorphosis, tension and contradiction, recognition and alienation, surface and depth: dualities that have long plagued the Indian psyche and constitute the self-questionings of Indian nationhood" (4).
3 Dwyer and Patel, 139–140.
4 This dominant reading of the film might well be attributed to the souvenir booklet released at the time, which explicitly reads the film as a celebration of Indian nationalism, including quoting from orientalist scholar Max Muller's celebration of Indian rural life and describing Radha "as a 'jewel of Indian womanhood,' with continual references to mythology and comparisons to Sita and Savitri" (Dwyer and Patel, 163–164).
5 Ganti, *Bollywood*, 31; see also Dass, "Cinetopia."
6 Rockwell, 114.
7 Mazumdar, 7.
8 Chopra, 7–8.
9 Mazumdar, 9.
10 Parts of the following discussion have been published in Anjaria, *Reading*, 105–107.
11 Vanita, *Dancing*, 9.
12 Vanita, *Dancing*, 182.
13 Sarkar, 34–36.
14 Some examples include *Garam Hawa* (1973), *Tamas* (1988), *Earth* (1998), and *Khamosh Pani* (2003). See also Sarkar, 98.
15 Daiya, 596.
16 Daiya, 592.
17 "Pulwama."
18 Vohra, "Love."

7. Gender and sexuality

1 Dudrah, 302.
2 Gopalan.
3 Mishra, 7.
4 L. Iyer, 83–84.
5 Vanita, *Dancing*, 6–7.
6 Oldenburg, 261.

7 Thomas, "Melodrama," 166.
8 In the Oxford Hindi-English dictionary, the first definition of "yaar" is friend, with the second being lover. The word originates in Persian, where yaar also means friend, lover, companion.
9 Vanita, Introduction, 6.
10 Vanita, Introduction, 9.
11 Banerjee.
12 But, as in *Chalti Ka Naam Gaadi* (1958), discussed earlier, fraternal relationships in the absence of parents often appear in Bollywood more like intense friendships than part of a biological family unit.
13 Portions of this discussion of *Silsila* have been previously published in Anjaria, "Relationships," 30–31.
14 Anjaria, "Relationships," 23.
15 Virdi, 117.
16 Thomas, "Melodrama," 159; Virdi, 119.
17 As Joshi (11) argues about *Deewaar*.
18 Joshi, 11.
19 Joshi, 11–12.
20 L. Iyer, 69.
21 Dudrah, 289; Vohra, "Bodily."
22 Gopinath, 286.
23 Butler, 174.
24 Shahani, 205.

8. The future of Bollywood

1 Prasad's discussion of "middle-class cinema" shows how the so-called gentrification of Bollywood that many scholars observe since the 1990s had its roots in earlier counter-trends within Bollywood itself (170–187).
2 Gopal, *Conjugations*, 138.
3 Ganti, *Bollywood*, 48–49.
4 Gopal, *Conjugations*, 138–139.
5 Kalra and Jamkhandikar.
6 Ganti, *Bollywood*, 43–55.
7 Gopal, *Conjugations*, 125–126.
8 https://boxofficeindia.com/hit-down.php?txtYearlyData=2000-2009, accessed April 30, 2020, and https://boxofficeindia.com/hit-down.php?txtYearlyData=2010-2019, accessed April 30, 2020.
9 Portions of this section were published in Anjaria, *Reading*, 121–127.
10 East.
11 East; Goyal; Perry.
12 Daniels, 159.
13 Raghavendra.
14 "When Masculinity Harms Men."
15 Mulvey, 19–20.
16 See also Dudrah, 293; Rao.
17 "The Making of Om Shanti Om," Bonus DVD.

Works cited

Ahuja, Shivani. "7 of the Biggest Film Sets Ever Built in Indian Cinema." *Book My Show*, April 26, 2018. https://in.bookmyshow.com/entertainment/movies/hindi/7-biggest-film-sets-ever-built-indian-cinema/, accessed January 10, 2020.

"Amitabh Better." *Times of India*, August 11, 1982, 1.

Anand, Mulk Raj. "The Montage Man." *Times of India*, October 29, 1961, A20–21.

Anjaria, Ulka. *Reading India Now: Contemporary Formations in Literature and Popular Culture*. Philadelphia: Temple University Press, 2019.

Anjaria, Ulka. "'Relationships Which Have No Name': Family and Sexuality in 1970s Popular Film." *South Asian Popular Culture* 10. 1 (2012): 23–35.

Arora, Sakshi. "Remembering Nirupa Roy, Indian Cinema's 'Goddess' who became its most popular mother." *The Print*, January 4, 2019. https://theprint.in/features/remembering-nirupa-roy-indian-cinemas-goddess-who-became-its-most-popular-mother/172765/, accessed March 11, 2020.

Bali, Karan. "The Break in the Script: How did Partition Affect the Film Industry?" *Hindustan Times*, August 14, 2016. www.hindustantimes.com/art-and-culture/the-break-in-the-script-how-did-partition-affect-the-film-industry/story-12NhRiWPYwiFKRJyb0ejgN.html, accessed May 8, 2020.

Banerjee, Rohini. "What You Might Not Have Noticed About Bromance in Bollywood." *Youth Ki Awaaz*, August 5, 2016. www.youthkiawaaz.com/2016/08/bromance-and-homoeroticism-in-bollywood/, accessed April 29, 2020.

Basu, Anustup. "Dharmendra Singh Deol: Masculinity and the Late-Nehruvian Hero in Hindi Cinema." *Indian Film Stars: New Critical Perspectives*. Ed. Michael Lawrence. London: Bloomsbury, 2020. 73–86.

Basu, Anustup. "*Filmfare*, The Bombay Industry, and Internationalism (1952–1962)." *Industrial Networks and Cinemas of India: Shooting Stars, Shifting Geographies, and Multiplying Media*. Ed. Monika Mehta and Madhuja Mukherjee. London: Routledge, 2020. 137–150.

Bhaumik, Kaushik. "A Brief History of Cinema from Bombay to 'Bollywood.'" *History Compass* 2 (2004): 1–4.

Braudy, Leo. "Genre: The Conventions of Connection." *Film Theory and Criticism: Introductory Readings*, 5th ed. Ed. Leo Braudy and Marshall Cohen. New York: Oxford University Press, 1999. 613–629.

Butler, Judith. *Gender Trouble: Feminism and the Subversion of Identity*. New York: Routledge, 1990.

Chakravarty, Sumita S. *National Identity in Indian Popular Cinema, 1947–1987*. Austin: University of Texas Press, 1993.

"Chammak Chalo Song Making." YouTube. www.youtube.com/watch?v=CAHa got7RIQ, accessed June 4, 2020.

"'Chingari' Dull Picture But Has Good Music." *Times of India*, April 10, 1955, 3.

Chintamani, Gautam. *Qayamat Se Qayamat Tak: The Film That Revived Hindi Cinema*. Noida: HarperCollins, 2016.

Chopra, Anupama. *Sholay: The Making of a Classic*. New Delhi: Penguin, 2000.

Cohan, Steven. "Introduction: Musicals of the Studio Era." *Hollywood Musicals, the Film Reader*. Ed. Steven Cohan. London: Routledge, 2002. 1–16.

Coppola, Carlo. "Politics, Social Criticism and Indian Film Songs: The Case of Sahir Ludhianvi." *Journal of Popular Culture* 10. 4 (1977): 897–902.

Creekmur, Corey K. "Remembering, Repeating, and Working Through *Devdas*." *Indian Literature and Popular Cinema: Recasting Classics*. Ed. Heidi R.M. Pauwels. London: Routledge, 2007. 173–190.

Daiya, Kavita. "Visual Culture and Violence: Inventing Intimacy and Citizenship in Recent South Asian Cinema." *South Asian History and Culture* 2. 4 (2011): 589–604.

Daniels, Christina. *I'll Do It My Way: The Incredible Journey of Aamir Khan*. Noida: Om Books, 2012.

Dass, Manishita. "Cinetopia: Leftist Street Theatre and the Musical Production of the Metropolis in 1950s Bombay Cinema." *Positions: Asia Critique* 25. 1 (2017): 101–124.

Dass, Manishita. "The Cloud-Capped Star: Ritwik Ghatak on the Horizon of Global Art Cinema." *Global Art Cinema: New Theories and Histories*. Ed. Rosalind Galt and Karl Schoonover. New York: Oxford University Press, 2010. 238–251.

"'DDLJ' Completes 23-Year Run at Maratha Mandir in Mumbai." *Outlook*, October 24, 2018. www.outlookindia.com/website/story/mumbai-ddlj-completes-23-year-run-a t-maratha-mandir/318953, accessed March 11, 2020.

Dean, Laura. "Forget Hollywood, Egyptians are in Love with Bollywood." *The World*, May 17, 2015. www.pri.org/stories/2015-05-17/forget-hollywood-egyptians-are-lo ve-bollywood, accessed May 6, 2020.

"Devdas, the Making." *India Times*, n.d. http://devdas.indiatimes.com/costumes.htm, accessed June 4, 2020.

Dickey, Sara. *Cinema and the Urban Poor in South India*. Cambridge: Cambridge University Press, 1993.

Dissanayake, Wimal. "Introduction." *Melodrama and Asian Cinema*. Ed. Wimal Dissanayake. Cambridge: Cambridge University Press, 1993. 1–8.

"Don't Call it Bollywood, Says Top Indian Film Star Amitabh Bachchan." *The Telegraph*, May 20, 2003. www.telegraph.co.uk/culture/film/bollywood/10068018/ Dont-call-it-Bollywood-says-top-Indian-film-star-Amitabh-Bachchan.html, accessed May 4, 2020.

Dudrah, Rajinder. "Queer as Desis: Secret Politics of Gender and Sexuality in Bollywood Films in Diasporic Urban Ethnoscapes." *Global Bollywood: Travels of Hindi Song and Dance*. Ed. Sangita Gopal and Sujata Moorti. Minneapolis: University of Minnesota Press, 2008. 288–307.

Dwyer, Rachel. *100 Bollywood Films*. New Delhi: Roli Books, 2005.

Dwyer, Rachel. "The Erotics of the Wet Sari in Hindi Films." *South Asia* 23. 1 (2000): 143–159.

Dwyer, Rachel. "The Hindi Romantic Cinema: Yash Chopra's *Kabhi Kabhie* and *Silsila*." *South Asia: Journal of South Asian Studies* 21. 1 (1998): 181–212.

Dwyer, Rachel. "*Yeh Shaadi Nahin Ho Sakti!* ('This Wedding Cannot Happen!'): Romance and Marriage in Contemporary Hindi Cinema." *(Un)tying the Knot: Ideal and Reality in Asian Marriage*. Ed. Gavin W. Jones and Kamalini Ramdas. Singapore: Asia Research Institute, 2004. 59–75.

Dwyer, Rachel. "Zara Hatke ('Somewhat Different'): The New Middle Classes and the Changing Forms of Hindi Cinema." *Being Middle-Class in India: A Way of Life*. Ed. Henrike Donner. London: Routledge, 2011. 184–208.

Dwyer, Rachel, and Divia Patel. *Cinema India: The Visual Culture of Hindi Film*. New Brunswick: Rutgers University Press, 2002.

East, Ben. "Aamir Khan, the Thinking Man's Hero." *The National*, November 26, 2015. www.thenational.ae/arts-life/film/newsmaker-aamir-khan-the-thinking-mans-hero, accessed June 5, 2020.

Elison, William, Christian Lee Novetzke, and Andy Rotman. *Amar Akbar Anthony: Bollywood, Brotherhood, and the Nation*. Cambridge, MA: Harvard University Press, 2016.

Fee, Annie. "Cinephilia." *Oxford Bibliographies*. Cinema and Media Studies, 2017. www.oxfordbibliographies.com/view/document/obo-9780199791286/obo-9780199791286-0278.xml, accessed May 20, 2020.

Ganti, Tejaswini. *Bollywood: A Guidebook to Popular Hindi Cinema*, 2nd ed. London: Routledge, 2013.

Ganti, Tejaswini. *Producing Bollywood: Inside the Contemporary Hindi Film Industry*. Durham, NC: Duke University Press, 2012.

Gehlawat, Ajay. "Main Hoon Farah: The Choreographer as Auteur." *Behind the Scenes: Contemporary Bollywood Directors and their Cinema*. Ed. Aysha Iqbal Viswamohan and Vimal Mohan John. New Delhi: Sage, 2017. 3–16.

Ghosh, Shruti. "Dancing to the Songs: History of Dance in Popular Hindi Films." *Salaam Bollywood: Representations and Interpretations*. Ed. Vikrant Kishore, Amit Sarwal, and Parichay Patra. London: Routledge, 2016. 93–111.

Gopal, Sangita. *Conjugations: Marriage and Film Form in New Bollywood Cinema*. Chicago: University of Chicago Press, 2012.

Gopal, Sangita. "Sentimental Symptoms: The Films of Karan Johar and Bombay Cinema." *Bollywood and Globalization: Indian Popular Cinema, Nation, and Diaspora*. Ed. Rini Bhattacharya Mehta and Rajeshwari V. Pardharipande. London: Anthem Press, 2011. 15–34.

Gopalan, Lalitha. *Cinema of Interruptions: Action Genres in Contemporary Indian Cinema*. London: British Film Institute, 2002.

Gopinath, Gayatri. "Queering Bollywood: Alternative Sexualities in Popular Indian Cinema." *Journal of Homosexuality* 39. 3–4 (2000): 283–297.

Goyal, Divya. "How Aamir Khan Followed the Calorie-Count Method to Lose around 25kg for *Dangal*." *Indian Express*, November 29, 2016. http://indianexpress.com/article/lifestyle/fitness/aamir-khan-weight-loss-story-secret-for-dangal-2857618, accessed June 5, 2020.

Hassan, Adeel. "Fatima Bhutto on the Surge of Bollywood, K-Pop and Turkish TV." *New York Times*, November 15, 2019. www.nytimes.com/2019/11/15/us/fatima-bhutto-new-kings-interview.html, accessed May 6, 2020.

"He-Man of the Golden Era, Dharmendra and His Love for 'Dillagi.'" *Bobby Talks Cinema*, August 23, 2009. www.bobbytalkscinema.com/recentpost.php?postid=postid082309071537, accessed March 11, 2020.

Hood, John W. *The Essential Mystery: The Major Filmmakers of Indian Art Cinema*. New Delhi: Orient Blackswan, 2000.

"Hum Aapke Hain Koun @ 20: Lesser Known Facts." *Times of India*, August 5, 2014. https://timesofindia.indiatimes.com/entertainment/hindi/bollywood/photo-features/hum-aapke-hain-koun-20-lesser-known-facts/hum-aapke-hain-koun-20-lesser-known-facts/photostory/39670287.cms, accessed March 11, 2020.

"I Can Never Cry With the Help of Glycerine: Sonam Kapoor." *Hindustan Times*, June 14, 2013. www.hindustantimes.com/bollywood/i-can-never-cry-with-the-help-of-glycerine-sonam-kapoor/story-sRRLHrT66mZ7wr3WswqcCJ.html, accessed April 20, 2020.

"I Feel Nice About Being a Gay Fantasy!" *Bombay Dost* 4. 2 (1995): 5.

Iyer, Anita. "Everywhere I Go, Bollywood Chat Becomes the Icebreaker." *Khaleej Times*, January 11, 2019. https://blogs.khaleejtimes.com/2019/01/11/everywhere-i-go-bollywood-chat-becomes-the-icebreaker/, accessed May 6, 2020.

Iyer, Lalita. *Sridevi: Queen of Hearts*. Chennai: Westland, 2018.

Iyer, Usha. *Dancing Women: Choreographing Corporeal Histories of Hindi Cinema*. Oxford: Oxford University Press, 2020.

Johnson, W.J. "Viraha bhakti." *A Dictionary of Hinduism*. Oxford: Oxford University Press, 2009. www-oxfordreference-com.resources.library.brandeis.edu/view/10.1093/acref/9780198610250.001.0001/acref-9780198610250-e-2691, accessed May 19, 2020.

Joshi, Priya. "Cinema as Family Romance." *South Asian Popular Culture* 10. 1 (2012): 7–21.

Kabir, Ananya Jahanara. "Allegories of Alienation and Politics of Bargaining: Minority Subjectivities in Mani Ratnam's *Dil Se*." *South Asian Popular Culture* 1. 2 (2003): 141–159.

Kabir, Nasreen Munni. "How Saroj Khan Approached Choreography: 'The Words Tell Us What the Story Is.'" *Scroll*, July 4, 2020. https://scroll.in/reel/966356/how-saroj-khan-approached-choreography-the-words-tell-us-what-the-story-is, accessed July 27, 2020.

Kalra, Aditya, and Shilpa Jamkhandikar. "Netflix and Amazon Face Censorship Threat in India." *Reuters*, October 17, 2019. www.reuters.com/article/us-india-streaming-regulation/netflix-and-amazon-face-censorship-threat-in-india-source-idUSKBN1WW1RX, accessed May 21, 2020.

Kalra, Nonita. "Ashok Row Kavi: The Real Maha Maharani." *Man's World*, June 2000. www.mansworldindia.com/currentedition/from-the-magazine/ashok-row-kavi-real-maha-maharani/, accessed May 21, 2020.

Kapur, Anuradha. "Love in the Time of Parsi Theatre." *Love in South Asia: A Cultural History*. Ed. Francesca Orsini. Cambridge: Cambridge University Press, 2006. 211–227.

Khubchandani, Kareem. "Snakes on the Dance Floor: Bollywood, Gesture, and Gender." *Velvet Light Trap* 77 (2016): 69–85.

King, Barry. "Articulating Stardom." *Stardom: Industry of Desire*. Ed. Christine Gledhill. London: Routledge, 1991. 167–182.

King, Christopher. *One Language, Two Scripts: The History of Hindi and Urdu*. Delhi: Oxford University Press, 1986.

Krishen, Pradip. "Knocking at the Doors of Public Culture: India's Parallel Cinema." *Public Culture* 4. 1 (1991): 25–41.

Laghate, Gaurav. "Indian Box Office Crosses Rs 10,000 Crore Mark in 2019." *Economic Times*, February 14, 2020. https://economictimes.indiatimes.com/industry/media/entertainment/indian-box-office-crosses-rs-10000-crore-mark-in-2019/articleshow/74139131.cms?from=mdr, accessed May 7, 2020.

Mahadevan, Sudhir. "*Dhan te Nan! Onomatopoeia and Other Deployments of Film Sound in Contemporary Multiplex Cinema.*" Presentation given at Brandeis University, April 22, 2013.

Majumdar, Neepa. "The Embodied Voice: Song Sequences and Stardom in Popular Hindi Cinema." *Soundtrack Available: Essays on Film and Popular Music.* Ed. Pamela Robertson Wojcik and Arthur Knight. Durham, NC: Duke University Press, 2001. 161–181.

Majumdar, Rochona. "Art Cinema: The Indian Career of a Global Category." *Critical Inquiry* 42. 3 (2016): 580–610.

Malhotra, Sheena, and Tavishi Alagh. "Dreaming the Nation: Domestic Dramas in Hindi Films Post-1990." *South Asian Popular Culture* 2. 1 (2004): 19–37.

Mandal, Manisha. "Know How the *Bajirao Mastani* Set Was Created From the Makers!" *Daily Bhaskar*, December 9, 2015. https://daily.bhaskar.com/news/ENT-BOW-exclusive-photos-know-how-the-bajirao-mastani-set-was-created-from-the-makers-5190343-PHO.html, accessed February 27, 2020.

Martin, Nancy M. "Rajasthan: Mirabai and Her Poetry." *Krishna: A Sourcebook.* Ed. Edwin F. Bryant. Oxford: Oxford University Press, 2007. 241–254.

Mazumdar, Ranjani. *Bombay Cinema: An Archive of the City.* Minneapolis: University of Minnesota Press, 2007.

Mendonca, Clare. "The Year's 'Bests' in Indian Films." *Times of India*, September 3, 1950, 10.

Mengying, Bi. "Bollywood Films' Popularity in China Opening Door for Cultural Exchange." *Global Times*, October 14, 2019. www.globaltimes.cn/content/1166842.shtml, accessed May 6, 2020.

Mishra, Vijay. *Bollywood Cinema: Temples of Desire.* New York: Routledge, 2002.

Mulvey, Laura. *Visual and Other Pleasures.* Bloomington: Indiana University Press, 1989.

Muyiwa, Joshua. "Growing Up Mixed-Race, Queer and Femme, How Saroj Khan Provided Me the Keys to the Vehicle of My Body." *Firstpost*, July 26, 2020. www.firstpost.com/art-and-culture/growing-up-mixed-race-queer-and-femme-how-saroj-khan-provided-me-the-keys-to-the-vehicle-of-my-body-8637921.html/amp?__twitter_impression=true&fbclid=IwAR2wf2TBvneiGw3jmT77Y8gFmFl705HqeFoXPQGals6AP-S6fVSMsIFv9HA, accessed July 27, 2020.

Nandy, Ashis. "The Popular Hindi Film: Ideology and First Principles." *India International Centre Quarterly* 8. 1 (1981): 89–96.

Nijhawan, Amita. "Excusing the Female Dancer: Tradition and Transgression in Bollywood Dancing." *South Asian Popular Culture* 7. 2 (2009): 99–112.

Oldenburg, Veena Talwar. "Lifestyle as Resistance: The Case of the Courtesans of Lucknow, India." *Feminist Studies* 16. 2 (1990): 259–287.

Orsini, Francesca. "Introduction." *Love in South Asia: A Cultural History.* Ed. Francesca Orsini. Cambridge: Cambridge University Press, 2006. 1–39.

Perry, Alex. "The Young Turk." *Time*, October 27, 2013. http://content.time.com/time/world/article/0,8599,2053802,00.html, accessed June 5, 2020.

Phukan, Vikram. "Bombay Dost, India's First LGBT Magazine, Turns 25!" *Mid-Day*, October 6, 2015. www.mid-day.com/articles/bombay-dost-indias-first-lgbt-magazine-turns-25/16587189, accessed May 21, 2020.

Pinto, Jerry. *Helen: The Life and Times of an H-Bomb.* New Delhi: Penguin, 2006.

Prasad, M. Madhava. *Ideology of the Hindi Film: A Historical Construction.* New Delhi: Oxford University Press, 1998.

"Pulwama Attack: Total Ban on Pakistani Actors and Artistes in India, Announces AICWA." *India Today*, February 18, 2019. www.indiatoday.in/movies/bollywood/story/pulwama -terror-attack-total-ban-pakistani-actors-artistes-india-aicwa-1458720-2019-02-18, accessed April 28, 2020.

Raghavendra, M.K. "Social Dystopia or Entrepreneurial Fantasy: The Significance of Kaminey." *Economic and Political Weekly* 44. 38 (2009): 15–17.

Raheja, Dinesh, and Jitendra Kothari. *Indian Cinema: The Bollywood Saga*. New Delhi: Roli & Janssen BV, 2004.

Rajadhyaksha, Ashish. "The 'Bollywoodization' of the Indian Cinema: Cultural Nationalism in a Global Arena." *Inter-Asia Cultural Studies* 4. 1 (2003): 25–39.

Rajagopalan, Sudha. *Leave Disco Dancer Alone! Indian Cinema and Soviet Movie-Going After Stalin*. New Delhi: Yoda Press, 2008.

Rao, R. Raj. "Memories Pierce the Heart: Homoeroticism, Bollywood-Style." *Journal of Homosexuality* 39. 3–4 (2000): 299–306.

Rockwell, Daisy. "Visionary Choreographies: Guru Dutt's Experiments in Film Song Picturisation." *South Asian Popular Culture* 1. 2 (2003): 109–124.

"Round and About the Film World." *Times of India*, August 1, 1954, 3.

Sahota, Inderpreet. "No Expense Spared in *Devdas* Remake." *BBC World*, July 12, 2002. http://news.bbc.co.uk/2/hi/entertainment/2119805.stm, accessed January 10, 2020.

Sarkar, Bhaskar. *Mourning the Nation: Indian Cinema in the Wake of Partition*. Durham, NC: Duke University Press, 2009.

Shahani, Parmesh. *Gay Bombay: Globalization, Love and (Be)Longing in Contemporary India*. New Delhi: Sage, 2008.

Sharpe, Jenny. "Gender, Nation, and Globalization in Monsoon Wedding and Dilwale Dulhania Le Jayenge." *Meridians* 6. 1 (2005): 58–81.

Siddiqui, Mehak. "Bollywood Fashion Through the Ages." *Culture Trip*. https://thecul turetrip.com/asia/india/articles/bollywood-fashion-through-the-ages/, accessed January 10, 2020.

Sinha, Lalita. *Unveiling the Garden of Love: Mystical Symbolism in Layla Majnun and Gita Govinda*. Bloomington: World Wisdom, 2008.

Srivastava, Neelam. "Bollywood as National(ist) Cinema: Violence, Patriotism and the National-Popular in Rang De Basanti." *Third Text* 23. 6 (2009): 703–716.

Subramaniam, Arundhathi. "Bollywood Dancing: Dance in Hindi Films in India." *Animated: The Community Dance Magazine*. www.google.com/url?sa=t&rct=j&q=&esrc=s& source=web&cd=&cad=rja&uact=8&ved=2ahUKEwj604HbgevpAhUBl3IEHSjVAbs QFjAEegQIBBAB&url=https%3A%2F%2Fwww.communitydance.org.uk%2Fcontent %2F29538%2FLive%2Fattachment1%2FArunundhathi%2520Subramaniam.pdf&usg=AO vVaw0sPv-Yltvz09shBvEWEUUg, accessed June 5, 2020.

Thomas, Rosie. "Indian Cinema: Pleasures and Popularity." *Screen* 26. 3–4 (1988): 116–131.

Thomas, Rosie. "Melodrama and the Negotiation of Morality in Mainstream Hindi Film." *Consuming Modernity: Public Culture in a South Asian World*. Ed. Carol Appadurai Breckenridge. Minneapolis: University of Minnesota Press, 1995. 157–182.

Tuli, Nidhi. *The Saroj Khan Story*, 2012. www.youtube.com/watch?v=ZikNLJeJ17M& fbclid=IwAR1_CbEwemLok1V24TDBK_dDk87vB87NEzP4JqGhnZrcYcPA71gc16 m77-w, accessed July 24, 2020.

Unny, Divya. "Internet Fan Clubs: Star Struck." *Open Magazine*, August 19, 2015. https:// openthemagazine.com/features/india/internet-fan-clubs-star-struck/, accessed March 11, 2020.

Vanita, Ruth. *Dancing With the Nation: Courtesans in Bombay Cinema*. New Delhi: Speaking Tiger, 2017.

Vanita, Ruth. "Introduction: Ancient Indian Materials." *Same-Sex Love in India: A Literary History*. Ed. Ruth Vanita and Saleem Kidwai. Gurgaon: Penguin, 2008. 3–35.

"Variety Show in Refugees' Aid." *Times of India*, July 24, 1950, 9.

Vasudevan, Ravi. "The Meanings of 'Bollywood.'" *Beyond the Boundaries of Bollywood: The Many Forms of Hindi Cinema*. Ed. Rachel Dwyer and Jerry Pinto. Oxford: Oxford University Press, 2011. 3–29.

Vasudevan, Ravi. "The Melodramatic Mode and the Commercial Hindi Cinema: Notes on Film History, Narrative and Performance in the 1950s." *Screen* 30. 3 (1989): 29–50.

Virdi, Jyotika. *The Cinematic ImagiNation: Indian Popular Film as Social History*. New Brunswick: Rutgers University Press, 2003.

Vohra, Paromita. "Bodily Fluid: The Movement of Bollywood Dance from Body to Body." https://parotechnics.blogspot.com/2020/07/bodily-fluid-essay-i-wrote-about-dance.html?fbclid=IwAR1IW5RbiQ0YeiTBq0yb1r9LNWfi7gb1BUwkVXt0MyuWJ79tySI5InE0Dx0, accessed July 24, 2020.

Vohra, Paromita. "Love, See Us Into A Hall of Mirrors." *Outlook*, July 13, 2009. www.outlookindia.com/magazine/story/love-see-us-into-a-hall-of-mirrors/250436, accessed May 28, 2020.

"When Masculinity Harms Men." Satyamev Jayate, season 3, episode 6, Star Plus. Aired November 9, 2014.

Wilkinson-Weber, Clare M. *Fashioning Bollywood: The Making and Meaning of Hindi Film Costume*. London: Bloomsbury Academic, 2014.

"Zoya Akhtar on How a Javed Akhtar and Divine Collaboration Led to 'Apna Time Aayega.'" *Film Companion*, February 7, 2019. www.filmcompanion.in/interviews/bollywood-interview/zoya-akhtar-on-how-a-javed-akhtar-and-divine-collaboration-led-to-apna-time-aayega/, accessed July 28, 2020.

Index

3 Idiots 95, 135, 198; cinephilia in 114, 118, 129, 134; critique of education in 165, 197, 204; international reception of 6; language in 10

adoption 28–31, 158, 184
Aiyyaa 10, 204; cinephilia in 124, 125, 135; sensuality in 22, 35, 41, 48, 79, 86, 200, 202
Akhtar, Javed 69–70, 102
Amar Akbar Anthony 100–101, 130; costumes in 92; critique of wealth in 22, 28; kinship in 28–29; language in 10; lost-and-found in 21, 24–26, 30–31; love in 51, 184–185; the mother in 119, 142, 145; music in 64, 87; secularism in 153–154; tableaux in 104–106; villainy in 23, 165
Anand, Dev 6, 92, 127
Andaz 119, 169; friendship in 177, 178; marriage in 54; and visual style 27, 108
Andaz Apna Apna 34, 48, 178; cinephilia in 119, 125, 131–133, 135; language in 10
Angry Indian Goddesses: friendship in 178, 195, 201; and sexual violence 195, 202; as a vigilante film 151
Aradhana 42, 85, 171; double role in 126, 183; kinship in 29; lost-and-found in 25–26, 31; love in 94–95; sexuality in 40, 48–49, 75, 109
art cinema 5, 9, 11, 155, 168, 195

Baazigar 25, 78, 109, 131; double role in 127; Shah Rukh Khan and Kajol in 119; villainy in 29, 85
Bachchan, Amitabh 3, 61, 118, 120; as angry young man 149–150; costumes of 92–93; stardom of 6, 116, 121, 128

Bajrangi Bhaijaan 68; India–Pakistan peace and 155, 196; queer family in 186
Bhonsle, Asha 60, 61
Bobby 120, 134, 184; costumes in 90–91; love in 36, 45, 52, 74; morality in 19, 24, 27, 51, 85, 97; secularism in 152
Bunty Aur Babli 112, 148, 201; cinephilia in 134; costumes in 94; the item song in 81–82

Chak De India 148, 152, 154, 197
Chalti Ka Naam Gaadi 67, 73, 105–106; cinephilia in 119, 130; friendship in 172; gender roles in 169; love in 37, 53; morality in 147
Chandni 85, 95–96; love in 38–40, 53, 110; love triangle in 80, 172–173; and masculinity 22
Chawla, Juhi 37, 125
choreography 59, 72, 79, 81, *96,* 110–114
cinephilia 26, 65, 99, 117–137; and the future of Bollywood 193; and morality 19, 206; and the star 107, 115; and visual style 84, 96, 98, 116
costumes 5, 86–94, 99, 114; and cinephilia *137*; circulation of 125; and parody 114–115; in song sequences 64, 71, 111, 112; and villainy 21
courtesan films 28, 45, 99, 112; and the erotic 61, 87; and gender roles 171–172; and secularism 153

Damini 23, 53–54, 128, 170–171
Dangal 6, 148, 197
Darr 52–53, 125; music in 59, 65, 66, 74, 134; sexual violence in 42–43; villainy in 23, 29

Deewaar 46, 69, 147–148; the mother in 28, 119, 145, 182, 183–184; repetition in 25; secularism in 152; and visual style 103–105, 107–108

Deewana 30, 32, 66, 118, 129; love in 34, 43, 75; villainy in 22, 27, 42; and visual style 96, 108

desire 11–12, 54, 57, 65, 76–81; and fandom 123; female desire 35, 46, 74–75, 76–79, 168, 196; impossible desire 44, 79–81, 182; and individualism 37; music and 58, 168; queer desire 63, 185; and romance 40, 73, 74; *see also* queer love; *see also* sexual intimacy

destiny *see* fate

Devdas 111, 134; cinephilia in 122–123; repetition in 24; separation in 45; and visual style 99–100, 110

Dharmendra 43, 121, 122–123, 128, 149

diaspora *see* NRIs

Dil Chahta Hai 135, 166, 198; cinephilia in 65, 114; love in 55, 176–177, 181; and masculinity 203; the music of 71, 94, 114; and visual style 91–92, 98

Dil Se; the music of 9, 63, 79, 95–96; and obsession 43–44, 161–162

Dilwale Dulhania Le Jayenge 37, 66, 85, 115, 119; cinephilia in 131–132, 166; desire in 74–75, 77–78, 79, 88, 171; love in 38; and the moral universe 19–20, 23–24, 51, 153, 167, 190; popularity of 120–121, 128; and visual style 95, 96, 106, 108–109

Dixit, Madhuri 61, 90–91, 123, 124; and dance 81, 111, 113, 126; *see also* *Main Madhuri Dixit Banna Chahti Hoon*

double roles *89*, 125, 126–128, 195

Duplicate 49–50, 127, 128, 186–187

Dutt, Guru 146, 169

editing 63, 107–110, 112

Ek Ladki Ko Dekha Toh Aisa Laga 35, 52, 129–130, 189–190, 195–196

An Evening in Paris 22, 130, 165; desire in 48; double role in 126; friendship in 177; love in 36, 170; the music of 10; villainy in 21; and visual style 88–90, 93, 96

the family 76, 108, 141, 166, 201; betrayal of 143–144, 182–184; as enemy of love 6, 33, 41–43, 51, 54, 116, 161, 171; gender and 169, 170, 172; and the moral universe 19–31, 84,

100, 105, 195; the queer family 184–186; and secularism 154, 158; *see also* kinship

Fan 125–126

Fanaa 31, 48, 75, 94, 110, 134, 170, 198; love in 35, 37, 38, 44–45, 159–160, 161–162

fandom 6, 13, 61, 117, 120–126; in *Om Shanti Om* 98, 135, 197, 206; queer fandom 125–126, 185

fate 12, 23, 38–39, 145, 175; and the moral universe 19–20, 24–25

friendship 24, 29, 55–56, 133, 149, 172–181, 195

Gabbar Is Back 59, 130–131, 150–151, 199

gender roles 169–172, 200–206

Guddi 24, 29, 74, 94, 110; cinephilia in 43, 77, 117–118, 122–123, 125, 128, 136

Guide 6, 10, 87, *92*, 111, 133, 182; erotics in 54, 74, 110, 170; and masculinity 169; morality in 22, 98

Gully Boy 70, 98, 111, 196

Gunday: cinephilia in 114, 132, 134, 136; friendship in 174–175; gender roles in 35, 81; morality in 199

hatke cinema 195–198, 201

hijras 30, 184–185

Hindi 3–4, 7–11, 59, 164; film magazines in 121; Hindi slang 70; in relation to English 68, 87, 196

Holi 80, 86, 134

Hum Aapke Hain Koun 37, 90–91, 121, 166; queerness in 81, 186, 189

Hum Dil De Chuke Sanam 9, 11, 97, 112, 129, 166; love in 23, 39, 77, 153; and masculinity 203–204

I Hate Luv Storys 56, 131, 195

intertextuality 18, 117, 130–134, 137

the item song 81–83, 136, 205–206

Johar, Karan 115–116, 117, 134, 197

Kabhi Alvida Naa Kehna 92, 115–116; sexual transgression in 37, 55, 201–202

Kabhi Kabhie 22, 42, 92–93, 119, 134; desire in 77; love in 55

Kabhi Khushi Kabhie Gham 51, 133, 171, 184; adoptive kinship in 29–30; erotics in 47–48, 75–76; the music of 9, 79, 94, 111; secularism in 152; stardom and

119, 134; and visual style 96–97, 107, 115–116

Kajol 76, 85, 115–116, 119, 128, 134

Kal Ho Naa Ho 37, 85, 94, *101*, 166; adoptive kinship in 30; cinephilia in 134; love in 41; the music of 10; queerness in 173, 180

Kaminey 127–128, 137, 148, 195, 199

Kapoor, Raj 6, 119, 120, 128, 147

Kapoor, Rishi 65, 92, 111

Kapoor, Shammi 111, 128

Kapoor & Sons 182, 184, 189, 195, 196

Karz 30, 92, 121; fate in 20; influence on *Om Shanti Om* 27–28, 64–65, 129, 133, 135; reincarnation in 25, 27, 64, 129, 133, 135; villainy in 22, 52

Kashmir 94, 159–160, 161, 198

Kashmir Ki Kali 66; adoptive kinship in 29; Kashmir in 159; love in 34, 36; villainy in 23, 52

Kati Patang 11, 21, 178; coincidence in 25; love in 32, 38, 53, 120

Khan, Aamir 37, 85, 125, 128, 132–133, 135; and the future of Bollywood 197–198; and new masculinities 202, 204–205; stardom of 6, 124

Khan, Farah 13, 205–206; and cinephilia 117, 128, 135, 136–137, 197

Khan, Salman 63, 118, 121, 124, 126, 129, 133

Khan, Saroj 102, 112–114

Khan, Shah Rukh 130, 132, 135; films based on 120, 125–126, 136; and Kajol 76, 115–116, 119, 128–129, 134; sexuality and 187, 205–206; stardom of 85, *101*, 119, 121, 124, 127, *129*

Khanna, Rajesh 122, 128, 136; and double roles 126, 171, 183; stardom of 121

kinship 27–31, 157, 163, 181–182; *see also* family

Kuch Kuch Hota Hai 11, 27, 91, 94, 110–111, 129, 130, 135, 201; adoptive kinship in 29; love in 36, 37, 80, 178; secularism in 153; Shah Rukh Khan and Kajol in 115, 119, 128, 134

Kumar, Dilip 7, 127, 155

Kumar, Kishore 60, 61, 62, 105, 119

Lagaan 67, 134, 154, 196, 198

Lamhe 67, 97, 165, 173; cinephilia in 134; double role in 126; love in 35, 37, 77

lip-synching 5, 59, 61, 62, 64; cinephilia and 124; *see also* playback singing

lost-and-found plot 21, 24–26, 30–32, 100, 127, 154

love 33–57, 168–172, 182, 185, 200–202, 203, 206; and cinephilia 118; the love song 12, 58–59, 65–67, 71–74, 94–95; the love triangle 178–181; and the moral universe 19–24, 26–27, 120, 130, 144; and the nation 142, 156–157, 159–162, 163–164, 167; and secularism 152; *see also* queer love

Love Aaj Kal 56–57, 98

Love in Tokyo 10, 28, 120, 165; love in 35, 36; queerness in 185; and visual style 105, 108

Ludhianvi, Sahir 67–68, 146

Mahal 85, 103, 130; love in 35, 38–9, 41, 45; the music of 61, 71

Main Hoon Na 8, 13; brothers in 28; cinephilia in 73–74, 128, 130, 131, 135, *137;* India-Pakistan peace and 20, 22, 155, 158, 196

Main Khiladi Tu Anari 23, 126, 135, 136, 172, 174

Main Madhuri Dixit Banna Chahti Hoon 122–123, 125, 136, 186

Mangeshkar, Lata 61–62

marriage 57, 75, 100–101, 157; critiques of 170, 178; in conflict with love 35–36, 41–42, 44, 52, 79–80, 122–123, 125, 147, 167, 200; love after 54–55, 201; *see also* weddings

masculinity 51, 78, 144, 169, 201, 202, 203–206

melodrama 12, 66, 103, 193, 197

Mirabai 43, 46, 122

Mom 30, 185, 199, 200, 202–203

the moral universe 17, 19–24, 27, 32, 45, 81, 143–146, 168, 182, 184; cinephilia and 119, 197, 206; family and 29, 30, 104; friendship and 174–175; gender and 171, 201; hatke films and 195; love and 26, 33, 35, 38, 51–54, 167, 190; secularism and 155–156; sexuality and 186, 188, 204; and the state 149–151; and visual style 84–86

the mother 104–105; adoptive kinship and 29–30; and the moral universe 19, 21, 27–28; Nirupa Roy as 119; nation as 142–145, 158; and sons 182–184; *see also* family; *see also* kinship

Mother India 47, 70–71, 109, 142–145, 182–183

Mr. and Mrs. 55 10, 146, 169; love in 52, 67; the songs of 72, 112

Mr. India 113, 148; cinephilia in 134; erotics in 79; references to 124, 132; Sridevi in 102–103; villainy in 21, 23, 121

Mughal-e-Azam 63, 86, 112; love in 34, 36, 51; sets of 97–98

Mukerji, Rani 116, 201–202

the multiplex 193–194, 200

My Name is Khan 115, 119, 152, 196

Nagina 97, 108, 165; adoptive kinship in 30; erotics in 36, 41–42, 74; love in 28, 185; Sridevi in 102; villainy in 51

Nargis 6, 119, 183

Netflix 6, 11, 194

NRIs (Non-Resident Indians) 21, 162–167

Om Shanti Om 71, 101; cinephilia in 65, 98, 114, 128–129, 133, 135–136, 197, 206; double roles in 126; fate in 20; kinship in 27–28; love in 45; reincarnation in 64; secularism in 152; sexuality in 205–206

orphans 29–30, 163, 179

Padosan 8, 96, 128–129, 160; friendship in 177–178; love in 36; music in 58, 60, 134; sexuality in 50

Pakistan 8, 201; conflict with 20, 197; love across border with 35, 40, 45, 156–157, 161; Partition and 7, 154–158; peace with 22, 141, 153, 155, 186, 196

parallel cinema *see* art cinema

parody 197; of Bollywood conventions 117, 135–136, 137, 195; and the future of Bollywood 194; of the love song 73; of visual style 114

Parsi theater 84, 100, 141

Partition 7, 8, 113, 154–158, 197

Paying Guest 19, 36, 127, 147, 169

Phalke, Dadasaheb 2, 7

playback singing 59–62, 122; *see also* lip-synching

Prem Kahani 148; erotics in 75; friendship in 172; love in 34, 35–36, 44, 160; love triangle in 80, 179; secularism in 151–152

Punjabi 9, 156, 178

Purab Aur Paschim 11, 130, 165; love triangle in 178; nationalism and 163–164; NRIs in 166; secularism in 153; villainy in 21, 28; and visual style 85, 108, 109

Pyaasa 111; kinship in 28; love in 35, 36, 45, 46, 52, 64; secularism in 169; social critique in 68, 146, 147, 152, 169

Qayamat Se Qayamat Tak 132, 135; female desire in 77; love in 34, 36–38, 45, 100; patriarchy in 24, 51

Queen 56–57, 130, 166, 178, 195–196, 200

queer: Bollywood dance as 63, 101, 102, 126; love triangles as 80–81; queer fandom 123, 125–126, 185, 204–206; queer friendship 172–182; queer kinship 30, 31, 184–190; queer love 43–44, 52, 79, 130, 132, 133, 168–169, 184–190, 196

Rafi, Mohammed 60–61, 62

Raja Hindustani 85, 107; cinephilia in 134; erotics in 40; kinship in 29, 30; love in 53, 72–73; marriage in 55; queerness in 188; secularism in 152–153; villainy in 22, 30, 164

Ram Aur Shyam 64, 67, 119, 133, 170; adoptive kinship in 29; cinephilia in 136; double role in 127; love in 37; villainy in 22

realism 5, 11–12, 84, 105, 193, 197

Rehman, Waheeda 9, 111, 128

reincarnation: in *Karan Arjun* 28; in *Karz* 20, 25, 27–28, 64, 129, 133, 135; in *Nagina 102*, 185; in *Om Shanti Om* 27–28, 129, 133, 135, 206

religion *see* secularism

Sahib Bibi Aur Ghulam 54, 77, 147, 169–170

Sangam 97, 100, 109, 155; erotics in 48; friendship in 177; love in 161; love triangle in 180–181; tableaux in 103–104

Sarfarosh 64, 93; item song in 81; love in 20, 67, 73; and Pakistan 20, 155, 197; secularism in 152, 155

secularism 8, 28, 105, 141, 145, 151–154, 155; failure of 21

Seeta Aur Geeta 22, 42, 71, 93, 134, 148; coincidence in 25, 32; double role in 127; gender roles in 170; kinship in 29; villainy in 21, 30

sexual intimacy 46–50, 74–79, 109–110, 179, 183, 187, 196

sexual violence 21, 162, 198; and #MeToo 202–203; and the moral

universe 42, 53, 170; and vigilante justice 185, 195, 199, 200, 203
Shamitabh 60, 124, 135, 136
Sholay 61, 69; fandom and 120–121; friendship in 175–176; Gabbar Singh in 21, 85, 112; love in 36; references to 129, 130–131, 133, 150; vigilante justice in 149–151; villainy in 23, 64, 81–83, 86, 165
Shri 420 119, 129, 134, 147
Shubh Mangal Zyada Saavdhan 67, 132, 189, 204
Silsila 69, 94, 103; coincidence in 25; love in 71, 109; marriage in 55; references to 134; sexuality in 46, 80, 179–180, 182
Sridevi 9, 59, 85, 170; and dance 103, 113, 124, 132; and double roles 126; as queer icon 102, 126, 185
the star 61, 119–122, 136; the aural star 60; costumes and 87; and double roles 126, 127; fandom and 6; Karan Johar and 115–116; obsession and 125; pleasure and 18, 85, 107; Shah Rukh Khan as 127
Swades 166, 198

Tagore, Sharmila 88–90, 126–127, 128, 183

Umrao Jaan 28, 61, 112–113, 134, 172

Urdu 70; Urdu poetry 9, 39, 41, 44, 67–68, 69, 161; Urdu script 8

Veer-Zaara 9, 201; India-Pakistan peace and 196; love in 35, 36, 37, 40–41, 45, 46, 67, 78–80; marriage in 54; secularism in 152, 153, 155–157, 158; villainy in 52
vigilante films 59, 148–151, 185, 195, 197, 199, 202, 203
villainy 21–23, 120, 122, 165; and cinephilia 127, 130, 131, 197, 206; and the enemy of love 33, 50–52, 162, 167; and friendship 172; and kinship 28; and the moral universe 12, 17, 150–151; and the police 148, 199; sexual violence and 42; stereotyping and 27; and visual style 84–85
viraha 33, 45–46

Waqt 11, 37, 48, 132; gender roles in 170; kinship in 29; lost-and-found in 30
weddings 56, 62, 101, 120, 143, 168, 195, 200, 201; queerness and 81, 168, 186, 189; secularism and 152, 153; sex and 77, 79; wedding songs 58, 59, 79, 134, 168, 186; *see also* marriage

Zanjeer 69, 118, 132, 149

Taylor & Francis eBooks

www.taylorfrancis.com

A single destination for eBooks from Taylor & Francis
with increased functionality and an improved user
experience to meet the needs of our customers.

90,000+ eBooks of award-winning academic content in
Humanities, Social Science, Science, Technology, Engineering,
and Medical written by a global network of editors and authors.

TAYLOR & FRANCIS EBOOKS OFFERS:

A streamlined
experience for
our library
customers

A single point
of discovery
for all of our
eBook content

Improved
search and
discovery of
content at both
book and
chapter level

REQUEST A FREE TRIAL
support@taylorfrancis.com

 Routledge
Taylor & Francis Group

 CRC Press
Taylor & Francis Group